The Inner Journey
Views from the Christian Tradition

Series Editor: Ravi Ravindra
Associate Series Editor: Priscilla Murray

The Inner Journey
Views from the Christian Tradition

Edited by Lorraine Kisly

PARABOLA Anthology Series

MORNING LIGHT
PRESS

Published by Morning Light Press 2006.

Editor: Lorraine Kisly
Series Editor: Ravi Ravindra
Associate Series Editor: Priscilla Murray

Morning Light Press
323 North First, Suite 203
Sandpoint, ID 83864
morninglightpress.com
info@mlpress.com

Printed on acid-free paper in Canada.

13 Digit ISBN: 978-1-59675-008-1
10 Digit ISBN: 1-59675-008-1
Philosophy
SAN: 255-3252

Library of Congress Cataloging-in-Publication Data

The inner journey : views from the Christian tradition / edited by Lorraine Kisly.
     p. cm. -- (Parabola anthology series)
  Includes bibliographical references.
  ISBN-13: 978-1-59675-008-1 (alk. paper)
  ISBN-10: 1-59675-008-1 (alk. paper)
  1. Spiritual life--Christianity. I. Kisly, Lorraine. II. Series.
  BV4501.3.I56 2006
  230--dc22
                                  2006006784

To the path makers
and the pilgrims on the path

General Introduction to
The Inner Journey: A Parabola Anthology Series

When *Parabola: Myth, Tradition, and the Search for Meaning* was launched in 1976, the founder, D. M. Dooling, wrote in her first editorial:

> *Parabola* has a conviction: that human existence is significant, that life essentially makes sense in spite of our confusions, that man is not here on earth by accident but for a purpose, and that whatever that purpose may be it demands from him the discovery of his own meaning, his own totality and identity. A human being is born to set out on this quest. ... Every true teaching, every genuine tradition has sought to train its disciples to act this part, to become in fact followers of the great quest for one's self.

For over thirty years, *Parabola* has honored the great wisdom traditions of every culture, turning to their past and present masters and practitioners for guidance in this quest. Recognizing that the aim of each tradition is the transformation of human life through practice supported by knowledge and understanding, *Parabola* on behalf of its readers has turned again and again to Buddhist and Christian monks, Sufi and Jewish teachers, Hindu scholars, and Native American and other indigenous peoples, evoking from each of them illumination and insight.

Over the years *Parabola*, in each of its issues devoted to a central theme of the human condition as it is and as it might be, has gathered remarkable material. "The Call," "Awakening," "Food," "Initiation," "Dreams and Seeing," "Liberation," "The Mask," "Attention": in these and in scores of other issues, a facet of the essential search is explored, always with the aim of casting light on the way.

The purpose of the *Parabola Anthology Series* is to gather the material published in *Parabola* during its first thirty years in order to focus this light, and to reflect the inner dimensions of each of these traditions. While every religious tradition has both external and inner aspects, the aim of each is the transformation of the whole being. The insights and understandings that ring true and carry the vibration of an inner meaning can provide guidance and support for our quest, but a mere mechanical repetition of forms which were once charged with great energy can take us away from the heart of the teaching. Every tradition must change and evolve; it has to be reinterpreted and reunderstood by successive generations in order to maintain its relevance and application.

Search carries a connotation of journey; we set out with the hope for new insight and experience. The aim of the spiritual or inner journey is transformation, to become more responsible and more compassionate as understanding and being grow. This demands an active undertaking, and insights from those who have traveled the path can provide a call, bring inspiration, and serve as a reminder of the need to search.

For this series, selections have been made from the material published in *Parabola* relating to each of the major traditions and teachings. Subtle truths are expressed in myths, poetry, stories, parables, and above all in the lives, actions, and expressions of those people who have been immersed in the teaching, have wrestled with it and have been informed and transformed by it. Some of these insights have been elicited through interviews with current practitioners of various teachings. Each of the great traditions is very large and within each tradition there are distinct schools of thought, as well as many practices, rituals, and ceremonies. None of the volumes in the present series claim to be exhaustive of the whole tradition or to give a complete account of it.

In addition to the material that has been selected from the library of *Parabola* issues, the editor of each volume in the series provides an introduction to the teaching, a reminder of the heart of the tradition in the section, "The Call of the Tradition," as well as a list of books suggested for further study and reflection. It is the hope of the publishers and editors that this new series will surprise, challenge, and support those new to *Parabola* as well as its many readers.

—*Ravi Ravindra*

CONTENTS

The Call of the Tradition

A new commandment I give to you, that you love one another;
even as I have loved you, that you also love one another.[1]

—John 13:34

Come to me, all who labor and are heavy laden, and I will give you rest.
Take my yoke upon you, and learn from me; for I am gentle
and lowly in heart, and you will find rest for your souls.
For my yoke is easy, and my burden is light.[2]

—Matthew 11:28–30

Ask, and it will be given you; seek, and you will find; knock,
and it will be opened to you.[3]

—Matthew 7:7

Seeing the crowds, he went up on the mountain,
and when he sat down his disciples came to him.
And he opened his mouth and taught them, saying:
"Blessed are the poor in spirit, for theirs is the kingdom of heaven.
"Blessed are those who mourn, for they shall be comforted.
"Blessed are the meek, for they shall inherit the earth.
"Blessed are those who hunger and thirst for righteousness,
for they shall be satisfied.

"Blessed are the merciful, for they shall obtain mercy.
"Blessed are the pure in heart, for they shall see God.
"Blessed are the peacemakers, for they shall be called sons of God.
"Blessed are those who are persecuted for righteousness' sake,
for theirs is the kingdom of heaven."[4]

—Matthew 5:1–10

I am the Alpha and Omega, the first and the last,
the beginning and the end.[5]

—Revelation 22:13

Therefore, let nothing hinder us,
nothing separate us,
nothing come between us.
Wherever we are,
in every place,
at every hour,
at every moment of the day,
everyday and continually, let all of us …
hold in our heart and love,
honor, adore, serve,
praise and bless,
glorify and exult,
magnify and give thanks …[6]

—Francis of Assisi

If man's eyes were but opened he should see God everywhere in his heaven;
for heaven stands in the innermost moving everywhere.[7]

—Jacob Boehme

Father, help me to realize that now is eternity and that there is only the
dimension of the now in which to awaken to Thy unquenchable love that
will not let me go. Strip me of all further evasion and postponement,
that this very hour I may abandon my heart to thee.[8]

—Bernard of Clairvaux

Let us, then, die and enter into the darkness;
let us impose silence upon our cares,
our desires and our imaginings.
With Christ crucified
let us pass out of this world to the Father
so that when the Father is shown to us,
we may say with Philip:
It is enough for us.
Let us hear with Paul:
My grace is sufficient for you.
Let us rejoice with David saying:
My flesh and my heart have grown faint;
You are the God of my heart,
And the God that is my portion forever.
Blessed be the Lord forever
And all the people will say:
Let it be; let it be,
Amen.[9]

—St. Bonaventure

The Inner Journey: Introduction

To *Parabola* readers over thirty years ago when the journal first was launched, and to readers in the West today, Christianity, among all the world's wisdom traditions, seems familiar and known. Most will acknowledge that Hinduism, for example, and even Buddhism, despite its recent eruption into contemporary culture, has something new to offer them. But don't we already know the essentials of the Christian tradition?

To those born to the teaching, it may be in adolescence that a "flaw" in a minister or doctrine is perceived, a judgment delivered, and an attitude formed that may take many years to dislodge. A single degree of the 360 that make up the tradition is taken for the whole, and the searcher moves on to another track. Even if not disaffected, many look no deeper, and perhaps do not even suspect the dimensions hidden within their own tradition.

Bede Griffiths in "Winding the Golden String" (Chapter One) relates that for him it was an experience during his adolescence of overwhelming beauty and mystery in nature that had the effect of turning him away from all religious institutions. "The religion in which I had been brought up," he writes, "seemed to be empty and meaningless in comparison to what I had found, and all my reading led me to believe that Christianity was a thing of the past." Griffiths, of course, ultimately became a Benedictine monk, and writes that it took thirty years for the full meaning of his early revelation to become clear to him.

It was disillusionment with the "return to nature" movement and with the apparent failure of civilization after the First World War that brought Griffiths to a serious study of the Bible, and to the unexpected discovery that Christianity "was just as much a living power now as it ever had been." It is the discovery of this living power to which the writers collected here direct us again and again.

For over three decades, *Parabola* has sought out those for whom the Christian Way is one of discovery and of questioning, rooted in a state of spiritual need. In "The Hidden Union" (Chapter Seven), Jacob Needleman, writing about what is required in order to approach the symbolic language of the noncanonical Gospel of Philip, reminds us that the inner meaning of all scripture, whether canonical or not, can be received only in this state of need and questioning. "If there is such a thing as transformational knowing (and this is the true meaning of the term, *gnosis*)," he tells us, "its first stage is the inner act of *not knowing*."

That said, there are essential qualities inherent in the tradition, some not often noted. Among these is the relationship between an elder and a disciple in which both are under the single Master, Christ. The only obedience is obedience to the Father's will, the only aim true human freedom. Paul Evdokimov has written of this that "a spiritual father does not engender his son, he engenders a son of God. Both, in common, place themselves in a school of truth … no obedience to human elements, no idolatry of a spiritual father, even if he is a saint. Every counsel of a starets leads a man to a state of freedom before the face of God."

There are other hallmarks very well expressed by Father Thomas Hopko, priest of the Orthodox Church in America in "Living in Communion (Chapter Five). "God is not removed from the world," he says in the interview, "but rather one who enters into the world and gets nailed to a cross. And unless we accept Christ crucified, which is a scandal to those who want God to be some kind of power figure, and total foolishness to those who want it all to fall into place intellectually in our terms, there's no Gospel." A scandal and foolishness the crucified Christ remains to many: that it is a reality reflecting the nature of reality itself is as difficult to comprehend and to accept today as it was 2,000 years ago, but there will never be a true Christian path that attempts to evade the cross and its burdens.

The primacy of desire is notable in the tradition as well: what we long for longs for us. The state of spiritual need has already been spoken of, and Christian practice aims to rouse that need and desire. "I came that they might have life, and that they might have it more abundantly," Christ said. To recognize this gift, offered at every moment, and to discover the obstacles that impede our ability to receive, form the heart of the Christian's lifelong search.

The articles collected here track this search through the great living realities of the tradition. Chapter One, "Turning Home," is centered on the parable of the prodigal son, the parable of freedom, loss, return, and joy at the very heart of the teaching. Paul Tillich's essay, "To Whom Much Was Forgiven," reveals what he terms the "shaking and liberating power" of the Christian message as expressed both in this parable and in the story of Jesus and the whore. "It is not the love of the woman that brings her forgiveness," Tillich writes, "but it is the forgiveness she has received that creates her love. ... Jesus does not forgive the woman, but he declares that she *is* forgiven." It is this that kindles the fire of love, opening the way to self-acceptance and the path home. Recognizing that the prodigal son's return is not once and for all but moment by moment, Christopher Bamford in "The Gift of the Call" writes that while we must each vow to change our lives, such a vow "is not made once, but must be renewed with every breath."

We remember only to forget again, and Chapter Two, "The Search for the Self," explores the tendencies that keep us from the realization of God's presence. Chapter Three, "Unseen Warfare," locates the ground of struggle toward this realization, evoking what D. M. Dooling calls "the reality of levels of 'worlds' in which the human being is called to live in more than one at a time, and moreover to participate—as no other living being is called to do—in an exchange between them." Here is the struggle against all the obstacles to that exchange for which we were created. It depends upon a will freed from selfishness, a will free to enter a life of ecstatic communion.

Chapter Four, "Attention and Remembrance," establishes the need for an inner state of vigilance and watchfulness amid all the powers of sleep and forgetting. And again, the watchfulness is not for its own sake but to bring us into the greater life for which Christ came. In the Aramaic of Jesus' time, Cynthia Bourgeault tells us in "The Gift of Life," there was no word for "salvation." "Salvation, she writes, "was understood as bestowal of life, and to be saved was 'to be made alive,'" and to participate in a "larger, more vivified and unified life made possible through the indwelling of the Spirit."

Communion, service, and love of neighbor are primary in the Christian tradition, and Chapter Five, "A Body of Beauty and Love," brings us nearer to the vision of humanity as members of the body of Christ. "The isolated individual is not a real person," says Bishop Kallistos Ware in "Image and Likeness." "A real person is one who lives in and for others. ... This idea of openness to God, openness to other persons, could be summed up under the word "love" ... By love, I don't mean merely an emotional feeling, but a fundamental attitude. In its deepest sense, love is the life, the energy, of God Himself in us."

Openness to the currents of earthly and divine life together is the focus of Chapter Six, and the radical vision of the Gnostic Gospels, brought to the attention of a nonspecialist public not long after *Parabola* was founded, leads us to the final chapter, "Fullness of Being." In James Cutsinger's "The Yoga of Hesychasm," we are brought, through his meditation upon "The Ladder of Divine Graces," to the glorious fulfillment of the Christian promise: not escape from the world or from the body but transfiguration of both in which all and everything is included, and nothing abandoned. "The body is not left behind in our approach to full union," he writes, "but is lifted up and drawn into its Divine prototype." By grace, a moment arrives when "the body, now thoroughly steeped in God, bears witness in its own substance to the realities it has seen."

A Church Father said Christ became man that man might become divine, pointing to the exchange of levels to which the human being is uniquely called: the divine incarnated in the human, the human granted a way into the heart of the living God.

Christian Imagery

The image of the body
of Christ in the arms
of his mother; upon
the cross; transfigured
in glory: in each is a
sign and promise that
our human nature is
permeated by the divine,
that our suffering and
death is redeemed in joy,
that nothing is lost and
all is gathered together.
The "holy and glorious
flesh" speaks directly to
us of the transformation
of matter by Spirit.

Through the depiction
in sacred art of Christ,
of the communion
of saints, of the Holy
Trinity, we are led again
and again in beauty to
the face of Love.

The image of God is found essentially and personally in all mankind. Each possesses it whole, entire and undivided, and all together not more than one alone.

In this way we are all one, intimately united in our eternal image, which is the image of God and the source in us of all our life.[1]

—Jan Ruusbroec (1293–1381)

Jesus said, "Let him who seeks continue seeking

until he finds. When he finds, he will become

troubled. When he becomes troubled, he will be

astonished, and he will rule over the All."[2]

—*The Gospel of Thomas (c 150)*

Inasmuch as we come near to him by love of Him,

so we become united by love with our neighbors,

and inasmuch as we are united with our

neighbors, so we become united with God.[3]

—Abba Dorotheus (sixth century)

You do well not to let drop from your hands the

polished mirror of the holy Gospel of your Lord,

for it provides the likeness of everyone who looks

into it. ...

There the kingdom of God is depicted,

visible to those who have a luminous eye.[4]

—*Ephrem the Syrian (303–373)*

If you want to see me in my uncreated Godhead,

you should learn to know and love me here in my

suffering humanity.[5]

—*Henry Suso (1300–1366)*

Holy, holy, holy, is the Lord of Hosts: the whole

earth is full of His glory.[6]

—Isaiah 6:3

I know that the immovable comes down;

I know that the invisible appears to me;

I know that he who is far outside the whole creation

    Takes me within Himself and hides me in His arms;

    And then I find myself outside the world.

I, a frail, small mortal in the world,

Behold the Creator of the world, all of Him, within myself.

    And I know that I shall not die,

    For I am within the Life.

I have the whole of life springing up as a fountain within me.

He is in my heart, He is in heaven:

Both there and here He shows Himself to me with equal glory.[7]

    —John Scotus Eriugena (810-877)

CHAPTER ONE

•

TURNING HOME

No one can come to me unless the Father draws him.[1]

—John 6:44

You must not imagine that you are drawn against your will,
for the mind can also be drawn by love. …
Show me a lover and he will understand what I am saying.
Show me someone who wants something, someone hungry,
someone wandering in this wilderness,
thirsting and longing for the fountains of his eternal home,
show me such a one and he will understand what I mean.[2]

—St. Augustine of Hippo

Parabola
Volume: 29.3
The Seeker

THE GIFT OF THE CALL

Christopher Bamford

> *I shall begin to sing what I must sing eternally,*
> *The mercies of the Lord.*
> —*Thérèse of Lisieux*

> *Draw me, we will run after thee …*
> —*Song of Solomon 1:4*

The call comes gradually, or so it seems. We must be called over and over before we hear its whisperings. Then we begin to notice. We begin to respond. Unconsciously, hesitantly, we start to listen. Incrementally, our response deepens. Finally, we realize that we ourselves are the call; that call and caller are one in life lived in obedience to the gift of the call. We come to recognize that we were called from the beginning, "from the foundation of the world," as St. Paul says. Looking back, we cannot remember a "first" call.

"Behind what we call the 'first' always lies a hidden sequence of other 'first' experiences," Allen Grossman writes of the poet's vocation. It is as if our lives were a palimpsest of memories, each experience collapsing back through other experiences to the beginning of conscious life; and reaching still further back, as Grossman says, "to the beginning of the world; and then, at last, to the great receptacle of all there is, the figure of no beginning."

If the call is without beginning, it is also without end. Every call seems to lie at the intersection of past and future. From one direction, it echoes up through time and memory from our source and origin, defining who we are, alerting us to whom we shall become. From the other, it comes toward us as destiny, drawing us toward an ineffable goal. You might say that to live is itself to be called. Perhaps that is why one of the meanings of *anthropos*, or human being, is "to look up," as one looks up when one hears one's name called. But how do you know your name? I think of the superfine rain masquerading as mist on certain northern islands. At first, you cannot tell whether it is raining or not, but after walking a while, say until midday, you come to your senses to find yourself soaked and you realize you have been wet forever.

Often, the call sounds first in childhood through nature and the senses, when the world is new, shining with the glory and the freshness of a dream, and the corn is orient and immortal wheat. First memories are frequently of light and color, or darkness and light, shadows, moving on the wall, or of pastel silks swaying in the breeze. The world seems luminous, though whether lit from within or without we cannot tell. Experience is unified. There is no need to question. Yet, if I remember it rightly, there is already a sense of a numinous other, though the ineffability is only intuited, not yet known. Beauty lies at the edge of consciousness, in the warm, dark, mothering embrace of a world in which we are one with all there is. Only later, when we have fallen into separateness, does beauty begin to draw us consciously from our isolation into the light. Then we begin to question and to hear the "something more," that luminous excess in nature that never quite arrives, but whispers of greater good than we can imagine.

The call of beauty is always intimate, one on one. She is our mother; she raises us to our feet, so that we may see her face to face. As we learn to move, we express our delight by running, jumping, climbing. She gives us language and thought, whose first form is imagination, so that we may praise her in our hearts and proclaim what we have found.

Not for nothing is the garden called a figure of the soul. The soul herself is a garden, and it is in a garden that we first learn her ways.

I, for one, found her there. My childhood garden was the kindergarten of the call, beauty's school. I loved her safe, enclosed spaces, filled with worlds and beings, each with its own alluring qualities. Dreaming my way in, I created houses, forts, caves, and tunnels—secret, hidden places in which to imagine magical encounters and make up stories, spontaneous prayers connecting me to the one whose breathing pulsed in its dark, embracing warmth. It was a complete universe, a whole. Each season called in its own way. Spring with its greening power of growth; summer with its expansive sense of immortality; autumn with its golden dying; winter with its solitude, darkness, and interiority. The garden is the first home. There is no horizon, and the call does not come from anywhere, it simply is.

The horizon, too, is a gift. I remember my first experience of it, standing on a beach, looking out at the vast expanse of ocean disappearing into the sky. When I looked up I thought I saw a second ocean, or perhaps the two were one, fire or water I couldn't tell. At my feet certainly was sand, but it too seemed to extend indefinitely as far as the eye could see. Standing at the center, I picked up a handful. Countless tiny grains glistened and sparkled up at me. Everything seemed poised on the cusp between familiar and unfamiliar, near and far, visible and invisible. Awe and an indescribable feeling of friendship flowed together in my heart. The world shone with an inner light. Later, the locus of that light shifted, so that I no longer saw it, though I still knew it was there.

Older, I would go into the hills behind our house, passing through a dark copse of oak and pine to reach the gentle curve of the open moors, dense with heather and marked by scattered gorse and stumpy, solitary trees. The wind soughed like a being's breath, caressing my cheek, now gently, now gusting. One evening I met a human figure, who told me many things. The next day I returned and met him again. On the third day, he was gone and I cannot tell if he was ever there.

I tasted freedom and learned that beauty in its heart-opening never-quite-arriving (or always eluding) presence communicated an undeniable, irresistible conviction of goodness and truth. I knew that the world was my home and that it was a blessed, sacred, holy place. The air, as Keats says, was my robe of state, the open sky sat upon my senses like a sapphire crown, the earth was my throne and the sea a mighty minstrel playing before it. Tiny rustling streams, silvery in the afternoon light, called me to their serpentine course. With clouds as my companions, I followed, and soon came upon some miniature waterfall, beside which I would lie down, eyeball to eyeball with the cascading drops.

We begin in dreams. Then we wake up. The world shrinks to the size of our own little selves. We become egotistic. The isolated, skin-bound, brain-bound, self-feeling being that has been growing within us since we recognized ourselves and proclaimed "me!" takes over. Anomalies appear in the interstices of wonder. Gradually, the paradigm changes, the call is muffled, the world becomes other. Like a sodden piece of paper that dries out, leaving only a ring, beauty, herald of the divine, seems to vanish, leaving behind only a memory, like a watermark in the soul. Where once as children we knew, growing into adolescence we struggle to hold to the memory of what we once experienced, but what we have left lives only as an inner conviction, vulnerable to the vagaries of doubt and despair. The possibility of faith is born in the growing darkness.

At first, people are like angels, bathed in light and goodness. We move without separation, as if all beings participated in a unique identity, a communion of perfect understanding. Somewhere, neither within us nor without us, we still hear the echo of the single name we all share. Echoing in the depths, it calls us to the common task of playfully, joyfully co-creating the world. We are busy with it. We understand the mutuality of being, of our interdependence. The world is a marvelous piece of music, and like an angelic choir we busy ourselves with performing the heavenly composition, knowing everyone is playing the same score.

Then comes the fall which, like the call itself, appears gradually, yet in fact paradoxically has always been there. Often it seems as if some single traumatic instance cuts the golden string by which we are woven into a higher tapestry. But, if we pay attention and push beyond the "remembered" trauma, we find we can no more locate a "first" fall than we can a "first" call. It seems that we are not only always called, but also always fallen, "from the foundation of the world." We know this because, though each of us experiences the fall subjectively, we also know that we are not alone in our pain. We are hurt but, as we turn our attention from our own pain, we recognize that the world is in pain, and that fallenness is a universal condition. Individually, we may feel violated or betrayed in different ways, but whatever the circumstances of our falling, we recognize the bitter teaching that the world is riven by violence and deception and that we are all complicit in it.

, Fall and call belong together. As the web of deception and death appears and the golden world fades, the memory of that world, which seemed once so safe and whole, continues to call. Nature remains beautiful. Though we no longer see its invisible source, we still intuit it at the edge of our perception. Fallen angels, we are still angels. The wonder and reverence that surrounded us, haloing parents and playmates alike, does not disappear. Transformed into curiosity, it becomes interest. People call us. They draw us. A glance, a smile, a touch are now redolent of the mystery the greater world once held. The wound of our fallenness becomes a school of empathy. We learn sympathy and compassion. The faces of others, their physiognomy, centered in the eyes, open us inwardly. From the eyes above all, "mirrors of the soul," we learn to acknowledge the depths of our own interiority. This is a time when two phrases, made trite by overuse, become like mantras: "Nothing human is alien to me"; "There but by the grace of God go I." Art, literature, and music become messengers, intermediaries of the call. The unity, though fallen, is still a unity. Meaning still occasionally pierces the clouds of fragmentation, drawing us on. The call, which seemed perhaps to echo from the past, now sounds from the future.

"Religion," if not a given religion, but one we make, is surely part of it. Equally surely, if given, we are also called to make it, for to respond to the call is to make it one's own. The way it comes is, of course, personal and subjective, depending upon imponderables, such as where we are born and to whom.

For me, there was always the sense of the divine ground, in whom "we live and move and have our being," and the corollary of this, that divinity "loved us first" and participates in our joys and sorrows. The unity, experienced in first love of beauty, seemed now to foreshadow the unity we could achieve by realizing God's identity with creation through the work of conscious human love and suffering. Thus, distorted though it may have been by its inflation and adolescent egotism, I understood somehow that what I suffered was not my own, nor in any sense for myself. Christ crucified seemed to me the image of the world. Only later would I realize that crucifixion without resurrection was meaningless; · and that the way, like the call itself, was only a *means*. For the moment, I realized only the suffering, the pervasiveness of the fall.

My father had been on the first convoy of soldiers into Auschwitz. Haunted by what he had witnessed, he bore and transmitted the mark of Cain. He felt compelled to return again and again to what he had learned: that human folly and inhumanity knew no bounds. I came to understand the "century of night" that stretched from before Sarajevo through the Holocaust to Hiroshima and beyond: perpetual wars, mass death, dehumanization, environmental destruction, social and psychological fragmentation, meaning reduced to domination and manipulation, sheer matter made autonomous and power given free reign.

The call to *metanoia*, transformation, and repentance, comes to us in · different ways. Yet we must all at some moment "hit bottom" and vow to change our lives. The "ego" crashes and the I AM, a light greater than the ego, breaks through the isolation and separation we have created. If the fall into ego lies on one side of the call, the vow to selflessness lies on the other. Such a vow is not made once, but must be renewed with every breath.

Called to a different way of knowing and being, we begin to read as if for the first time. We do not read for information, but to know ourselves and be changed. We want to know where we have come from, where we are, and where we are going. We want to know what it is to know and whether and how we can change. We seek testimonies of those who have done so. We seek evidence that we can make our own. We read philosophy, psychology, history, mythology. We read the great texts of the world's esoteric and wisdom traditions. But such untutored reading, no matter how passionate and committed, is not sufficient. We must learn to read differently. We must learn to think differently, to be differently. There is no mystery about this. We are given the world we think. For the world to change, our thinking must become different, selfless, endlessly responsive, ethical. We must learn not to consume a text, but to allow it to call us. We must learn to listen, to receive and respond. Meaning becomes a gift that we allow to live within us and return to the giver with our whole being.

We are called to a new interiority, a new solitude; and a new kind of community. We discover that books and written words are only signs, as the body is the sign of the soul. We learn to read meditatively, to rise from the letter to the spirit. Perhaps we learn to do so from Guigo the Carthusian who laid down the steps of "sacred reading," or from some other teacher, or perhaps the texts themselves teach us. We read the words before us slowly, reflectively, sentence by sentence, to understand exactly what is meant. As if called by name, we read with a heart filled with empathy and love, straining to hear what is really being said and demanded of us. With each reading, the meaning sinks deeper into our body, as we discover level upon level of meaning and apply it to our lives. We ponder, associate, seeking insight wherever we can find it. We rest in awe at the richness we have been given. Entering a meditative state, we sit with our attention completely focused, as if the speaker understood us perfectly and the words were calling us and only us directly. Then, we stop thinking, surrendered to the invisible author with open heart. Finally, we let go of everything and, enveloped in a vast body of silence and inner peace, rest in emptiness, in pure, listening receptivity. A greater universe of consciousness, worlds within worlds, opens before us, filled with beings and their relationships, constituting a lineage and community in which we are called to participate.

We discover that, despite its suffering and despair, earthly existence has a meaning. Working through history, there are traditions of those who have sought to enhance it. These traditions now call us one by one, individually, for we are no longer called simply by birth and geography. As we are called, we realize the reality of the invisible worlds. For we are called home, and home is not an exclusively earthly place, but more like what St. Paul calls "a cloud of witnesses." In Christianity, this is called the "community of saints," a body that encompasses the living, as well as the so-called dead. In Buddhism it is called the *Sangha*, the community of practitioners; in Islam, the *Ummah*, or body of believers. Each communion has its own way of speaking of the precious gift of human birth and to what it calls us. Whichever path we take, once we take it, life becomes a pearl of great price, the receiving of which is the giving of ourselves to it.

Answering the call, one becomes a seeker. In my own case, following the call to live otherwise, I sought a different approach. Seeking to awaken from the nightmare of sleep, of egotism run amuck in the world, I studied alternative ways of knowing. I began time-tested practices of meditation, prayer, and attention. I steeped myself in esoteric theologies, cosmologies, and philosophies.

I explored many paths. One, the Western Christian, finally called me. Inwardly, as my interest grew, I found I knew much more than I thought. It was as if gifts, spontaneously accepted in earlier life, were seeds planted in the soul, which, if watered in the right way at the right time, could germinate into gifts of another kind.

Grace taught me much, not the least of which was that the human state and the striving native to it are universal and that the call, though it takes different forms, is always one: to realize the unity of creation, the nonduality of reality, and thereby to transfigure the world. I learned, too, especially in human relationships and above all in love, that if I become a question, if I shift from being an "I" to become a "who?," then experience begins the process of answering. It is a path from the monotony of the sameness of the ego to perpetually becoming "other," nonjudgmental, without boundaries, an open door. The way is unrestricted.

Having been called, one begins to call, and need only pay attention to the little prompting of one's heart and the apparently trivial events of the day to begin to receive the gift of a response. I called and Christ called me in return. He called first inwardly, then through scripture and tradition, until finally all of life was one great call.

Irresistibly, by choice, or by necessity of grief or gratitude, I was drawn into churches. In the often shabby, dusty darkness, prayer called on prayer. In the silence that wrapped the dark interior and muffled and made distant the voices and footsteps of others, a presence called. Mary stood in a small alcove at the back, her feet upon the moon, a star of crowns upon her head. Or she had her hands before her heart, palms touching, in an immaculate gesture of infinite compassion as in her appearance at Lourdes. Or she bore in her arms the infant Jesus, or in her lap, as in Michaelangelo's *Pietà*, her crucified son. She gestured toward me in an aura of prayer, illumined by the tiny, flickering flames of innumerable votive candles.

Kneeling at the prayer rail for the first time, it was her sweetness I recognized. It was not in the stone or the plaster, which were often quite ordinary. It was not physical at all, yet it was visible, like the invisible that surrounds and penetrates the edges of the beauty we see. She radiated waves of patience, selflessness, and a tender, loving humility. Suddenly I understood in a different way who Mary was and how she had given birth, not once, but again and again, and still. I felt my heart melt at her approach. Her gentleness seemed to answer my question. I understood why I had to walk in her footsteps, become like her, and like her give birth and more. An answering silence descended and thickened. Somewhere in the distance the faint praise sounds of an organ could be heard.

To Mary's right, also in a small alcove, stood a statue of Jesus. His arms were raised slightly in a welcoming gesture like an old friend not seen for many years. He seemed about to move toward me, but hesitated, as if waiting to be invited in. I experienced great closeness, but also distance. I realized that the distance was the lightning flash from my heart to his. His was open to me. Warmth and light streamed from it. He was risen, truly he was risen. What a paradox that this fallen world should be redeemed. Turning to the crucifix that hung above the altar, I understood why. Redemption, like creation, was continuous. Emmanuel meant what it said: "God with us." Jesus still hung on the Cross, as he was still being born. He was still teaching, healing, suffering, dying, uniting with the earth, rising, and ascending. He would do so to the end of the world. Life was nothing but that. We were nothing but that, called for nothing but that, while remaining imperfect creatures to become perfect, to become co-creators, co-sufferers, co-healers, co-redeemers.

Somewhere, in the bowels of the church, I could hear Mass beginning. A stranger, uncertain of the invitation, I joined a small group of worshippers, mostly older women, scattered in the pews. Without expectation, but inwardly quieted, willing to receive, the readings flowed through me like a cleansing stream. I felt a presence like an ocean of love. Now the priest was blessing the Eucharist. He held it up, saying, "Behold, the feast of the lamb, blessed are those who are called to his supper." The congregation responded: "Lord, I am not worthy to receive you, but only say the word and I shall be healed." Taking my place in line, I approached the host. Here was the whole perfection of the universe hidden in a tiny, white, almost tasteless wafer. If the creator of all, who was all, and united with the sufferings of all for their sake, could become so small as to enter into me, who was so thick with matter and dense with imperfection, then surely there was nothing that could not be penetrated, that was not already permeated.

We seek and we are found. We call and we are called. We give and we are given. We study, we form groups, we meditate. We pray. All this is good, but the heart of the matter lies elsewhere. There is only one universe, one search, one call, one love, one gift. Returning it in the form of the gift of ourselves, we recover not only what we have lost, but the seed of the world yet to come. Then the way is clear and simple. Chosen from the foundation of the world, we are called "to the praise of the glory of his grace."

Parabola
Volume: 1.3
Initiation

The Return

Luke 15:11–32

A certain man had two sons; and the younger of them said to his father, "Father, give me the portion of goods that falleth to me." And he divided unto them his living. And not many days after, the younger son gathered all together and took his journey into a far country, and there wasted his substance with riotous living.

And when he had spent all, there arose a mighty famine in that land; and he began to be in want. And he went and joined himself to a citizen of that country; and he sent him into his fields to feed swine. And he would fain have filled his belly with the husks that the swine did eat; and no man gave unto him.

And when he came to himself, he said, "How many hired servants of my father's have bread enough and to spare, and I perish with hunger! I will arise and go to my father, and say unto him, 'Father, I have sinned against heaven, and before thee, and am no more worthy to be called thy son; make me as one of thy hired servants.'"

And he arose, and came to his father.

But when he was yet a great way off, his father saw him, and had compassion, and ran and fell on his neck and kissed him. And the son said unto him,

"Father, I have sinned against heaven, and in thy sight, and am no more worthy to be called thy son."

But the father said to his servants, "Bring forth the best robe, and put it on him, and put a ring on his hand, and shoes on his feet. And bring hither the fatted calf, and kill it; and let us eat and be merry. For this my son was dead, and is alive again; he was lost, and is found."

And they began to be merry. Now his elder son was in the field, and as he came and drew nigh to the house, he heard music and dancing. And he called one of the servants and asked what these things meant. And he said unto him, "Thy brother is come; and thy father hath killed the fatted calf, because he hath received him safe and sound."

And he was angry, and would not go in. Therefore came his father out, and entreated him. And he, answering, said to his father,

"Lo, these many years do I serve thee, neither transgressed I at any time thy commandment, and yet thou never gavest me a kid, that I might make merry with my friends; but as soon as this thy son was come, which hath devoured thy living with harlots, thou hast killed for him the fatted calf."

And he said unto him, "Son, thou art ever with me, and all that I have is thine. It was meet that we should make merry and be glad, for this thy brother was dead, and is alive again; and was lost, and is found."

Parabola
Volume: 19.1
The Call

Winding the Golden String

Bede Griffiths

I give you the end of a golden string;
Only wind it into a ball,
It will lead you in at heaven's gate,
Built in Jerusalem's wall.

—*William Blake*

One day during my last term at school I walked out alone in the evening and heard the birds singing in that full chorus of song, which can only be heard at that time of the year at dawn or at sunset. I remember now the shock of surprise with which the sound broke on my ears. It seemed to me that I had never heard the birds singing before and I wondered whether they sang like this all the year round and I had never noticed it. As I walked on I came upon some hawthorn trees in full bloom and again I thought that I had never seen such a sight or experienced such sweetness before. If I had been brought suddenly among the trees of the Garden of Paradise and heard a choir of angels singing I could not have been more surprised. I came then to where the sun was setting over the playing fields. A lark rose suddenly from the ground beside the tree where I was standing and poured out its song above my head, and then sank still singing to rest. Everything then grew still as the sunset faded and the veil of dusk began to cover the earth. I remember now the feeling of awe which came over me. I felt inclined to kneel on the ground, as though I had been standing in the presence of an angel; and I hardly dared to look on the face of the sky, because it seemed as though it was but a veil before the face of God.

These are the words with which I tried many years later to express what I had experienced that evening, but no words can do more than suggest what it meant to me. It came to me quite suddenly, as it were out of the blue, and now that I look back on it, it seems to me that it was one of the decisive events of my life. Up to that time I had lived the life of a normal schoolboy, quite content with the world as I found it. Now I was suddenly made aware of another world of beauty and mystery such as I had never imagined to exist, except in poetry. It was as though I had begun to see and smell and hear for the first time. The world appeared to me as Wordsworth describes it with "the glory and the freshness of a dream." The sight of a wild rose growing on a hedge, the scent of lime tree blossoms caught suddenly as I rode down a hill on a bicycle, came to me like visitations from another world. But it was not only that my senses were awakened. I experienced an overwhelming emotion in the presence of nature, especially at evening. It began to wear a kind of sacramental character for me. I approached it with a sense of almost religious awe, and in the hush which comes before sunset, I felt again the presence of an unfathomable mystery. The song of the birds, the shapes of the trees, the colors of the sunset, were so many signs of this presence, which seemed to be drawing me to itself.

As time went on this kind of worship of nature began to take the place of any other religion. I would get up before dawn to hear the birds singing and stay out late at night to watch the stars appear, and my days were spent, whenever I was free, in long walks in the country. No religious service could compare with the effect which nature had upon me, and I had no religious faith which could influence me so deeply. I had begun to read the Romantic poets, Wordsworth, Shelley, and Keats, and I found in them the record of an experience like my own. They became my teachers and my guides, and I gradually gave up my adherence to any form of Christianity. The religion in which I had been brought up seemed to be empty and meaningless in comparison with that which I had found, and all my reading led me to believe that Christianity was a thing of the past.

An experience of this kind is probably not at all uncommon, especially in early youth. Something breaks suddenly into our lives and upsets their normal pattern, and we have to begin to adjust ourselves to a new kind of existence. This experience may come, as it came to me, through nature and poetry, or through art or music; or it may come through the adventure of flying or mountaineering, or of war; or it may come simply through falling in love, or through some apparent accident, an illness, the death of a friend, a sudden loss of fortune. Anything which breaks through the routine of daily life may be the bearer of this message to the soul. But however it may be, it is as though a veil has been lifted and we see for the first time behind the façade which the world has built round us. Suddenly we know that we belong to another world, that there is another dimension to existence. It is impossible to put what we have seen into words; it is something beyond all words which has been revealed.

There can be few people to whom such an experience does not come at some time, but it is easy to let it pass, and to lose its significance. The old habits of thought reassert themselves; our world returns to its normal appearance and the vision which we have seen fades away. But these are the moments when we really come face to face with reality; in the language of theology they are moments of grace. We see our life for a moment in its true perspective in relation to eternity. We are freed from the flux of time and see something of the eternal order which underlies it. We are no longer isolated individuals in conflict with our surroundings; we are parts of a whole, elements in a universal harmony.

This, as I understand it, is the "golden string" of Blake's poem. It is the grace which is given to every soul, hidden under the circumstances of our daily life, and easily lost if we choose not to attend to it. To follow up the vision which we have seen, to keep it in mind when we are thrown back again on the world, to live in its light and to shape our lives by its law, is to wind the string into a ball, and to find our way out of the labyrinth of life.

But this is no easy matter. It involves a readjustment to reality which is often a long and painful process. The first effect of such an experience is often to lead to the abandonment of all religion. Wordsworth himself was to spend many years in the struggle to bring his mystical experience into relation with orthodox Christianity and it may be doubted whether he was ever quite successful. But the experience is a challenge at the same time to work out one's religion for oneself. For most people today this has become almost a necessity. For many people the very idea of God has ceased to have any meaning. It is like the survival from a half-forgotten mythology. Before it can begin to have any meaning for them they have to experience his reality in their lives. They will not be converted by words or arguments, for God is not merely an idea or a concept in philosophy; he is the very ground of existence. We have to encounter him as a fact of our existence before we can really be persuaded to believe in him. To discover God is not to discover an idea but to discover oneself. It is to awake to that part of one's existence which has been hidden from sight and which one has refused to recognize. The discovery may be very painful; it is like going through a kind of death. But it is the one thing which makes life worth living.

I was led to make this discovery myself by the experience which I have recorded at school. This was the beginning for me of a long adventure which ended in a way for which nothing in my previous life had prepared me. If anyone had told me when I was at school or at Oxford that I should end my life as a monk, I would have doubted his sanity. I had no idea that any such thing as a monastery existed in the modern world, and the idea of it would have been without meaning to me. I have tried to show, however, that the steps which led to this revolution in my life, though they were in some way exceptional, nevertheless followed a logical course, and I hope therefore that they may be found to have more than a personal interest.

I was one of those who came of age in the period after the first world war, and I shared its sense of disillusionment at the apparent failure of our civilization. In an effort to escape from the situation in which we found ourselves I was led, with two Oxford friends, to make an attempt to "return to nature," and to get behind the industrial revolution. The attempt was, of course, in one sense, a failure, but it led to the unexpected result that I made the discovery of Christianity. I read the Bible seriously for the first time, and I found that the facts were quite different from what I had supposed and that Christianity was just as much a living power now as it had ever been. I then had to find a Church in which I could learn to practice my new-found faith, and after a long struggle, which cost me more than anything else in my life, I found my way to the Catholic Church. From that it was but a short step to the monastic life, and so by successive stages a radical change in my life was effected.

That search for God which began for me on that evening at school has gone on ever since. For the more one discovers of God, the more one finds one has to learn. Every step in advance is a return to the beginning, and we shall not really know him as he is, until we have returned to our beginning, and learned to know him as both the beginning and the end of our journey. We are all, like the Prodigal Son, seeking our home, waiting to hear the Father's voice say: "This my son was dead and is alive again; was lost and is found."

It is only now after thirty years that the full meaning of that which was revealed to me that day at school has become clear to me. That mysterious Presence which I felt in all the forms of nature has gradually disclosed itself as the infinite and eternal Being, of whose beauty all the forms of nature are but a passing reflection. Even when I was at school I had been fascinated by that passage of Plato in the Symposium, where he describes the soul's ascent on the path of love; how we should pass from the love of fair forms to the love of fair conduct, and from the love of fair conduct to the love of fair principles, until we finally come to the ultimate principle of all and learn what Beauty itself is. But I have learned what Plato could never have taught me, that the divine Beauty is not only truth but also Love, and the Love has come down from heaven and made his dwelling among men. I know now the meaning of St. Augustine's words, "O thou Beauty, so ancient and so new, too late have I loved thee, too late have I loved thee." I know now that God is present not only in the life of nature and in the mind of man, but in a still more wonderful way in the souls of those who have been formed in his image by his grace. I had sought him in the solitude of nature and in the labor of my mind, but I found him in the society of his Church and in the Spirit of Charity. And all this came to me not so much as a discovery but as a recognition. I felt that I had been wandering a far country and had returned home; that I had been dead and was alive again; that I had been lost and was found.

Reprinted from Bede Griffiths, *The Golden String* (Springfield, Ill.: Templegate Publishers, 1980), pp. 9–13, 16–17. Reprinted by permission of Templegate Publishers.

Parabola
Volume: 12.3
Forgiveness

To Whom Much Was Forgiven

Paul J. Tillich

One of the Pharisees asked him to eat with him, and he went into the Pharisee's house, and sat at table. And behold, a woman of the city, who was a sinner, when she learned that he was sitting at table in the Pharisee's house, brought an alabaster flask of ointment, and standing behind him at his feet, weeping, she began to wet his feet with her tears, and wiped them with the hair of her head, and kissed his feet, and anointed them with the ointment. Now when the Pharisee who had invited him saw it, he said to himself, "If this man were a prophet, he would have known who and what sort of woman this is who is touching him, for she is a sinner." And Jesus answering said to him, "Simon, I have something to say to you." And he answered, "What is it, Teacher?" "A certain creditor had two debtors; one owed five hundred denarii and the other fifty. When they could not pay, he forgave them both. Now which of them will love him more?" Simon answered, "The one, I suppose, to whom he forgave more." And he said to him, "You have judged rightly." Then turning toward the woman he said to Simon, "Do you see this woman? I entered

your house, you gave me no water for my feet, but she has wet my feet with her
tears and wiped them with her hair. You gave me no kiss, but from the time
I came in she has not ceased to kiss my feet. You did not anoint my head with
oil, but she has anointed my feet with ointment. Therefore, I tell you, her sins,
which are many, are forgiven, for she loved much; but he who is forgiven little,
loves little.”
—Luke 7:36–47

The story we have heard, like the parable of the prodigal son, is peculiar to the Gospel of Luke. In this story, as in the parable, someone who is considered to be a great sinner, by others as well as by herself, is contrasted with people who are considered to be genuinely righteous. In both cases Jesus is on the side of the sinner, and therefore he is criticized—indirectly in the parable, by the righteous elder son; and directly in our story, by the righteous Pharisee.

We should not diminish the significance of this attitude of Jesus by asserting that, after all, the sinners were not as sinful, nor the righteous as righteous, as they were judged to be by themselves and by others. Nothing like this is indicated in the story or in the parable. The sinners, one a whore and the other the companion of whores, are not excused by the ethical arguments which would remove the seriousness of the moral demand. They are not excused by the sociological explanations which would remove their personal responsibility; nor by an analysis of their unconscious motives which would remove the significance of their conscious decisions; nor by a statement of man's universal predicament which would remove their personal guilt. They are called sinners, simply and without restriction. This does not mean that Jesus and the New Testament writers are unaware of the psychological and sociological factors which determine human existence. They are keenly aware of the universal and inescapable dominion of sin over this world, of the demonic splits in the souls of people, which produce insanity and bodily destruction; of the economic and spiritual misery of the masses. But their awareness of these factors, which have become so decisive for *our* description of man's predicament, does not prevent them from calling the sinners sinners.

Understanding does not replace judging. ... In story and parable the sinners are seriously called sinners.

And in the same way the righteous ones are seriously called righteous. We would miss the spirit of our story if we tried to show that the righteous ones are not truly righteous. The elder son in the parable did what he was supposed to do. He does not feel that he has done anything wrong, nor does his father tell him so. His righteousness is not questioned, nor is the righteousness of Simon the Pharisee. His lack of love toward Jesus is not reproached as a lack of righteousness, but it is derived from the fact that little is forgiven to him.

Such righteousness is not easy to attain. Much self-control, hard discipline, and continuous self-observation are needed. Therefore, we should not despise the righteous ones. In the traditional Christian view the Pharisees have become representatives of everything evil, but in their time they were the pious and morally zealous ones. Their conflict with Jesus was not simply a conflict between right and wrong; it was, above all, the conflict between an old and sacred tradition and a new reality which was breaking into it and depriving it of ultimate significance. It was not only a moral conflict: it is also a tragic one, foreshadowing the tragic conflict between Christianity and Judaism in all succeeding generations, including our own. The Pharisees—and this we should not forget—were the guardians of the law of God in their time.

The Pharisees can be compared with other groups of righteous ones. We can compare them, for example, with a group that has played a tremendous role in the history of this country—the Puritans. The name itself, like the name Pharisee, indicates separation from the impurities of the world. The Puritans would certainly have judged the attitude of Jesus to the whore as Simon the Pharisee did. And we should not condemn them for this judgment nor distort their picture in our loose talk about them. Like the Pharisees, they were the guardians of the law of God in their time. ...

The sinners are seriously called sinners, and the righteous ones are seriously called righteous. Only if this is clearly seen can the depth and the revolutionary power of Jesus' attitude be understood. He takes the side of the sinner against the righteous although he does not doubt the validity of the law, the guardians of which the righteous are. Here we approach a mystery which is the mystery of the Christian message itself, in its paradoxical depth and in its shaking and liberating power. And we can hope only to catch a glimpse of it in attempting to interpret our story.

Simon the Pharisee is shocked by the attitude of Jesus to the whore. He receives the answer that the sinners have greater love than the righteous ones because more is forgiven them. It is *not* the love of the woman that brings her forgiveness, but it is the forgiveness she has received that creates her love. By her love she shows that much has been forgiven her, while the lack of love in the Pharisee shows that little has been forgiven him.

Jesus does not forgive the woman, but he declares that she *is* forgiven. Her state of mind, her ecstasy of love, show that something has happened to her. And nothing greater can happen to a human being than that he is forgiven. For forgiveness means reconciliation in spite of estrangement; it means reunion in spite of hostility; it means acceptance of those who are unacceptable; and it means reception of those who are rejected.

Forgiveness is unconditional, or it is not forgiveness at all. Forgiveness has the character of "in spite of," but the righteous ones give it the character of "because." The sinners, however, cannot do this. They cannot transform the divine "in spite of" into a human "because." They cannot show facts because of which they must be forgiven. God's forgiveness is unconditional. There is no condition whatsoever in man which would make him worthy of forgiveness. If forgiveness were conditional, conditioned by man, no one could be accepted, and no one could accept himself. We know that this is our situation, but we are loath to face it. It is too great as a gift and too humiliating as a judgment. We want to contribute something, and if we have learned that we cannot contribute anything positive, then we try at least to contribute something negative—the pain of self-accusation and self-rejection. And then we read our story and the parable of the prodigal son as if they said: These sinners were forgiven *because* they humiliated themselves and confessed that they were unacceptable; because they suffered about their sinful predicament, they were made worthy of forgiveness. But this reading of the story is a misreading, and a dangerous one. If that were the way to our reconciliation with God, we would have to produce within us the feeling of unworthiness, the pain of self-rejection, the anxiety and despair of guilt. There are many

Christians who try this in order to show God and themselves that they deserve acceptance. They perform an emotional work of self-punishment after they have realized that their other good works do not help them. But emotional works do not help either. God's forgiveness is independent of anything we do, even of self-accusation and self-humiliation. If this were not so, how could we ever be certain that our self-rejection is serious enough to deserve forgiveness? Forgiveness creates repentance: this is declared in our story, and this is the experience of those who have been forgiven.

The woman in Simon's house comes to Jesus because she was forgiven. We do not know exactly what drove her to Jesus. And if we knew, we would certainly find that it was a mixture of motives, spiritual desire as well as natural attraction, the power of the prophet as well as the impression of the human personality. Our story does not psychoanalyze the woman, but neither does it deny human motives which could be psychoanalyzed. Human motives are always ambiguous. The divine forgiveness cuts into these ambiguities, but it does not demand that they become unambiguous before forgiveness can be given. If this were demanded, then forgiveness would never occur. The description of the woman's behavior shows clearly the ambiguities of her motives. Nevertheless, she *is* accepted.

There is no condition for forgiveness. But forgiveness could not come to us if we were not asking for it and receiving it. Forgiveness is an answer, the divine answer, to the question implied in our existence. An answer is answer only for him who has asked, who is aware of the question. This awareness cannot be fabricated. It may be in a hidden place in our souls, covered by many strata of righteousness. It may reach our consciousness in certain moments. Or, day by day, it may fill our conscious life as well as its unconscious depths and drive us to the question to which forgiveness is the answer.

In the minds of many people the word "forgiveness" has connotations which completely contradict the way Jesus deals with the woman in our story. Many of us think of solemn acts of pardon, of release from punishment—in other words, of another act of righteousness by the righteous ones. But genuine forgiveness is participation, reunion overcoming the powers of estrangement. And only because this is so does forgiveness make love possible. We cannot love unless we have accepted forgiveness, and the deeper our experience of forgiveness is, the greater is our love. We cannot love where we feel rejected; even if the rejection is done in righteousness. We are hostile toward that to which we belong and by which we feel judged, even if the judgment is not expressed in words.

As long as we feel rejected by him, we cannot love God. He appears to us as an oppressive power, as he who gives laws according to his pleasure, who judges according to his commandments, who condemns according to his wrath. But if we have received and accepted the message that he *is* reconciled, everything changes. Like a fiery stream, his healing power enters into us, we can affirm him and, with him, our own being and the others from whom we were estranged, and life as a whole. Then we realize that his love is the law of our own being, and that is the law of reuniting love. And we understand that what we have experienced as oppression and judgment and wrath is in reality the working of love, which tries to destroy within us everything which is against love. To love this love is to love God. Theologians have questioned whether man is able to have love toward God; they have replaced love by obedience. But they are refuted by our story. They teach a theology for the righteous ones but not a theology for the sinners. He who is forgiven knows what it means to love God.

And he who loves God is also able to accept life and to love it. This is not the same as loving God. For many pious people in all generations the love of God is the other side of the hatred for life. And there is much hostility toward life in all of us, even in those who have completely surrendered to life. Our hostility toward life is manifested in cynicism and disgust, in bitterness and continuous accusations against life. We feel rejected by life, not so much because of its objective darkness and threats and horrors, but because of our estrangement from its power and meaning. He who is reunited with God, the creative Ground of life, the power of life in everything that lives, is reunited with life. He feels accepted by it and he can love it. He understands that love is greater, the greater the estrangement which is conquered by it. In metaphorical language, I would like to say to those who feel deeply their hostility toward life: Life accepts you; life loves you as a separated part of itself; life wants to reunite you with itself, even when it seems to destroy you.

There is a section of life which is nearer to us than any other and often the most estranged from us—other human beings. We all know about the regions of the human soul in which things look quite different from the way they look on its benevolent surface. In these regions we can find hidden hostilities against those with whom we are in love. We can find envy and torturing doubt about whether we are really accepted by them. And this hostility and anxiety about being rejected by those who are nearest to us can hide itself under the various forms of love: friendship, sensual love, conjugal and family love. But if we have experienced ultimate acceptance, this anxiety is conquered, though not removed. We can love without being sure of the answering love of the other one. For we know that he himself is longing for our acceptance as we are longing for his, and that in the light of ultimate acceptance we are united.

He who is accepted ultimately can also accept himself. Being forgiven and being able to accept oneself are one and the same thing. No one can accept himself who does not feel that he is accepted by the power of acceptance which is greater than he, greater than his friends and counselors and psychological helpers. They may point to the power of acceptance, and it is the function of the minister to do so. But he and the others also need the power of acceptance which is greater than they. The woman in our story could never have overcome her disgust at her own being without finding this power working through Jesus who told her with authority: "You *are* forgiven." Thus, she experienced, at least in *one* ecstatic moment of her life, the power which reunited her with herself and gave her the possibility of loving even her own destiny.

This happened to her in one great moment. And in this she is no exception. Decisive spiritual experiences have the character of a breakthrough. In the midst of our futile attempts to make ourselves worthy, in our despair about the inescapable failure of these attempts, we are suddenly grasped by the certainty that we are forgiven, and the fire of love begins to burn. That is the greatest experience anyone can have. It may not happen often, but when it does happen, it decides and transforms everything.

And now let us look once more at those whom we have described as the righteous ones. They are really righteous, but since little is forgiven them, they love little. And this is their unrighteousness. It does not lie on the moral level, just as the unrighteousness of Job did not lie on the moral level where his friends sought for it in vain. It lies on the level of the encounter with ultimate reality, with the God who vindicates Job's righteousness against the attacks of his friends, with the God who defends himself against the attacks of Job and his ultimate unrighteousness. The righteousness of the righteous ones is hard and self-assured. They too want forgiveness, but they believe that they do not need much of it. And so their righteous actions are warmed by very little love. They could not have helped the woman in our story, and they cannot help us, even if we admire them. Why do children turn from their righteous parents, and husbands from their righteous wives, and vice versa? Why do Christians turn away from their righteous pastors? … Why do people turn away from righteous Christianity and from the Jesus it paints and the God it proclaims? Why do they turn to those who are not considered to be the righteous ones? Often, certainly, it is because they want to escape judgment. But more often it is because they seek a love which is rooted in forgiveness, and this the righteous ones cannot give. Many of those to whom they turn cannot give it either. Jesus gave it to the woman who was utterly unacceptable. The Church would be more the Church of Christ than it is now if it did the same, if it joined Jesus and not Simon in its encounter with those who are rightly judged unacceptable. Each of us who strives for righteousness would be more righteous if more were forgiven him, if he loved more, and if he could better resist the temptation to present himself as acceptable to God by his own righteousness.

From *Best Sermons*, edited by G. Paul Butler (New York: McGraw-Hill, 1955). Reprinted by permission.

Parabola
Volume: 23.4
Birth and Rebirth

THE NIGHT JOURNEY OF NICODEMUS

Philip Zaleski

The words are magisterial, even harsh:

> *Verily, verily, I say unto thee, Except a man be*
> *born again, he cannot see the kingdom of God.*
> *—John 3:3*

Astonishing idea, to be born again! This cryptic teaching, given by Jesus in Jerusalem at the beginning of his ministry, bewilders Nicodemus, a pious Jew and member of the Sanhedrin, who has come to the celebrated Rabbi for guidance. Nicodemus has approached Jesus "by night": that is to say, in spiritual darkness, but as a seeker of the light ("If a man walk in the night, he stumbleth, because there is no light in him" John 11:10). Bewildered by Jesus' remarks, he blurts out his confusion, "How can a man be born when he is old? Can he enter the second time into his mother's womb, and be born?"

To these questions—epitomizing for all time the cry of the man in whom reason overrules the heart—Jesus answers in riddles and symbols:

> *Verily, verily I say unto thee, Except a man be*
> *born of water and of the Spirit, he cannot enter*
> *into the kingdom of God. That which is born of the*

flesh is flesh; and that which is born of the Spirit is spirit. Marvel not that I said unto thee, Ye must be born again. The wind bloweth where it listeth, and thou hearest the sound thereof, but canst not tell whence it cometh, and whither it goeth; so is every one that is born of the Spirit.

These words constitute the heart of Christian teaching on spiritual rebirth; indeed, it can be argued that they constitute the very essence of Christianity. For the night journey of Nicodemus, according to tradition, reveals the means for saying no to complacency, yes to self-struggle; no to evil, yes to good; no to ego, yes to God; no to darkness, yes to light, "the true Light, which lighteth every man that cometh into the world" (John 1:9). The passage teems with pun and paradox; thus "again," *anothen* in the original Greek, has a second meaning: "from above." To be born again is to be born from above, to receive divine life, to hear the call of God, and to be recast in His image and likeness. This rebirth, Christ emphasizes, is in "the Spirit," not in the flesh. On one level, of course, Christ is simply offering a corrective to Nicodemus' literal-minded understanding of rebirth; but there is a second meaning as well. For flesh signifies all that is bound by gravity, dead weight, ruled by desire and the ego. Against flesh stands the Spirit, giver of life, guardian of all that is ruled by truth and love.

This rebirth in the Spirit constitutes a radical transformation of the human being on every level. St. Paul describes it vividly in his letter to the Colossians:

Ye have put off the old man with his deeds; And have put on the new man, which is renewed in knowledge after the image of him that created him. ...

Put on therefore, as the elect of God, holy and beloved, bowels of mercies, kindness, humbleness of mind, meekness, longsuffering; Forbearing one another, and forgiving one another, if any man have a quarrel against any: even as Christ forgave you, so also do ye.

And above all these things, put on charity, which is the bond of perfectness. And let the peace of God rule in your hearts. ...
—Col. 3:9–10, 12–15

Who doesn't long to be so renewed, to live in mercy and meekness, charity and peace? But such dramatic change does not take place overnight. To be born "from above" is a more complicated matter than the transformation that overtakes Ebenezer Scrooge in *A Christmas Carol* or Jimmy Stewart in *It's a Wonderful Life*. There is much work to be done, and in order to grasp the nature of this work, it is necessary to understand that Christian tradition speaks not of one rebirth, but of two. One unfolds within church walls, the other in the labyrinth of the heart; one is common, the other rarer than gold; one freely given, the other fiercely won; one takes place under the sign of water, the other under the sign of fire.

There are, to my knowledge, no icons of Nicodemus, that enigmatic figure from the third chapter of John, no images that would help us to gauge his spiritual state. I picture a thin man with a long beard and sorrowful eyes, a man of little imagination but good heart. Let us envision Nicodemus returning home from his night journey to ponder the words of Christ. Perhaps he looks at his wife, children, possessions; perhaps he goes outside, lies upon a straw mat, and stares up at the stars. He recalls his victories and retreats, his kindnesses and cruelties; he turns within and weighs his life. To be born again. ...

Sooner or later, all men and women who awaken to the life of the spirit must engage in a similar self-examination. I trace the course of my life, its twistings and turnings, its peaks and valleys. I look long and hard; I see that a decision must be made. I must die to what I have been; I must begin anew. This special look, waxing and waning, may go on for years. Then at last something energizes the soul, and the first step, tentative and feeble, is taken towards "the light that enlightens everyone that comes into the world." The catalyst for this initial *metanoia* ("change of mind"), as it was known in the early Church, may be almost anything: a death in the family, a chance encounter, a brilliant sunset. A justly famous example comes to us from the life of St. Antony of the Desert, the fourth-century founder of Western monasticism. As a young man, Antony overheard, while praying in church, the following words of Christ read from the pulpit:

> *If thou wilt be perfect, go and sell that thou hast, and give to the poor, and thou shalt have treasure in heaven: and come and follow me.*
>
> *—Matthew 19:21*

"Immediately," reports Athanasius in his *Life of Antony*, written just four years after the saint's death in 356 C.E., the young man "went out from the Lord's house and gave to the townspeople the possessions he had … and devoted himself from then on to the discipline";[1] that is to say, to an intense life of study, prayer, and psycho-physical exercises in search of God. Antony's conversion may be dramatic, but from its earliest days, the Church recognized the revolutionary nature of this metanoia and sanctified it with the sacrament of baptism. Frithjof Schuon speaks of "the essentially initiatory character of Christianity"; baptism is the Christian initiation par excellence. Recall Jesus' words to Nicodemus: "Except a man be born of water and of the Spirit, he cannot enter the kingdom of heaven." Here Jesus proclaims water to be the physical analog or manifestation of Spirit, in accordance with Biblical tradition: in the Book of Jeremiah, God defines Himself as "the fountain of living waters," while in Revelations, a "pure river of water of life, clear as crystal," flows out of the throne of God. Even evolutionary biology declares water to be the womb of life. Jesus' baptism in the Jordan River signifies his self-emptying, his submission to the Spirit; just so, immersion of the spiritual acolyte (or "catechumen") into a pool of holy water has always been the mark of spiritual renewal and rebirth, of death and resurrection through Christ. The profound significance of these "awe-inspiring rites," as St. John Chrysostom termed them, can be discerned in St. Paul's declaration that "we are buried with him by baptism into death … as Christ was raised up from the dead by the glory of the Father, even so we also should walk in newness of life" (Romans 6:4), and in St. Justin's contention, a few centuries later, that "this bath is called *enlightenment*, because those who receive [it] are enlightened in their understanding."

Nowadays, infant baptism is the norm. Whether one reads the sacramental regeneration of those too young to understand what is happening to them as inspired solicitude or as a tragic loss of meaning, there is no doubt that one result has been the suppression, if not the obliteration, of the initiatory aspects of this ritual process. To understand baptism fully, one must study it as it was practiced in the early Church, when the first rebirth involved a complex initiatory process that took months to reach its culmination in the waters of renewal.

As practiced in the fourth or fifth centuries C.E., Christian initiation was too intricate to be described here in detail. It abounded in symbolic gestures, many carrying hidden meanings known only to the initiated. Two examples will suffice: Soon after beginning his training, the catechumen received a handful of salt to signify his search for truth, in accordance with Jesus' teaching that "ye are the salt of the earth," elaborated by the sixth-century writer John the Deacon in his comment that "the mind, sodden and soft as it is from the waves of the world, is seasoned by the salt of wisdom and of the preaching of the word of God."[2] Again, one of the most important stages in Christian initiation was the *Apertio* or "Opening," during which the bishop anointed the catechumen's eyes, ears, and nostrils, preparing these sensory organs to receive spiritual impressions, divine truths ("He who has ears, let him hear").

In time, the catechumen was deemed ready to receive the esoteric truths of the Tradition, known in ancient times as the *Disciplina Arcani.* That such secret teachings existed and were passed from teacher to pupil in initiatory rites may surprise modern readers, but the evidence is beyond dispute. The imprimatur for post-Apostolic hermeticism comes from Christ's saying that "Unto you it is given to know the mystery of the kingdom of God; but unto them that are without, all these things are done in parables." A passage from Dionysius the Areopagite offers one reason for this secrecy:

> *The things that are bestowed uniformly and all at once, so to speak, on the Blessed Essences dwelling in Heaven, are transmitted to us as it were in fragments. ... Since these truths had to be translated into the usages of the Church, the Apostles expressed them under the veil of symbols and not in their sublime nakedness, for not everyone is holy, and, as the Scriptures say, Knowledge is not for all.*[3]

One must be prepared to receive the mysteries; to approach them unprepared is to cheapen both them and oneself. Moreover, one whose senses have not been exalted through the *Apertio* or other divine rites will never be able to distinguish ambrosia or nectar from ordinary, earthly foods.

Initiation into the Christian mysteries began during Lent. These secret teachings included much that is now broadcast indiscriminately, including the text of the Creed and the Lord's Prayer, as well as their inner meaning. The transmission of these sacred formulae was known as the *Traditio Symboli* ("Handing over of the Creed"); the candidates, after proper contemplation of these mysteries, had to recite their contents in a ceremony entitled the *Redditio Symboli* ("Giving back of the Creed"). If practiced faithfully and attentively, this arduous routine of memorization and recitation instilled the truths of the tradition into one's innermost being. The process took months, under the tutelage of a spiritual adept (an office still found here and there in the Orthodox Church, in the person of the *staretz*). The climax of the first rebirth came with the Easter immersion of the catechumen into the baptismal font, an event that Dionysius the Areopagite called "initiation to theogenesis"—that is to say, "initiation into the generation of God," the beginning of divinization, the transformation of the individual from a man into a god-man.

In the Byzantine Museum in Athens hangs an icon, tempera on wood, by the sixteenth-century master Michael Damaskinos, of St. Antony of the Desert. In keeping with the hagiographic iconography of the era, Antony's eyes are sad but serene, gazing beyond the viewer into eternity; his brows and cheeks are gouged with wrinkles, marks of spiritual combat; his nose is elongated, indicating his sensitivity to spiritual aromas. Behind him shimmers a golden backdrop, suggesting both the brilliance of sanctity and the duskiness of the desert where he lived for most of his life. Antony's expression is composed, benevolent, tinged with sadness: here is a man who has taken the measure of himself and the world, a man who embodies the fundamental Christian teachings of birth and rebirth.

The spiritual accuracy of Damaskinos's portrait is confirmed by Athanasius' *Life of Antony*. Here we read that, after hearing Christ's call to "come and follow me," Antony strode into the Egyptian desert, where he retreated into an abandoned tomb for twenty years of inner work. After this extraordinary gestation, he emerged reborn:

> *Antony came forth as though from some shrine, having been led into divine mysteries and inspired by God. … The state of his soul was one of purity, for it was not constricted by grief, nor relaxed by pleasure, nor affected by either laughter or dejection. Moreover, when he saw the crowd, he was not annoyed any more than he was elated at being embraced by so many people. He maintained utter equilibrium, like one guided by reason and steadfast in that which accords with nature.*[4]

This tranquillity, Athanasius makes clear, was not easily won. For twenty years Antony engaged in what we may call the second rebirth, under the sign of fire. This second rebirth is not a one-time affair, but rather a continual movement of the heart away from self-love and toward love of God. Christ's injunction, it's worth noting, is not "come to me" but rather "come and follow me"; one cannot escape the labor, travel, lifetime of effort contained in that concluding phrase. The second rebirth never ends; even while preparing for death, Antony "departed from the monks in the outer mountain" and "entered the inner mountain." His journey was ever inward, toward his true self, toward Christ.

The second rebirth stands under the sign of fire for it is a continual purgation, a refining in the furnace—or the desert—of self-struggle and self-sacrifice. Immediately after his own baptism, Jesus was "led by the Spirit" into the desert, where Satan tempted him for forty days. The three famous temptations—that Jesus turn stone into bread, that he worship Satan in return for the kingship of the world, and that he cast himself from a pinnacle and be saved by angels—represent the three universal temptations of greed, power, and pride, answerable only by the three virtues of poverty, obedience, and humility. We are all heirs to these ancient temptations; we all must enter the desert—a sojourn that may last a lifetime, as it did for Antony, and that may demand more struggle and suffering than we bargained for.

The fourteenth-century Orthodox monks Callistus and Ignatius, of Xanthopoulos, in their *Directions to Hesychasts, in a Hundred Chapters,* write of the second rebirth: "Have you understood the travail of our complete spiritual regeneration after we leave the holy font [of baptism]? … Do you see how much it lies in our power to increase or to diminish this supernatural grace, that is, to show it forth or to obscure it?"[5] According to Christian tradition, nothing erases the mark of the first rebirth, for baptism "imprints on the soul an indelible spiritual sign" (*Catechism of the Catholic Church*). But the second rebirth is necessary to allow this sign to shine forth, to ensure that it not be buried under our pettiness and self-love.

In ancient Christian writings, the process of the second rebirth is often likened to ascending a ladder. Like an ordinary ladder, one's risk increases as one ascends—the Tradition emphasizes that no one fell further than Satan, once the most glorious of angels—yet it is a paradoxical ladder as well, for the more one lowers oneself, through humility, obedience, and poverty, the higher one climbs, until finally, as Christ explained, "he who is last shall be first." The process entails more than the acquisition of knowledge about oneself and the world, although that is essential. Eventually, a transformation in being takes place, which the ancients called *theopoesis*, or deification. This change is effected from above—that is to say, one is reborn from above. All the exercises of spiritual combat, lasting a lifetime, prepare the ground for a metanoia so radical that finally one is no longer what one was; one is now an aspect of God, in the classic words of St. Paul: "For I through the law am dead to the law. … I live, yet not I, but Christ liveth in me" (Gal. 2:19–20).

And how does one ascend this ladder? Perhaps the best manual to the second rebirth remains the *Philokalia*, a collection of texts composed between the fourth and sixteenth centuries and compiled about two hundred years ago, fittingly enough, by St. Nicodemus of the Holy Mountain, the most venerated namesake of our Biblical Nicodemus. The complete *Philokalia* is being translated into English as I write; the first four volumes, now available, offer an extraordinary abundance of spiritual exercises and insights. One hesitates to summarize, but it can perhaps be said that the keynotes are the acquisition, in the spiritual aspirant, of attention, discrimination, and stillness. One must learn to see, to assess, and to absorb. These verbs suggest contemplation rather than action.

In his talk with Nicodemus, Jesus commented that "the wind bloweth where it listeth." Wind here doubles as Spirit (the Greek *pneuma* carrying both meanings). The Spirit "listeth," a lovely archaism derived from the Indo-European *las*, or "eager," a root that also gives rise to "lust." The Spirit hungers for our enlightenment. The Spirit is the active principle, we the passive; our job is to be prepared to receive the Spirit when it comes ("But as many as received him, to them gave he power to become the sons of God," John 1:12).

And what of Nicodemus, with whom we began? Did he heed the words of Jesus, did he undergo the first and second rebirths? After his night journey, he appears twice more in the Gospel of John. In a cameo appearance in chapter seven, he urges the temple priests to give Jesus a hearing before judging his mission. Far more significant is Nicodemus's final appearance in chapter nineteen. Jesus has been crucified and his body removed from the cross by Joseph of Arimathea. Then Nicodemus arrives with "a mixture of myrrh and aloes, about a hundred pound weight." Together, he and Joseph sprinkle the body with spices, wrap it in linen cloths, and lay it in the Holy Sepulchre—the final act in the New Testament before the Resurrection. The spices brought by Nicodemus carry great symbolic weight: myrrh is the first spice mentioned by God in his instructions to Moses in Exodus 30:23 to anoint the tabernacle and the ark, and it is the chief constituent in what the Psalmist calls "the oil of gladness" (Psalm 45:7–8). Aloe, too, comprises part of this oil of gladness. Nicodemus bears, literally, the weight of Christ's body upon his shoulders; he has advanced far enough to be able to anoint, or bless, Christ with the sacred herbs. It would seem that Nicodemus has indeed heeded the words of Christ, that he has been reborn from above. He thus stands as an example to us all, demonstrating that the smallest approach to Truth, uttered in the darkness of confusion, can lead in time to spiritual rebirth.

Notes:

1   Athanasius, *The Life of Antony*, translated by Robert C. Gregg (New York: Paulist Press, 1980), pp. 31–32.

2   Quoted in Edward Yarnold, S. J., *The Awe-Inspiring Rites of Initiation* (Slough: St. Paul Publications, 1971), p. 6. The author of this article is greatly indebted to Fr. Yarnold's study, a key source for anyone studying the early Christian mysteries.

3   Quoted in Frithjof Schuon, *The Transcendent Unity of Religions* (New York: Pantheon, 1953), pp. 155–156.

4   Athanasius, *The Life of Antony*, p. 42.

5   Quoted in *Writings from the Philokalia on Prayer of the Heart*, translated by E. Kadloubovsky and G. E. H. Palmer (London: Faber and Faber, 1951), p. 167.

•

CHAPTER TWO

The Search for the Self

I am the way, the truth, and the life.[1]

—John 14:6

Lord! Teach me to seek thee and show thyself to me as I seek: for I cannot seek thee unless thou teach me, nor find thee unless thou show thyself.[2]

—St. Anselm

Parabola
Volume: 19.4
Hidden Treasure

Am I the Innkeeper?

Richard Temple

It is said that truth can only be given in the form of a lie. A lie, in this case, means not a falsehood, but an artificial arrangement of ideas that seems to mean one thing while, for certain people, it may also mean something else. By combining pictorial elements in a certain way, such as images and colors in a certain sequence, associations can be created in the mind of the beholder. From there, discoveries of hidden treasure within the paintings can be made, but not by the ordinary mind whose thought process actually belongs to the senses. This kind of knowledge limits us to literalism and rationalism. It is the mentality of "seeing is believing" and could never lead us to what lies beyond the wall.

Access to hidden knowledge can only be gained through initiation in a school. In ancient times schools for the study of higher knowledge were sometimes concealed within schools of art and architecture. Medieval religious art in Europe was rich in such traditions, as we can see in the art of Hieronymous Bosch. A successor to the tradition was the Northern Renaissance master Pieter Brueghel the Elder. Brueghel's masterpiece, *The Numbering at Bethlehem*, was painted in 1566 and can be seen today at the Beaux Arts Museum in Brussels.

The painting shows, apparently, a typical event from contemporary Flemish village life. A tax official has set up his desk at a prominent inn where a green wreath is displayed. A number of peasants are already formed in a disorderly crowd around him while others, singly or in groups of two or three, arrive from further afield. The season is winter, and in the snow and on the frozen river, villagers and children are snowballing, skating, and tobogganing.

Other details depict events of everyday life. We see that outside another inn a fire has been lit, possibly as a counter attraction to the tax office at the rival establishment. A group of peasants crowd around it warming themselves. At the principal inn a delivery of wine is being made and two great barrels on carts are parked in front. The innkeeper expertly slaughters a pig for roasting while his wife, holding out a pan to catch its blood, instinctively flinches from the act of butchery.

There are other random details: a woodsman unloads a tree trunk from his cart, organizing his strength under its weight; a tiny child asserts his influence over a couple of geese by waving his arms; a man in a red cap leans out of a window to close the shutters; a woman sweeps a path through the snow; a crow perches on the top of a leafless tree. Oblivious of all the bustle and activity, three chickens peck away in the snow. It is evening and through the branches of the tree we see that the sun has already begun to set.

In the foreground, approaching the crowd around the inn, is a family group. The man is on foot while after him comes an ox and a young woman wrapped in a shawl riding on a donkey. They are integrated into the composition so as to pass unnoticed. They do not appear, at first, to have any special significance.

In the background are, on one side, a ruined castle and, on the other, a church.

The picture compels our interest; we feel there must be some purpose, some overall plan, in the arrangement of the various elements and details. For instance, the attitudes and gestures of the peasants grouped around the tax office express a grim and lively observation of human nature. We see ignorance, greed, stupidity and doubt; we see vanity and self-importance, flattery and folly; we see people's childlike simplicity, their inability to change their lot or to see beyond the ends of their noses.

In depicting character, Brueghel shows the psychology of humanity in all its common aspects. The painting can be seen as an allegory of human life and its one hundred and fifty figures, in the sum total of their behavior, represent all people. It shows the human struggle against nature, striving to gratify immediate physical needs for warmth, food, shelter, money. Life here means material life, the level of worldly values; it is the everyday life that we all know.

In the background of the picture is a ruined castle: a symbol of emptiness. It is usually interpreted as a reference to the destructive and oppressive forces of the Spanish military occupation of the Netherlands; at the same time it may have another more psychological meaning. In medieval country life, the local castle played an important part in the mind of the peasants, signifying security in contrast to the precarious conditions of the life of ordinary people. The castle offered protection in times of war and food in times of want; its lord owned the land on which the villagers worked and could influence the individual direction of anyone's life. Thus, both actually and symbolically, the castle stood as a bastion of strength, security, and authority. But now the castle is in ruins, destroyed by man's folly and greed, and the people are leaderless, with no one to direct their lives, with no immediate discipline and authority.

It is interesting to see how Brueghel depicts the innkeeper. We do not see his face, but his attitude expresses his character. He is a man with a grasp on life. He and his wife and their two sturdy children are comparatively well dressed; he is probably something of a disciplinarian and certainly commands their respect if not fear. He runs a thriving business and we see him at a peak moment of trade with a great number of customers to keep satisfied. Probably he has some deal arranged with the tax officials for the increase in business they bring: perhaps a percentage of the takings and free bed and board while they are there. We know from the testimony of the gospels that all the rooms are let on this particular night.

So, yes, certainly we can say he knows his business; he is up to every trick in the book, not what you would call dishonest, just very capable of looking after himself. In fact, he is good at his job. We can imagine what sort of place he has: well run, clean and with good service. And yet this man, so much a man of the world, a good citizen, a good father, an honest tradesman, misses the greatest opportunity of his life; the greatest opportunity ever offered to an innkeeper in all history.

On this scenario of the human condition, the sun sets. It is the end of the day, the last day of the ancient order. In a few hours the greatest drama in history will begin. When the sun rises tomorrow, it will be the dawn of a new era. All nature is hushed as if holding its breath to see if anyone will notice, if anyone will turn or even glance up for a second. The sun, the earth, and all the planets, including a new star to be seen for the first time tonight, align themselves in readiness for the great event of which only humanity is oblivious.

The moment passes, and no one, neither the innkeeper nor anyone else, is aware of it. People are oblivious because they are intent on the immediate moment to which they give themselves up entirely. They are the blind slaves of circumstances that dictate life but which cannot be questioned.

The perennial truths about humanity's fall and search for redemption, and the questions to which they relate, are outside time. Brueghel succeeds in bringing us this perennial vision because, in the picture, time has stopped: suddenly and at an unexpected moment with everyone frozen into the attitude held at that moment. It gives Brueghel—and us—an opportunity to see people exactly as they are. It has the effect of reminding us that the situation is a constant one and that the problem it reveals is as relevant today as it was on the first Christmas Eve. In other words, by updating the environment of the first Christmas Eve, Brueghel makes it contemporary and relevant for us as a real and personal question and not just a historical event. We have to ask ourselves: *am I the innkeeper?*

Bethlehem and its inhabitants can be interpreted as standing for contemporary humanity and, since each one of us typifies humanity, it can be thought of as a representation of ourselves: all the different figures in the picture represent our own characteristics. None of us is free from the doubt, vanity, self-importance and so on that are portrayed here. All these characteristics are to be found in the multiplicity of our own nature and they are capable of breaking out at any time. We try to hide this of course, from ourselves as well as from others, but if we seek reality, we need to face this truth.

In occult and traditional sacred literature, a city, such as Jerusalem, or a town, such as Bethlehem, are symbols for a person, its inhabitants denoting different sides of his or her character. On a later occasion Christ will enter the city of Jerusalem in triumph; here Christ, or the idea of the "Christ within" arrives not in triumph but unnoticed. The people do not see what is in their midst.

An effective and mysterious element is the man in a red cap closing the shutter of his window. This cannot be an incidental detail; the moment is too powerful. There is something about the half-seen figure and the mystery of the darkened room behind him that fills us with curiosity. There is intent and purpose in the gesture with which he shuts himself into darkness at the approaching sacred event.

The carts with hogsheads of wine occupy a central place in the composition and we shall see that what they symbolize is also central to the painting's hidden meaning. In Germany and Flanders there still exists the ancient custom of decorating the wine houses with green branches for the festival of new wine which occurs in December. This is almost certainly the explanation of the green wreath outside the inn. The arrival of the new wine, in itself quite an event, may be a symbol for the arrival of the new testament. In this connection it is interesting to remember that the first of Christ's miracles is the changing of water into wine at the marriage feast at Cana, thus establishing himself at the outset of his ministry as the higher truth.

The figure of Mary is in contrast to everything else in the picture. Her presence reflects the stillness of the evening, and the idea of what she represents, what she holds within her, adds an altogether new dimension to the whole scene. She appears in the world as the bringer of a reality whose origin issues from a point in the cosmos beyond the one where humanity exists. Yet this possibility exists in life at all times; that is why the literal understanding of time is suspended here. What happened "then" is also happening "now" and "now" always exists. •

Nobody sees her; indeed almost everyone's back is turned to her. All are engaged in individual activity, oblivious of anything else. Only in the movements of the little donkey on which she sits and the gentle ox that accompanies them do we sense an atmosphere that corresponds to her modesty and stillness.

Even Joseph has his back to Mary. Joseph's position in the Nativity is a difficult one to occupy. We recognize his type: he intends well but seems uncomprehending. He is full of movement, agitated, fussing, responsible, and yet ineffectual as his group approaches the full, round swollen shapes of the wine barrels whose rich pregnancy echoes that other, richer pregnancy.

I have found that other paintings by Brueghel (*The Harvesters, The Fall of Icarus, The Adoration of the Kings*) evoke in me similar intuitions. Others will not necessarily find exactly the same meanings. But I am sure that, beyond our individual associations, beyond the small scale of our subjectivity, there lies universal truth. Brueghel makes his vision available to everyone. He brings us treasure, hiding it perhaps from the surface mind with its ceaseless preoccupations, but not from the heart.

Parabola
Volume: 15.1
Time and Presence

AWAKENING TO THE PRESENT

Interview with Father Thomas Keating

Father Thomas Keating is a monk of the Cistercian order at St. Benedict's Monastery in Snowmass, Colorado. He is best known as an advocate of centering prayer, a personal practice of contemplative silence through the use of a sacred word (such as "God," "Jesus," "peace," "silence," "open," or "presence") or a sacred image (such as resting in the arms of God). Unlike a mantra, the word or image is not repeated continuously, but is more of a focal point to which to return when the ordinary clamor of thoughts becomes insistent.

*Father Keating is also the author of several books, includ-*ing The Mystery of Christ *and* Open Mind, Open Heart *(Amity House). In the mid-1980s he founded Contemplative Outreach, a program to offer information about the contemplative life to all Christians, not just those in monastic orders, through intensive centering prayer retreats at Snowmass and ongoing programs at affiliated regional centers. One such center is Chrysalis House, near the village of Warwick, New York, in the wooded hill country about fifty miles northwest* *of New York City, where this interview took place on an Indian summer afternoon in late October.*

—*Cynthia Bourgeault*

Cynthia Bourgeault: *You've talked in your book,* The Mystery of Christ, *about living in two kinds of time, ordinary time and eternal time. Can you tell us what you mean by these two times?*

Father Thomas Keating: Eternal time implies the values of eternity, which transcend ordinary time, breaking into linear time. Besides the three-dimensional world of time and space, there is the *source* of it that is always present, too, as the chief aspect of every reality. And its values are totally encompassing and embrace all time as if in an eternal embrace. So all of eternity is present in each moment of time for the person or seeker who has interiorized those values.

CB: The moment itself takes place in chronological time?

TK: Yes, chronological time keeps moving. Now in this context you could also conceive of it as circular time. Chronological time is a favorite view of the Western world; circular time, which is perhaps closer to the natural cycles, is more in honor in the Eastern religions. But in either case—whether you conceive of it as circular or linear, going toward an end point—eternal time, since it transcends the space/time continuum, is present in every moment. And this is what makes every moment of ordinary time extraordinary.

CB: *We don't seem to* feel *it as extraordinary very often.*

TK: That's because our perception of it is ordinary, meaning nothing is happening. But in actual fact, everything is happening in every moment—

CB: *—if we could only wake up to it?*

TK: That's what awakening really is. It's awakening to the full value of each moment of time, as penetrated by eternal values. And along with eternity, of course, go all the intuitive and unitive values of oneness that are covered over by the perception of categories and divisions on the mental-egoic, or rational, levels—especially in cultures cut off from their contemplative traditions and roots. At a deeper or higher, or what I prefer to call a more *centered* level, a movement toward our own center is really a movement toward everybody's center, which is the oneness of the ultimate unifying source of all creation. In other words, individuals are bound together by a unifying force which is present but not normally perceived, given the human condition, without the discipline of a practice that penetrates the mystery of ordinary time.

CB: *Are you speaking only of our present Western culture here, or of the human predicament?*

TK: The human predicament. All world religions seem to agree that our present state of evolutionary consciousness is a mess. We suffer from illusion—not knowing what true happiness is—and from concupiscence, which is a desire for the wrong things, or too much of the good things. And then if we ever discover the path to true happiness, our will or energy is too weak to pursue it anyway. This is classically what Christians mean by "the consequences of original sin," but in Hinduism you have *maya*—the same basic understanding that something is radically missing or wrong with the present state of consciousness that everybody, the human family, seems to have. Some religions depict this by the story of a fall from some happier or grace-filled state. So in the desperate need to find happiness which seems to be deeply rooted in every human being, we begin to develop emotional programs to shore up the fragile ego, to compensate for the happiness we can no longer find in the intimate experience of the source of our life. When a sense of connection to that source has been lost, almost anything seems better than to endure the emptiness, boredom, alienation—perhaps existential dread—that goes with feeling one's sense of isolation in a potentially hostile universe.

CB: *Isn't there some part of us which actively resists this reconnecting? Is there something in us that clings to our usual sense of time? Do we have to fight our way down to the unitive source?*

TK: I would think that it's usually experienced that way. That's why you get images in the different traditions of the warrior, or the spiritual combat—because it *is* a war. The false sense does not just drop dead on request; it's very firmly grounded in the subconscious—so much so that even when we buy into the spiritual journey and its values consciously, the false self just laughs at them and keeps right on going. And hence one experiences this battle between what one wants to do and what one actually does, still under the influence of the unconscious. So the heart of the *ascesis*, really, is in trying to dismantle the unconscious values, and these do not change unless you go after them deliberately. That's why you can have people in religious circles or on the spiritual journey who have given up all kinds of things and have changed to a new lifestyle, but unless you ask the false self to change, nothing really changes. It's the same worldliness under perhaps a more respectable façade.

CB: *So what's needed is a change in attitude.*

TK: Yes, and this is hard to come by, because the false self is so firmly in place when we begin to be self-conscious. And so its influence in our lives is extremely powerful and subtle unless we directly confront it and try to dismantle it—unless, as the Buddhists say, we "try to develop a mind that clings to nothing."

CB: *Earlier you spoke of the need for "the discipline of a practice that penetrates the mystery of ordinary time." Were you thinking specifically of centering prayer here?*

TK: Centering prayer is a method to introduce the dynamic of contemplation in the Christian tradition. By bracketing, so to speak, the ordinary flow of thoughts for a designated period of time in order to seek God at the intuitive level, it gives the practitioner a rest from the usual flow of thoughts which tend to reinforce or strengthen the objects of desire of the false self system. So it's a way of beginning to wake up to the eternal values that were always there but just drowned out by this racket of restless desires and desperate needs.

CB: *I wonder if this doesn't exist in almost every tradition, this stilling and stopping in the present moment.*

TK: It's essential in every tradition in some form, and there are a variety of forms to reach it. By the very act of letting go of the usual flow of thoughts during a regularly repeated time of prayer, one is experiencing some silence, some solitude, a certain simplicity in one's life, and a discipline of prayer. In every tradition these are the four ingredients of a contemplative lifestyle, and in actual fact they have a certain spontaneous capacity to express themselves in a change in daily life by accessing a level of rest, of well-being, that is deeper than ordinary sleep. But in the Christian tradition one has a personal relationship with Christ or with God. One is praying not just for an experience of rest, but to deepen one's relationship with God, which in turn prepares one to be able to face the dark side of the unconscious. Unless we are inwardly translating that experience of rest into practice and an inner freedom, then the experience is simply a high-class tranquilizer.

CB: *Does this, in turn, have anything to do with Saint Paul's injunction to "pray without ceasing?"*

TK: The real meaning of praying without ceasing, it seems to me, is that the divine presence or eternal values in the present moment begin to become more transparent; they become a kind of fourth dimension of the three-dimensional world. The awareness of God's presence at the subtlest level of all realities begins to be a kind of spontaneous addition to ordinary awareness, not through a thought or through any effort of ours at the time, but simply because it's there, and our capacity to perceive it has awakened through progress in contemplative prayer. Accessing the divine presence within ourselves seems to unlock the capacity to perceive it in all events, however opaque they may seem to the ordinary human perceptions. So to pray without ceasing is to be aware of the divine presence all the time as a spontaneous part of all reality.

CB: *So far we've spoken of contemplative prayer as an individual's personal relationship to God. Isn't there a similarity in the way that a religious com-*

munity as a group can make that relationship through liturgy, particularly the Eucharist?

TK: Oh, absolutely. Perhaps for most of us it is regular participation in worship that puts us in touch with eternal values on a regular, recurring basis. In the Old Testament the Sabbath seems to have had this purpose in view, and the Sunday for Christians is simply another way of celebrating a kind of peak moment in ordinary time in which the access to eternal time is particularly strong, usually because of the congregation of worshipping individuals who are trying to be in touch with divine energy.

CB: *Is liturgy for the community, or is it also for the individual? And what does it give the individual that contemplative prayer couldn't?*

TK: Fortunately, they have a friendly relationship, so that any growth in one is a growth in the other and they tend to reinforce each other; in other words, the best preparation for Eucharist is a deepening contemplative attitude. And actually contemplation is itself a social event because it's a real participation in the interior passion and death of Christ, which is the paradigm of what's going on within us. In other words, we, too, are experiencing the death of the false self, which Christians believe is what's meant by Christ taking on the human condition, becoming flesh. Flesh means the human condition in its fallen state, and this is what we believe the Son of God has taken on himself.

CB: *Can you say a little more about the liturgical year—how that deepens and expands the various moments of the liturgy on a regular, cyclic basis?*

TK: Each moment of time, obviously, is fairly brief, at least from our perspective. So even though the whole of the mystery of Christ is contained in one Eucharist, it helps if you can "open the package" somewhat and separate the parts so as to concentrate on one aspect of this living and dynamic mystery which can be totally communicated in one moment but, given the human faculties, can be much better assimilated by a gradual initiation into each mystery as it appears in a cycle.

Depending on where you are in your own process, you are also going to perceive in the liturgy and identify with one process more than another because that's the one that's going on in you at this time. When that mystery recycles, it deepens awareness. Eventually you have integrated or assimilated them all, and then you *become* the word of God; in other words, you've heard it now at ever-deepening levels. Ultimately, the gospel is addressed to our inmost being and really hasn't been heard until that final level has been engaged. And then all the other levels become awakened and enriched because once it has reached the center and penetrated the mystery, all the symbols become more transparent and all other forms of prayer are enriched without one depending on them as a substitute for the mystery itself.

There's a marvelous wisdom in the liturgical year which teaches the whole of spiritual theology in a practical, dramatized way. Only unlike any other kind of drama, you're not just watching it—you are in the drama and the drama is in you. Thus in the drama of the death and resurrection of Christ, first comes the purification that Lent represents: a confrontation with the false self in order to dismantle it, with the help of grace.

After Lent, one has been purified to enter into the Easter and Pentecost mysteries, which are resurrection experiences of the fruit of having been freed from some degree of our false self through the Lenten practice. And year by year as this goes on, one is celebrating in the liturgy one's interior experience both of purification and resurrection.

Pentecost celebrates the completion of the cycle. Pentecost is the fullness of the Holy Spirit, the full illumination of the Pentecostal grace, which is to see reality from the perspective of divine wisdom, which is love. And remember that the liturgical year reads the gospel in the light of Pentecost, not in the light of the synoptic Gospels themselves.

CB: *But doesn't the liturgical calendar use the phrase "ordinary time" for the period between Pentecost and Advent?*

TK: Yes, that's what it's called. But all time is extraordinary when seen from the perspective of the Spirit.

CB: *But just as we lose or ignore the importance of ordinary time in our everyday life, it seems that we also downplay the importance of ordinary time in the liturgical year. We wait around for the big feast days of Christmas,*

Easter, and Pentecost, and the rest of the year we feel we don't have to go to mass; it's not a "peak experience."

TK: But the whole purpose of the big feasts is to awaken us to the importance of ordinary time. And you see that in contemplatives. After awhile they prefer the ferial days of ordinary time because these days don't have the sharp focus of a particular feast, but rather communicate the simple fact of the whole of the reality given you in the humble symbols of bread and wine, of eating and drinking.

In other words, all of life is to be transformed. The Eucharist really means that the whole universe is the body of God, so whatever its manifestation, you're always touching, seeing, sensing, feeling God. And the consciousness that is spontaneously aware of this deepest level of reality is totally present to these simple things because now everything is a total revelation of God, whether you're in church or outside of church. So the real reason to go to church is to be able to get along without it; that is to say, you have become the temple of God. Corporate worship is then a celebration of the ongoing experience.

Parabola
Volume: 27.2
Dying

Consumed by Either Fire or Fire

Kim Coleman Healy

Thomas Merton (1915–1968), an American Trappist monk and priest, made a life's work of the art of dying. His spirituality, which echoes *The Cloud of Unknowing* and St. John of the Cross, addressed the twentieth century with a fresh vision of the Christian apophatic tradition.

> *Contemplation is always beyond our own knowl-edge, beyond our own light, beyond systems, beyond discourse, beyond dialogue, beyond our own self. To enter into the realm of contemplation one must in a certain sense die: but this death is in fact the entrance into a higher life. It is a death for the sake of life, which leaves behind all that we can know or treasure as life, as thought, as experience, as joy, as being. ...*
>
> *In the actual experience of contemplation, all other experiences are momentarily lost. They "die" to be reborn again on a higher level of life.[1]*

From his adult baptism in 1938 until his accidental death in Bangkok on December 10, 1968, Merton sought this contemplative "death for the sake of life"—which, he was to learn in correspondence with D. T. Suzuki, has kinship to the "Great Death" of Zen enlightenment. Yet his desire to die to his false self and embrace God in the dark night of the soul warred with and was sometimes confused with a false dying to self, a desire to "deny himself for the love of himself,"[2] as he puts it in *The Sign of Jonas*.

Both baptism and monastic vows "kill" the old self of a disciple to make way for a new life in Christ. According to Mircea Eliade, baptism re-enacts the story of Noah's flood, which destroyed the accumulated results of human sin to give the world a new beginning. Merton's autobiography *The Seven Storey Mountain*, published early in his monastic life, shows that he felt he had a burdensome history to relinquish. The book's relentless self-judgment ("Did I know that my own sins were enough to have destroyed the whole of England and Germany?")[3] seems disproportionate to the details it narrates; the disproportion arises from what it does *not* narrate. In 1934, as an undergraduate at Cambridge, Merton had become an unwed father. Though his superiors in the Order asked him not to publish this fact, it had engendered the guilt that drove him to both his conversion and his vows. The will he made before solemn profession left a share of his property to the mother and child, who are rumored to have died in the Blitz.

Determined to do lifelong penance, Merton decided three years after his baptism to join the Cistercians of the Strict Observance; in a journal of the period he cites:

> *... the arguments in Saint Thomas [Aquinas]: that the man who has repented of great sins should forsake even lawful things and give up even more than those who have always obeyed God, and sacrifice* everything. *Nothing was ever so near certain.* Deo Gratias![4]

Authorized biographer Michael Mott observes,

> *There was a certain romance, if a chilling one, in the idea that this [the Trappist Order] was the Foreign Legion of the Church, into which a man could plunge, losing his name and every tie with the world, going into a silence within high walls that must be a living death. For God, yes; but a living death.*[5]

In *The Seven Storey Mountain* Merton narrates his departure by train in December 1941 from St. Bonaventure's College (where he had taught

English after completing a master's degree at Columbia) toward the Abbey of Our Lady of Gethsemani in Kentucky: "It was nothing less than a civil, moral death."[6] He later recounts a "last meal" of scrambled eggs, cheese, milk, and chocolate in the abbey guesthouse on the eve of his reception as a novice.

Merton envisioned the "moral death" of his monastic initiation preeminently as a death of *identity*. He writes of a fellow postulant:

> *Practically the first thing you noticed, when you looked at the choir, was this young man in secular clothes among all the monks.*
>
> *Then suddenly we saw him no more. He was in white. They had given him an oblate's habit, and you could not pick him out from the rest. The waters had closed over his head, and he was submerged in the community. The world would hear of him no more. He had drowned to our society and become a Cistercian.*[7]

Throughout the earlier narrative of *The Seven Storey Mountain*, Merton had condemned his own attachment to his independent judgment. The vow of obedience, he felt, would kill that attachment. "Excellence, here, was in proportion to obscurity: the one who was best was the one who was least observed, least distinguished. Only faults and mistakes drew attention to the individual."[8] One may see in this statement both a desire for the unselfconscious transparency of *participation mystique* and an expectation that the children of Mother Church should be seen and not heard.

Merton intended initially that his nascent writing career should drown in the Order with the rest of his individuality; he saw publication as both a breach of Cistercian silence and an affirmation of the worldly self. His superiors disagreed.

> *By this time I should have been delivered of any problems about my true identity. I had already made my simple profession [temporary vows at the end of the novitiate]. And my vows should have divested me of the last shreds of any special identity.*
>
> *But then there was this shadow, this double, this writer who had followed me into the cloister.*

He is still on my track. He rides my shoulders, sometimes, like
the old man of the sea. I cannot lose him. He still wears the name of
Thomas Merton. Is it the name of an enemy?
He is supposed to be dead. ...
And the worst of it is, he has my superiors on his side. They won't
kick him out. I can't get rid of him.
Maybe in the end he will kill me, he will drink my blood.
Nobody seems to understand that one of us has got to die. [9]

Because abbot Dom Frederic Dunne refused to choose between
Merton the writer and Merton the monk—a refusal perpetuated by his
successor Dom James Fox—those lines reached print.

As soon as I had renounced all earthly things, I was called into
Father Abbot's room and he presented me with a contract with Har-
court, Brace for the publication of The Seven Storey Mountain.
So after making my will I put my living signature on this contract.
The royalties of the dead author will go to the monastery. [10]

The "dead author," though repeatedly buried in the private journals that
gave rise to *The Sign of Jonas*, was repeatedly resurrected. His superiors'
refusal to countenance authorial death forced Merton to reexamine his
motives for trying to renounce writing. "It seems absurd for a man to be
sanctified by things he naturally likes,"[11] he complains in the February 2,
1949 entry of *The Sign of Jonas*. By September 1, however, he had accepted
the necessity to die to himself *by* writing rather than to die *to* writing.

Writing, far from being an obstacle to spiritual perfection, has
become one of the conditions on which my perfection will depend. ...
To be as good a monk as I can, and to remain myself, and to write
about it: to put myself down on paper, in such a situation, with the
most complete simplicity and integrity, masking nothing, confusing
no issue: this is very hard, because I am all mixed up in illusions and
attachments. These, too, will have to be put down. But without exag-
geration, repetition, useless emphasis. No need for breast-beating and
lamentation before the eyes of anyone but You, O God, who see the

depths of my fatuity. To be frank without being boring. It is a kind of crucifixion [emphasis added].*[12]*

In accepting the vocation to work out his salvation on paper, Merton began to turn away from the desire of self-annihilation for its own sake, and toward the crucifixion—less dramatic, less painful, more necessary—of accepting himself as he was rather than as he felt he ought to be.

From this point on, Merton grew in the ability to distinguish between the false self-loss of wounded pride and the true self-loss that receives God into one's emptiness. "It is when we are angry at our own mistakes," he writes, "that we tend most to deny ourselves for love of ourselves."[13] It is difficult not to see in this statement an acknowledgment of the undercurrent of self-hatred in *The Seven Storey Mountain.* In *Thoughts in Solitude* (composed in 1953–1954 and published in 1958) he develops the distinction further:

> *What does it mean to know and experience my own "nothingness"?*
> *It is not enough to turn away in disgust from my illusions and faults and mistakes, to separate myself from them as if they were not, and as if I were someone other than myself. This kind of self-annihilation is only a worse illusion, it is a pretended humility [in] which, by saying "I am nothing" I mean in effect "I wish I were not what I am."*[14]

The false humility of "I wish I were not what I am" partakes of what Mark Epstein calls "the *klesha* [compulsion] of 'I am not'."[15] This pervasive sense of unworthiness, which Epstein asserts is the central modern obstacle to spiritual growth, arises from childhood emotional traumas. Pertinently, Merton recalls his mother Ruth as "cold and cerebral," concerned with intellectual discipline at the expense of emotional nurture; he lost her to stomach cancer when he was six years old. His monastic life represented, among other things, a quest for filial attachment to Mother Church, to the Virgin Mary, and to the Redeemer whom Julian of Norwich addressed as "Our Mother Jesus."

Merton continues his discussion of nothingness with a radical departure from his early self-repudiations.

> *To love our nothingness in this way, we must repudiate nothing*
> *that is our own. … We must see and admit that it is all ours and that*
> *it is all good: good in its positive entity since it comes from God: good*
> *in our deficiency, since our helplessness, even our moral misery, our*
> *spiritual, attracts to us the mercy of God. … To love our nothingness*
> *we must love* ourselves.[16]

Michael Mott comments, "There is something magnificent about this passage, even though it starts questions at once. … He had repudiated himself over and over. Now he was repudiating the repudiator, the self-hater."[17]

Dying to self-hatred opened the way for Merton to die to his former contempt of the world, in his "Louisville Vision" of March 18, 1958.

> *In Louisville, at the corner of Fourth and Walnut, in the cen-*
> *ter of the shopping district, I was suddenly overwhelmed with the*
> *realization that I loved all these people, that they were mine and I*
> *theirs, that we could not be alien to one another even though we were*
> *total strangers. It was like waking from a dream of separateness, of*
> *spurious self-isolation in a special world, the world of renunciation*
> *and supposed holiness. … My happiness could have taken form in the*
> *words: "Thank God, thank God that I am like other men, that I am*
> *only a man among others."[18]*

What Merton calls the "illusion" of being holier than other people by reason of monastic renunciations is really his illusion of being *more sinful* than other people, turned inside out. His sense of singular sin had driven him to a renunciation that felt singular; relinquishing the inverted pride of self-despite removed the need for compensatory pride in piety.

Merton's initial attempts to die to the "false self" of worldly and egotistical attachments apparently had given rise to another "false self" of ecclesiastical compliance. Biographer Monica Furlong suggests that between 1950 and 1960 Merton died to this compliant self, giving up his early unquestioning submission for a greater interior independence. His words in *New Seeds of Contemplation* may hint at such an ordeal:

> *For every gain in deep certitude there is a corresponding growth*
> *of superficial "doubt." This doubt is by no means opposed to genuine*
> *faith, but it mercilessly examines and questions the spurious "faith"*
> *of everyday life, the human faith which is nothing but the passive*
> *acceptance of conventional opinions. This false "faith" which is what*
> *we often live by and which we even come to confuse with our "reli-*
> *gion" is subjected to inexorable questioning. ...*
>
> *What a holocaust takes place in this steady burning to ashes of old*
> *worn-out words, clichés, slogans, rationalizations! The worst of it is*
> *that even apparently holy conceptions are consumed along with all*
> *the rest.[19]*

Among those apparently holy conceptions was Merton's determination to renounce his desire for solitude. From his novitiate forward,
Merton had struggled with the sense that Gethsemani was too active a
community for one with a purely contemplative vocation.

> *Every day I kill Isaac—my beautiful dream about a silent, soli-*
> *tary, well-ordered life of perfect contemplation and perfect monastic*
> *observance, with no intrusion from the world, no publicity, no best-*
> *selling books, just God and that nice archaic little Carthusian cell![20]*

The death of this "Isaac" gave life to Merton's books and to the monks
he taught in his years as Master of Scholastics (trainees for priesthood)
and Novice Master. Yet Merton's growing inner freedom allowed "Isaac"
to revive. Despite his vow of stability, he repeatedly inquired into the
possibilities of joining the Carthusians or the Camaldolese, participating
in the founding of a new community, or becoming a hermit.[21] Though
permission to leave Gethsemani was denied, Dom James did make an
important concession. He gave Merton restricted use of "St. Anne's," a
former tool shed, as solitary space. Merton exclaimed in his journal:

> *It seems to me that St. Anne's is what I have been waiting for*
> *and looking for all my life and now I have stumbled into it quite*
> *by accident. ... With tremendous relief I have discovered that I no*
> *longer need to pretend. ... I do not have to buy St. Anne's. I do not*
> *have to sell myself to myself here. Everything that was ever real in*

me has come back to life in this doorway wide open to the sky! I no longer have to trample myself down, cut myself in half, throw part of me out the window, and keep pushing the rest of myself away.[22]

Merton here revokes the violence he has done to his inner hermit, in forthright language he would have found scandalous as a novice. "Isaac," resurrected, would lead him in the 1960s to a full-time hermitage on Gethsemani land, with the blessing of Dom James and the community.

The dying to the false self that impelled the mature Merton to turn toward the world, to risk the displeasure of the hierarchy by his outspokenness against nuclear war, and to insist on his vocation to solitude, also impelled him to risk interfaith dialogue. *The Seven Storey Mountain*'s parochial judgments upon Protestant Christianity and Asian religions were sacrificed and transmuted into an openness to truth wherever it could be found. In his letters to Zen master Daisetz T. Suzuki, recognition of a kindred spirit overwhelms his syntax.

Christ himself is in us as unknown and unseen. We follow Him, we find Him (it is like the [Zen] cow-catching pictures) and then He must vanish and we must go along without Him at our side, why? Because He is even closer than that. He is ourself. *O my dear Dr. Suzuki I know you will understand this so well, and so many people do not, even though they are "doctors in Israel."[23]*

In late 1968 Merton traveled to Asia to meet with religious leaders including Chatral Rinpoche (who pronounced him *rangjung Sangay*, a natural Buddha)[24] and the Dalai Lama and ultimately to attend a conference of Asian abbots in Bangkok, sponsored by the Benedictine organization *Aide à l'Implantation Monastique*. After delivering his talk, "Marxism and Monastic Perspectives," to the Bangkok conference on December 10, 1968, he was found dead during the midafternoon break, electrocuted by touching an electric fan as he emerged from the shower. His body was returned to the U.S. in the bay of a SAC bomber, alongside those of soldiers killed in the Vietnam war he had protested in print. At Gethsemani's funeral Mass an excerpt from *The Sign of Jonas* was read: "The Voice of God is heard in Paradise. ... Have you had sight of Me,

Jonas my child? Mercy within mercy within mercy."[25] Merton's monastic youth was fraught with self-conscious preparations for death; his actual death came unexpectedly when he had relearned to love life—but to love it without fearing death. "The King of Death," says a Buddhist poem, "does not see you if you do not see any self in yourself."[26]

Notes:

1   Thomas Merton, *New Seeds of Contemplation* (New York: New Directions, 1961), p. 2.

2   Thomas Merton, *The Sign of Jonas* (New York: Harcourt, Brace, 1953), p. 242.

3   Thomas Merton, *The Seven Storey Mountain* (New York: Harcourt, Brace, 1948), p. 128.

4   Thomas Merton, *Run to the Mountain: The Story of a Vocation (Journals, 1939–1941)*, edited by Patrick Hart, O.C.S.O. (San Francisco: HarperSanFrancisco, 1995).

5   Michael Mott, *The Seven Mountains of Thomas Merton* (New York: Houghton Mifflin, 1984), p. 168.

6   *The Seven Storey Mountain*, p. 369.

7   Ibid, p. 325.

8   Ibid, p. 330.

9   Ibid, p. 410.

10 *The Sign of Jonas*, p. 25.

11 Ibid, p. 154.

12 Ibid, p. 234.

13 Ibid, p. 242.

14 Thomas Merton, *Thoughts in Solitude* (New York: Farrar, Straus & Giroux, 1958; reprinted 2000), p. 34.

15 Mark Epstein, *Going On Being* (New York: Broadway Books, 2000), pp. 132–147.

16 *Thoughts in Solitude*, p. 34.

17 *The Seven Mountains of Thomas Merton*, p. 317.

18 Thomas Merton, *Conjectures of a Guilty Bystander* (New York: Image, 1966), pp. 156–157.

19 *New Seeds of Contemplation*, pp. 12–13.

20 Thomas Merton, *Entering the Silence: Becoming a Monk and Writer (Journals 1941–1952)*, edited by Jonathan Montaldo, O.C.S.O. (San Francisco: HarperSanFrancisco, 1995). Entry of May 1, 1949.

21 Mott discusses these stability crises in detail in the "Mount Purgatory" chapter of *The Seven Mountains of Thomas Merton*.

22 Journal entry of February 16, 1953, quoted in *The Intimate Merton: His Life from His Journals*, edited by Patrick Hart and Jonathan Montaldo (New York: HarperSan-Francisco, 1999), p. 110.

23 Letter from Thomas Merton to D. T. Suzuki, April 11, 1959, in *Encounter: Thomas Merton and D. T. Suzuki*, edited by Robert E. Daggy (Monterey, Ky.: Larkspur Press, 1988).

24 *The Seven Mountains of Thomas Merton*, p. 352.

25 *The Sign of Jonas*, p. 361.

26 *Conjectures of a Guilty Bystander*, p. 230.

CHAPTER THREE

•

UNSEEN WARFARE

Very truly, I tell you, unless a grain of wheat falls into the earth and dies,
it remains just a single grain; but if it dies, it bears much fruit.
Those who love their life lose it, and those who hate their life in this world
will keep it for eternal life. Whoever serves me must follow me,
and where I am, there will my servant be also.[1]

—John 12: 24–26

Parabola
Volume: 7.4
Holy War

BECOME WHAT YOU ARE

Interview with Brother David Steindl-Rast

*I met Brother David Steindl-Rast, of the Roman Catholic
Benedictine Order, at the San Francisco Zen Center's Edward
Conze guest house, where he was staying briefly on his way
to a monastery in Big Sur. The setting was apt: Conze was
a Westerner who became one of the century's great authori-
ties on Buddhism, and the Victorian house has an inviting
spaciousness, an unpretentious elegance and absence of clutter,
yet real warmth—all of which fit the monk with whom I was
to speak. To those who encounter Brother David now and
again, he seems very much a man on the move, remarkably
mobile for a monk. Yet despite all this travelling and speaking, he always appears a calm eye at the center of any storm
of activity. To a passing observer, he might look disturbingly
gaunt and ascetic, confirming popular prejudices about monks
being world-haters. But as soon as he greets you, the illusion of severity vanishes: he is so warm and effervescent that
you really want to learn how he packs so much alertness and
delight into his life.*

Originally from Vienna, Austria, Brother David has a

doctorate in psychology and has been a monk for twenty-six years now; he cur-
rently lives in a small community, called the Grange, in Connecticut. He says
that he is as much at home in a Zen monastery as in a Catholic one, and it's
hard to think that he would not be at home anywhere. For he has a remarkable
ability to be joyfully and wholly present: when he listens, he does nothing else;
when the phone interrupts, he takes the call with full attention and delight;
when he answers questions he does so with the kind of care and élan that make
an interviewer's task a joy. More than many teachers I've met, the man is his
message, and it is hard to imagine a more persuasive and attractive advocate
for the Catholic monastic tradition.

Many people ask him whether the spirituality he embodies and presents
is really the Catholicism that they've found so difficult to appreciate in other
forms which they've encountered. But it may be that few people have so appro-
priated that tradition that they can express it with such simple grace.

—John Loudon

John Loudon: *What does "holy warfare" mean to you?*

Brother David Steindl-Rast: Today the notion of warfare is inseparable from that of alienation, whereas the very essence of spiritual warfare in the monastic tradition is the overcoming of alienation—what we call nowadays pulling or getting yourself together. And the monastic symbol for pulling yourself together is the belt, which monks wear in many different traditions. The aim is to overcome alienation from yourself, from others, and from God.

JL: *What forces need to be overcome in this struggle against alienation?*

BD: Well, in the classical discussion of holy warfare in the writings of the Eastern Fathers of the early church, these forces are personified as demons. Even in the New Testament Paul says that it is not against "flesh and blood" that we are struggling, but against principalities and powers of evil. But it's not necessary to take these powers literally, in a fundamentalist way, and in fact to do so we probably would do an injustice to the early Fathers who wrote in those terms. They were no doubt as alert to the metaphorical nature of this imagery as we are, just as Buddhists have long known that the different hells in their tradition are best understood as mental or psychological states, not actual places.

JL: *Can you give examples of some of these personified forces and some indication of how you might express them today?*

BD: The three great forces that the Latin Fathers identified as the enemies against which we're battling are anger, lust, and laziness. The third one is called the noonday devil. It is in the middle of everything—of a day, of a life—that you can lose your resolve, that torpor can set in. When you're in the middle of swimming across a river, it's too far to go back and seems too far to reach the other side, and you are tempted to give up. Well, these three elements—anger, lust, and laziness—are precisely the three ways that we can fail to be present where we are, and the whole idea of getting yourself together is to be present where you are and, in the Christian context, to respond to the presence of God.

Anger really means impatience (as opposed to the righteous anger that is desirable in many circumstances). Impatience makes us get ahead of ourselves, reaching out for something in the future and not really being content with where we are, here and now.

Lust extends much wider than the sexual sphere, and essentially means attachment, attachment to something that is not present, or is not the appropriate thing right now.

And one by-product of laziness, of being victimized by the noonday devil, is sadness—not the genuine sorrow of compassion, but the lifeless ennui of never really being involved in the present, with what's happening.

If you would like another contemporary interpretation of the idea of spiritual warfare, there is C. S. Lewis's *The Screwtape Letters*, in which he translates the tradition with great wit and insight into a modern idiom. It's all about struggling with the forces that are all around us in the world and within us and that distract us from being really unified, in one piece.

JL: *When I was thinking about the theme of holy warfare, it occurred to me that there are military virtues—such as discipline, strength, courage, resolve, fidelity, and so on—which are also vital to spiritual growth. And especially the aspect of discipline, involving training and regular practice. What are the disciplines that have been developed that can be used against these devils today?*

BD: The word discipline is very significant in this context, since it is not primarily a military term. The corresponding military term is regimentation. Discipline is a school term: the *discipulus* is the disciple, the pupil. Even the word pupil is apt here, because it is related to the pupil in our eye, the *pupilla*—the little doll, the little image of oneself that one sees in another's eye. This eye-to-eye contact is the essence of discipline: discipline is the attitude that you have when you see eye-to-eye with your teacher. Today especially people reject external regimentation, and are looking for a teacher that gives discipline eye-to-eye. The drill sergeant doesn't care if you are eye-to-eye with him or anybody else, just that you do what you are told. But discipline involves bringing out what is already within you. That's what the true teacher does. And the other virtues you mentioned have similar parallels. Fortitude or courage, for instance, is simply the resolve to overcome obstacles. Spiritual warfare involves the acquiring and implementation of the strengths and virtues needed to overcome obstacles.

JL: *Discipline suggests to me habits of behavior and regular practices that the teacher would presumably teach. How does this dimension relate to overcoming anger, lust, laziness?*

BD: Within the monastery, which is my background and the essential environment that I feel comfortable with and know well, there is a particularly highly developed tradition of such training. In fact, the monastery can be understood precisely as a setting in which this discipline is cultivated. It is a place to which people go in order to get themselves together, again in the sense of uniting with themselves, with others, with God.

The two realms in which this discipline is cultivated are space and time, and the aim is that the whole of life should be brought together from alienation to fullness. With regard to time, for instance, there are in monasteries all sorts of bells, gongs, clappers, drums, and so on—all kinds of signals that tell you what it is time for. The struggle is within yourself to overcome your laziness, your attachments, your impatience in order to be truly wherever you need to be at any particular time. T. S. Eliot speaks of "Time, not our time," and he explicitly says this in relation to the Angelus bell that, in monastic life, rings three times a day—at sunrise, at sunset, and at high noon. The sun doesn't rise again or wait for you if you oversleep and don't get up when the bell rings. The sun rises and the bell rings, and you are to be there: your impatience can't make it happen before the right time; your attachment to staying in bed can't delay it; and you'll miss it if you're up but not really present, alert, attentive. If this sort of timeliness appeals to you, as it does to me, these signals are not a torturing regimentation but musical invitations, celebrations of particular moments.

The difficult aspect, of course, is the one expressed by St. Benedict in his Rule: "When the bell rings, stop everything. Don't even cross your t's or dot your i's, but go quickly." The challenge is to learn to respond immediately to whatever it is time for. Not to wonder whether you have time for it or whether you like it, but simply to respond when it is time. And the truth of this discipline is universal. For instance, in Taoism, the flow goes on and you can either be in tune with the flow or not. All these signals are simply means to get you into the flow, and the less you are in tune the more difficult the immediate responding is, the more obstacles you have to overcome to get with it.

With regard to space, the monastery is organized in such a way that there is a place for everything, and relatedly that everything is there, the monastery is self-contained. The ideal is wonderfully expressed in the Benedictine tradition by the famous plan of St. Gall, which is reflected more or less in many medieval monasteries. With everything there and a place for everything, you can be at home in your world, in the place where you belong. And belonging and getting yourself together are closely related. This sufficient world, which St. Benedict calls a workshop for the spiritual life, affords the spaces and the tools for working on yourself, transforming yourself, and in turn the world around you.

Novices always have difficulties with both aspects—time and space. When it is time for something, they often want to do something else; when this is the place to be, they often want to be somewhere else. And isn't this how it is for most people? The monastery also emphasizes neatness and orderliness; most visitors notice this immediately. There is a close relation between the struggle to put things in order within your self, within your life, and the ordering of the space around you. But novices find this hard to understand. They say, "We came here to learn spiritual matters, and what I'm told to do is how to put my shoes on, when to put them on and take them off, to put them down with the right one on the right side, the left one on the left, and parallel, not toed in. What does that have to do with the spiritual life?" It has everything to do with it. That is the spirituality; it isn't something that you do just as a novice, and then graduate to spirituality. But it takes a long time to see that orderliness and cleanliness is not just cleaning the room, but it is getting your life in order.

So bringing things into order is the goal. Order is the disposition of things in which each gives to the other its room, its own proper place. That's the external aspect. The other is that order that springs from love: there's no other way of establishing order except through love. So spiritual warfare is radically unlike what we know as warfare, which is rooted in hate and alienation and leads to chaos.

JL: *Besides the imagery of warfare, some people have compared spiritual discipline to athletic training. There is the talk, for instance, about becoming an athlete of Christ.*

BD: Both the athletic imagery and that of spiritual weaponry occur in St. Paul, but the weapons he speaks of are faith, hope, and love. I am convinced that in the present world, in which peace and order are no longer possible through arms, it is best to change our spiritual vocabulary, because misunderstandings do arise on the popular level. I am much more comfortable with speaking about spiritual struggle, since that does not necessarily involve struggling against someone else. You can struggle up a mountain, or struggle to get your body in shape. It even applies to animals: a chick struggling to get out of the eggshell. Plants struggle to break through cracks in the concrete, and amazingly they manage to. And similarly, I prefer to speak of obstacles rather than enemies. *The struggle against obstacles*, I think, puts the essentials of the tradition of spiritual warfare into contemporary language that is proper and helpful.

JL: *Do you think the spiritual path demands a special way of life?*

BD: If by a special way of life, you mean a special place like a monastery, I would say no. But if the question implies making an effort, having to struggle, I would say yes. The difference between other animals around us and ourselves seems to be that dogs and cats and birds and other animals don't have to struggle to be good at what they are. But we human beings somehow have to struggle to become what we are.

JL: *Our being is to become.*

BD: Yes. We experience ourselves as unfinished, and we have to struggle to become a finished product. Actually, we're never completely finished; that's our glory and our agony. We remain open-ended.

JL: *In contemporary Catholicism, and in the past as well, there seem to be two divergent paths: there is that of those who emphasize spirituality, spiritual disciplines and growth, and then there is the more general, popular path in which salvation is available through regular participation in the sacraments and the life of the church generally. The former way sees* becoming *a Christian as a lifelong task; the latter stresses fidelity to* being *a good Catholic. Can you say something about this?*

BD: You speak of participating in the sacraments. At the heart of all the sacraments, especially the eucharist and baptism, is the celebration of the struggle of Christ through death to resurrection. If you really participate in the sacrament, it is impossible not to enter into that struggle. The whole idea of the sacrament is to go through that struggle yourself in communion with the struggle of Christ, to participate day by day and hour by hour in the struggle of dying into greater fullness of life. And the real issue is not whether there is one kind of life that allows for this acceptance of death that leads to fuller life, and so is a spiritual life rather than a run-of-the-mill life. No, the real question is to what extent within ordinary life we can wake up to the essential inner struggle of realizing the fullness of life. Going to church, sending your kids to Catholic schools, and so on, by themselves don't do anything; they're worthless, unless they lead you into, wake you up to that struggle.

JL: *Since you participate in both the Christian and the Zen communities, do you think there is an ultimate difference between Christianity and Buddhism, and what kinds of differences do you see between the two?*

BD: The point is, how ultimate is "ultimate"? There are many different levels. On one level there are great cultural differences: the two traditions grew up in entirely different settings, and so are dissimilar in many respects. But the moment that you penetrate through the accidental cultural differences, you find a remarkable similarity. Sometimes now I cannot remember if I'm in a Christian or a Buddhist monastery. The atmosphere is very similar. Then you go deeper still, and you discover profound differences in approach, although it's difficult to put them into words. Basically, the Biblical tradition centers on the Word in the widest sense: the divine speaks to us, approaches us, and we have to respond; we're burdened with *respons*ibility.

JL: *The Bible also emphasizes hearing over seeing.*

BD: And the reason for the emphasis on hearing is the call to live by the word of God, being nourished by it, responding to it. In Zen the stress is not on the word, but on the silence—the silence that is so profound that you can go down into it forever and ever. Openness, emptiness, void—all this permeates Zen. Of course, in the Christian tradition, the Word comes out of the silence and returns to the silence. But despite the teaching of the dark night of the soul and the like, the Christian tradition still stays very close to the Word. Though there are lots of words in Buddhism, they aim at silence. After everything is said and done, the Zen teacher will say, "Ah yes, but what a pity that we have to say anything at all." The saying doesn't really effect anything; what counts is the silence of practice. But then, if you go still deeper down, to what I think might well be the deepest level, you can experience communion and unity between the traditions, the complementarity of the Word and the silence.

JL: *What is the connection between the life of contemplation and the call to social action in the world?*

BD: You can't really be a contemplative, unless you also want to change the world. You want to change yourself, and that's where the struggle comes in. By changing yourself, you're beginning to change the world. In fact, you're changing the world much more by changing yourself than if you're running around blindly, involved in one cause after another. But the difference between what we call the apostolic and the contemplative orders, or vocations, is that the apostolic approach says, "We live in this world, we're responsible for it, and we have to do something to change the world for the better." The monastic answer is, "We are not strong enough to change the world in general. Let's change that little spot where we are. And let's put a wall around it and say this is as far as we go, as far as our strength reaches. And now within that narrow confine, let's change the world, make it more what it's supposed to be." That approach has its drawbacks, too, because it can become ingrown, its own private little affair. And the apostolic approach has its limitations, because it can become so watered down that nothing spiritual remains. So we need the two; they are the poles of one continuum. People who are now engaged in apostolically changing the world need to come back periodically to a monastic environment where what they are trying to achieve everywhere is to a certain extent achieved already. And if the world could gradually become what a good monastery or Zen center is, that would be fine. The monastic communities can provide the strength, the encouragement to realize that true order can be achieved.

JL: *Traditionally, Catholicism has emphasized that the contemplative life is valuable in and of itself, even if the effect on the outside world is not very immediate or direct, but with the faith that spiritual service of God would redound ultimately to the benefit of all of humankind. How would you translate that idea into contemporary terms?*

BD: The problem is that all too easily you can think of the spiritual as the opposite of the material. But in authentic Christianity, the material is completely integrated with the spiritual. The essence of Christianity is incarnation. Spiritual is not opposed to material, but to the unspiritual. It's better to speak of alive and dead. Spirit, "breath," means life. The unspiritual or "the flesh," as the New Testament puts it, does not mean the material, the bodily. Flesh stands for that which is dead and in the process of decay. So it's best to think of death not in the sense of negating life, denying life. Life-affirming and life-denying are what spiritual and unspiritual mean. So from that viewpoint, there is a struggle for more and more spirituality, but this spirituality does not deny the world and material things, but expresses itself in more and more beautiful transformation of the material world. Now and then you see a place where every roof tile and every door knob speaks of spirituality, and it reminds you that material things can be completely transformed.

JL: *I asked you earlier if a spiritual life demanded a special way of life, and in the light of the distinctions that you've made, I'm beginning to think that what it actually comes down to concretely is how you spend your day. Of course, monks spend their day differently than people who drive trucks or work in offices and so on. How do you spend your day? And what principles that the monastic life has taught you might apply to people who live in the "ordinary world"?*

BD: One doesn't go to the monastery to lead a different kind of life from the rest of people. The challenge of living according to certain principles is the same for everyone, and we all need to lead a special kind of life if we want to come truly alive. The monastic day starts with getting up earlier than most of us would like to get up. So the struggle is right there at the start.

JL: *Do you get up earlier because it is difficult, or because it's good to be up when the sun comes up?*

BD: You never do anything, theoretically or ideally, just because it's more difficult. You do it in spite of it's being difficult, but for a good reason. The reason for getting up early is that these early morning hours provide a setting, a quiet, a silence that never comes again later in the day; there is something special going on in those early hours. And you're also there for the sunrise, dawn, which is very important: you celebrate the dawning of each new day. But it's a struggle to get up and to remain alert.

Then during the day, there are several times for prayer and times when we get together to celebrate important points in the day—high noon, sunset, night prayers at the end of the day. The rest of the time is spent studying or in manual labor. Manual labor is significant and everybody in the monastery takes part in it, including the abbot. It's simply a part of life. It keeps you humble, down to earth (*humus*—the word that also gives us humor and human). Essentially, then, monastic life is dedicated to prayer, manual labor, and study.

JL: *How much of this regimen can you take with you when you travel?*

BD: It's very difficult, and that's why monks don't usually travel. The kind of prayer that I find most helpful, in place of the divine office that is chanted seven times a day in the monastery, is the prayer of the heart from the Eastern Christian tradition, which involves a kind of mantric repetition of the name of Jesus. But I try to restrict my travel, because it's so hard to take much of the monastery with you, although it's fine if I can stay in another monastery, such as Zen or Camaldolese [one of the Benedictine orders in the Roman Catholic church with a monastery in southern California].

JL: *And how would you suggest that the values of that sort of structure be translated to people who live their whole lives in the situation you find your-self in when you're not in the monastery?*

BD: There's no point in just imitating the externals. What one should and can take out of the monastic life is its very essence, and that is the grateful approach to life moment by moment, being grateful in every-thing you do. That means, for instance, an alertness to the character of every moment as a given moment, a gift. Every moment demands a response, and the basic Christian response is trust in the giver.

JL: *But you can't have awareness just by wanting it, can you? There are people here at the Zen Center who have spent years and years of their lives trying to be more awake.*

BD: That's true. But there are degrees of wakefulness. And people who have practiced for years and years may not realize that they have made great steps toward greater wakefulness. The difficulty in speaking about wakefulness is that when you are asleep you can't just wake yourself up.

But if you focus on thankfulness, it is easier, since being grateful is within your power. If you do it again and again, you remind yourself that every moment is a given moment. Gratefulness is an experience that everyone has, and seems very natural when cultivated. Actually, it is emphasized more explicitly in Buddhist monasteries, where there are so many formal bows. It is a form of teaching us to receive everything—a cup of tea, another person—with gratitude.

JL: *So this rhythm of gift and response is a spiritual practice, or at least a way that anybody can practice in any circumstances.*

BD: Yes, and I don't think spiritual practice is too grandiose a term for it. If you really explore its larger implications, it is at the core of every spiritual practice, although it may be expressed in quite different ways.

JL: *What is the importance of the dialogue between Christianity and Zen?*

BD: These are traditions that seem to me to have a lot of future and that complement one another well. And what really interested me in Buddhist-Christian dialogue was the monastic dimension. I wanted to know in what sense Buddhists are monks like I am. And ultimately I've come to see that the monastic life isn't something that is especially connected to Buddhism or to Christianity, but is related to one's frame of mind, one's own inner bent.

JL: *So it's an essential human vocation or option; in any culture or society there are going to be people who want to live this way?*

BD: Right, and you could even think of it as an externalization of a dimension that is in every human being and is sometimes very strong in people who do not externalize it because of their life circumstances.

JL: *You spoke about our always becoming and never reaching the end. What is it that one is supposed to become? What's the struggle for?*

BD: As the Christian tradition sees it, each one of us is a unique word that is spoken, or a unique way of saying the one eternal Word of God. Each one of us is a word, and we become the word that we are by our response to all the other words around us, human or otherwise. Thus we become the word that we are meant to be. If the word is in the process of being spoken, you can never really say it's finished. In a certain sense, the word is completed with my death, when all that I have made of my life is rounded off. But even then, the Cappadocian Fathers in the early church taught that heaven is not a static state, but a dynamic experience of moving deeper and deeper into the ultimate, and the ultimate can never be completely discovered.

JL: *If you're playing tennis, I suppose that one person eventually wins in the end, but the joy of playing is not just getting to the end.*

BD: That's a good point. The spiritual struggle is like learning to play tennis, with the muscle pain, the awkwardness, the frustration, and so on at the beginning. The element of playing is very important in spirituality, because otherwise you begin to wonder what all this struggling is for. The goal is partly the enjoyment; it doesn't come later, but within the very process of the struggle.

JL: *What about the people who aren't even playing the game?*

BD: I tend to be very trusting and to believe that even in people in whom we least see it, deep down there is that aliveness, that longing, that struggle, and it's just well covered over. My world view is not that there are a few people who really struggle and that the masses haven't awakened to their real calling. My view is that in some the process is more obvious and in others the process is more hidden. And that is a common view in monastic traditions, East and West. Both have stories of the spiritual master who is very accomplished and is having trouble finding a teacher of his own. And he is directed, in a dream or a vision or in some other way, to someone who is more advanced than he is, but is the last person you would have expected. In Buddhism it's a butcher for example, someone way down the spiritual line, whom you'd expect to have no spiritual consciousness at all. And in the Christian tradition it's often a merchant with a big family and no time to pray, just buying and selling all day. And all of a sudden the searching teacher discovers this is it, this is the one.

And the most urgent spiritual task today is one being waged by just such "ordinary people"—the struggle against nuclear arms, the struggle for peace, which means harmony among all things.

JL: *What do you regard as your special vocation?*

BD: Strangely enough, I really joined the monastery to spend the rest of my life there, and I am perfectly happy to stay there without going out at all. But I do accept invitations to speak or participate in events when there are not that many people available who are interested and experienced in an area, such as the Buddhist-Christian dialogue. And these days I'm more and more involved in working with people who are quite alienated from the Christian tradition, even though many of them were raised as Christians. I very much enjoy, for instance, workshops with New Age people, many of whom come out of a Christian back-ground but have been away from it for a long time and are now ready to give Christianity a new look. They have a real need and longing to be reconciled with their roots. Much has to be thrown out and forgotten for good, but there also is a lot in the Christian tradition, if you grew up in it, that cannot readily be replaced by anything else. So you have to come to terms with it. Essentially, my vocation is simply to be a monk, but part of that is this sort of healing mission that not too many others are involved in.

JL: *So your vocation is to live the Christian monastic life, and then to com-municate what you discover in it?*

BD: Really the latter part is more a matter of exposing myself to other people who have the monk within them, and haven't discovered it. One doesn't need to say much; it seems to be a help to find a monk who can be a catalyst for the monastic bent of mind that is in all of us.

Parabola
Volume: 10.4
The Seven
Deadly Sins

Fire Proveth Iron

D. M. Dooling

> *I have set before thee this day life and good, and death and evil ... therefore choose life, that both thou and thy seed may live.*
>
> *—Deuteronomy 30:15, 19*

The problem of evil has baffled mankind since Eden; perhaps because it can only be approached through facing the mystery of good, and we do not like to acknowledge that good is a mystery. In our times especially, people dislike the thought of what is nevertheless inescapably true: the existence of scale; the idea of relativity in any more humanly personal sense than Einstein's; the reality of levels of "worlds" in which the human being is called to live in more than one at a time, and moreover to participate—as no other living being is called to do—in an exchange between them. Without a sense of this process, the understanding of good and evil, except in the most limited and subjective way, remains forever beyond our possibility even to approach.

We feel uneasily that we are surrounded by evil, that our world is indeed "sinful," although our therapists are constantly telling us for the sake of our "positive self-image" that we are good people—even if we don't often stop to ask ourselves what this means. We deplore violence, certainly; in or out of church or temple, we wish to be forgiven for our own occasional sins; we mean well. Something in us knows—vaguely, because it is mostly unrealized—that we have value; but *goodness?* "Why callest thou me good?" asked Jesus of Nazareth. "There is none good but one, that is, God."[1] Even on the human level, can I say that I am wise and compassionate, as the Buddha taught, or that I love my enemies, as Christ commanded? Goodness and love: the two seem inseparable, a state of being and the action which is its manifestation; but who can say what that state of goodness is, or define the action of love? Is it really love we speak of when we say "I love my parents but I don't want to be around them," or "I love my children so much I can't help spoiling them"? These formulas leave one with a question, and lead to the confession that love, seen as action, is indeed a mystery; it is unknowable, for it is not of the nature of our plane of existence, and so it is incommensurable with the creatures and events of our level.

Nevertheless it manifests somehow on this level; I have some relation with it. Something in me strongly affirms that I can, I even must, approach it. What then could be the way toward this mysterious "good" that is forever above and beyond me, and how does it show itself, how does it relate with my human life?

Perhaps the greatest of all formulations of the human situation, as it is and in its possibility of transformation, is what we call the Lord's Prayer—the Pater Noster, so often repeated by those who profess and call themselves Christians that it has given rise to the word "patter," which defines a mechanical recitation by rote. Yet the depth of meaning and possible understanding in those same words, if one listens to them, is unfathomable. Thousands have pondered them and hundreds, perhaps, have written down and shared their ponderings; and each time, there is more to be said, more to be understood.

The triple structure of the prayer has often been recognized; it is a triad of triads, of which the first and third are sometimes thought of as salutations, a ritual approach and withdrawal, and the middle one as the heart of the matter, that which has to do with man. But in my view, the whole prayer, from the first word to the last, is an examination of the process of exchange between levels in which the human person lives and moves and has his actual as well as his potential being. In the first two words, the relationship is established: Our Father; and in the next four, the distance—the necessary condition for the relationship to be valid. The first plea of the prayer is that we may remember that distance, that we may not lose the dimension of the sacred. "Hallowed be Thy name": it is the first necessity for us "to remember to keep it holy," not to forget the relationship nor the distance—to preserve the mystery. Otherwise we are imprisoned for a brief and meaningless moment on this earth, in this body, and our days indeed are as grass; our participation in the cosmic exchange is reduced to our bodies' nourishment of the earth itself.

"Hallowed be Thy name, Thy kingdom come, Thy will be done—in earth, as it is in heaven"; the exchange again, the necessity of the resonance of the higher within the lower. It is not enough that the Most High should be praised from afar; it must be "resurrected," incorporated, incarnated in fallible mortal clay; and in the process of striving to reflect the "good," somehow we are fed. We are fed even by our mistakes, by our sins. Sin is implicit in human being: in our lack of completion, the partiality of our nature; it is "imperfection," that which is unfinished, and it is the way we were made—intentionally, if we believe in a conscious Creator or creative process. The words *sin* and *to be* have the same root, and incompleteness—unrealized relationships, gaps of understanding and communication, blind spots, within and without—is the law of our being. "The strength of sin is the law," wrote St. Paul; but his message was that through the challenge and the discipline of temptation and resistance, sin and repentance, trial and error and trial again, man's possibility is to go beyond the law of his natural being, beyond death and its sting of unfinished business to the completeness of union with the source of life itself.

So we are told that there is a reason for sin; it might be said that there is nothing wrong with sin, if it takes its right place in a positive process. "Betimes," says Meister Eckhart, "it is the will of God that I commit sin";[2] and one of his Talks of Instruction is entitled "How the inclination to sin is always beneficial"[3] to the just man, the man of *good will*—which does not, I think, mean simply the man who means well.

For man was given will, but not much wisdom; he must choose, without knowing how; so it is inevitable that he make mistakes, but possible that he learn from them. He was also given a conscience, which is the heart of his possible consciousness; but like the rest of his being, will and conscience are also unfinished, rudimentary. Potentially the infallible knower of good and evil (is this, perhaps, our legacy from that tree in Eden?), conscience, like will, is actually small, weak, and uncertain; but it is a very fine instrument, and perhaps its weakness comes mostly from disuse. It is the central compass for our functioning throughout life, the one thing on which the development of our real humanity depends; yet it never enters into our considerations that the use of this instrument is a skill that has to be educated. As children, we are given vast amounts of information and of the most varied impressions (especially with the help of television), but not the slightest guidance, at least not in our schools, in learning how to appreciate or discriminate between the differences of levels in all this wealth of material. We don't learn that there is an "up" and a "down," a life and death, a good and evil, on a scale beyond ourselves and our concerns but between which we have inevitably to choose. And it is only conscience that discriminates truly and makes a correct choice possible.

Without conscience, will is our greatest danger; our choosing is fatally liable to self-indulgence, which "errs" from the direction of the higher. Sin is the error of a wrong choice which often is injurious to ourselves and others; we do a great deal of harm unintentionally. But we are forgivable—by which I understand that the harm may turn to inner profit: food for conscience, new knowledge, finer valuations—to the extent that we acknowledge our kinship with other makers of mistakes, other committers of injury. Forgive us our sins, our debts, our trespasses, as we forgive others; yes, that depends on us. But only You can deliver us from evil!

Here where the "problem of evil" makes its appearance, it is generally agreed that even the text of the prayer becomes a problem. "Lead us not into temptation." Some say: How can goodness itself lead us into temptation? My difficulty is the opposite; I do not see how it can fail to do so, since choice is our destiny and our privilege as humans, and every choice is a temptation; so it would seem to me an unbelievable weakness, in this strongest of all declarations of an aim, to ask to be excused from the means of going toward it. But the phrase can be understood differently: not cut off from the words which follow it but taking them together, as seems to me logical and as the threefold structure of the prayer seems to demand. Lead us not into temptation *except* You deliver us from the "unforgivable," from total destruction. Lead us into temptation if You must—and it seems You must, since we can learn only through challenge, and the very movement of our life depends on this process of choosing; but allow us to profit by the mistakes we make that we recognize, the sins we fall into and repent of, as well as by the strength we acquire when we resist them. "Fire proveth iron, and temptation a just man. We know not oftentimes what we are able to do, but temptation showeth us what we are," wrote Thomas à Kempis.[4] We need the battle, we even need to be defeated sometimes, but not to lose our lives; deliver us, therefore, from evil.

The difference between sin and evil is not, it seems, just one of degree, although the degree of distance is certainly an element in the process. We cannot go too far, too deep into our errors, take on too long their shape and coloration, without the risk of losing sight of the indubitable if mysterious existence of the good. "By becoming unlike, thou hast gone far away," said St. Augustine; "by becoming like, thou drawest near."[5] We are alive, and so we are in a continual movement, going now in one direction and now in the other, in a constant choosing, a constant "temptation," which, if we were aware of it, could also be our daily bread. But in the comatose state of our consciences, we don't notice this continuing inner situation, nor do we open the eyes of our mind to it; we imagine that our changes of direction are imposed on us by something outside, and are oblivious to the fact that everything takes place within ourselves. We are taken over by the habit of the self-indulgent impulse into what seems like another life-movement but which is in fact inertia, and can lead only to a running down.

In this process there is a point of no return, a moment when the starved conscience finally disappears; all sight and even memory of the original direction vanishes. One is entirely lost to it and captured by the attraction of another magnetic pole. There the ego, always an eager candidate for power, has no rival in sight; and then indeed sins become "deadly," for they have entered the domain of evil, in which good, by being forgotten, is denied existence and nothing is left but the gravity pull to entropy, disintegration, and death.

Good is not the mere absence of evil, however easy our present-day attitudes would like to make it. Good is the "one"; it is completeness, unity, the give and take of all the levels in harmony. It is evil that is partial, for it is the banishment of good, the dismissal of the possibility of a process leading to wholeness. Evil is incompleteness by choice, a willed, because consented-to, disintegration; it is vice "embraced," as Pope puts it. And joined with the human will, it becomes a force, although in itself it is really nothing. "I enquired what iniquity was," wrote St. Augustine, "and found it to be no substance, but the perversion of the will, turned aside from Thee, O God, the Supreme, towards these lower things."[6] It is man's will, his consent, that gives it its power, and its power is great and its presence everywhere: on every street corner, on every page of the newspaper. And behind that consent, without which it would be impotent, there is also nothing real, not even a devil—only the absence of something: a forgetting, a not-seeing. I used to wonder why stupidity—my own and others,—was not counted among the seven deadly sins; but I now believe that it is because it is not one but all of them.

The Buddhists call it ignorance, which we tend to condone: it is not our fault if we don't know something! No one told us, no one taught us that! And that is dangerous, like all half-truths; but what is more dangerous is that we don't know that we are ignorant, we don't see that we don't see. We believe in our one-dimensional, evil world with its strange ego-god, and if someone tries to tell us of a different truth, we refuse to listen or—worse—say yes, that is exactly what I think too.

The fact is that we don't ever really see good or evil; we see "good things" and "bad things," or what we judge to be so, but we don't see their source or their goal. With more attention to our weak consciences (thereby strengthening and educating them) we could see at least the direction from which impulses and events come and toward which they tend, and draw from that knowledge some conclusion on which could be based a more intelligent choice. For choose between them we must. The will we were given by whatever force created us destines us to choose. But our will is not free; it is bound by our conditioning, by fear, by imagination, by habits of all sorts. Perhaps we are here just to free that will and take the blindfold off of conscience; perhaps the reason for human existence is that we should come to be responsible for the gifts that make us different from the animals, and whose full use could give us a different destiny from theirs.

In the words of one of the Upanishads:

> *Man is a creature of will. According to what his will is in this world, so will he be when he has departed this life. Let him therefore have this will and belief:*
>
> *The intelligent, whose body is spirit, whose form is light, … who never speaks, and is never surprised,*
>
> *He is my self within the heart … smaller than a canary seed or the kernel of a canary seed, … greater than the earth, greater than the sky, greater than all these worlds …*
>
> *He, my self within the heart, is that Brahman. When I shall have departed from hence, I shall obtain him.*[7]

"Let him have this will and belief"—again, it is our choice. It is possible to begin to value the fact that "man is a creature of will" and appreciate ourselves for our real potential worth, our possibility of becoming instead of a taken-for-granted, imaginary "goodness." The human will could be free—we have examples of it; free to coincide with a higher will ("Thy will be done") instead of the self-will of the ego. There could be a will to obey the law and to stop our offenses against nature; a will on the side of life and the completion of its relationships, inner and outer—a movement toward wholeness. For will is action, a movement toward; it is close to being the equivalent of love. Certainly real love is not possible without it. "The seat of love is the will alone," Meister Eckhart wrote. "Love depends altogether on the will; to have more will is to have more love."[8] For this kind of free will would be open to the light of conscience and the sense of responsibility for one's choice.

Notes:

1 Matthew 19:17

2 *Meister Eckhart: A Modern Translation* by Raymond Bernard Blakney (New York: Harper & Bros., 1941), p. 50.

3 Ibid., p. 12.

4 *The Imitation of Christ*, I–13.

5 *The Confessions of St. Augustine*, translated by E. B. Pusey (Everymans Library), p. 134.

6 Ibid., Book 7, XVI.

7 Chandogya Upanishad, III, 14. In *Upanishads: English Selections*, translated by Max Muller. Sacred Books of the East. (New York: Dover, 1962).

8 *Meister Eckhart: A Modern Translation*, p. 14.

Parabola
Volume: 15.2
Attention

Silence of the Heart

Richard Temple

Almost unknown in the West there exists an extensive literature from the Christian mystics of the East. The writings, contained in the anthology known as the Philokalia ("love of the good"), date from the fourth to the fourteenth century. They are the advice and practical teaching of the Byzantine monastic spiritual tradition, the actual techniques of mysticism from spiritual guides to their direct followers. Unlike Western and most other mystical writings, those in the Philokalia are neither poetic nor self-consciously literary; they are private documents of a technical nature, preserved within the Mount Athos monasteries purely for the use of monks of later generations. To enter the thought of these writings, it is necessary to be sincerely in search of true meaning in one's life. At the same time they are not exclusive. Although not everyone is on the way, the way is in everyone.

The foreword, written by the English translators, begins promisingly: "The 'Philokalia' ... shows the way to awaken attention and consciousness," and further, "the primordial condition and absolute necessity is to know oneself. To gain this knowledge the beginner must be alive to the many-sided possibilities of the ego."[1] Bishop Theopan the Recluse, the nineteenth-century translator of the Russian version, and himself a hesychast (from the Greek *hesychia*, "silence"), refers to the "secret life in our

Lord Jesus Christ, which is the only truly Christian life."[2] By the "secret life" he means the practice of the ideas given in the book which he calls the "essence of Christianity." Writers in the Philokalia make the following promises: "I will impart to you the science of eternal heavenly life,"[3] and "if you wish … to acquire within you your own lamp shedding the mental light of spiritual knowledge … I will show you a marvellous spiritual method not requiring physical labour or exertion, but demanding spiritual work—attention of mind and thought."[4]

But the present-day reader of the Philokalia will not find in it a basic introduction to spirituality laid out step by step in easy stages. It is not a primer. In antiquity and in medieval times, readers of the church fathers were people who had already passed through the stages of questioning and doubting the values of the existing material world; they had renounced the world and were already on the path towards spiritual knowledge. The Philokalia texts are writings shared among people who were working together on themselves towards a spiritual ideal. But the missing first steps can be reconstructed from the many passing references in the text.

The ideas in these writings are based on traditional and ancient esoteric teachings about human beings: what they are and what they can become. According to these ideas man is regarded as a "tripartite being" consisting of mind, body, and soul. Sometimes the term "spirit" replaces "mind." Each of these three aspects is in turn subdivided into various categories; for example, one of the subdivisions of the soul is the "thinking part." This terminology comes from Platonism and is standard Hellenistic thinking; it is an example of how we have to be careful of certain words that today are differently understood. For instance, we think of the term "mind" as meaning the function of thought, whereas here "mind" is the same as "spirit" and is understood as something much higher than mentation. Elsewhere we read that the soul is subdivided into "three powers": the "thinking part" (which we could call the mind), the "excitable (or energetic) part," and the "desiring part."[5] The mind (or spirit) is similarly subdivided into three parts.

The student of the Philokalia also sees that the terminology is not always consistent; sometimes the same word is employed to convey different meanings—we have seen that we have to be particularly careful of the word "mind"—and sometimes there are different words having the same meaning. But behind this apparent lack of precision we can sense a far more important aspect of the teaching than verbal accuracy. The truth of the ideas in these writings can only be reached through practice and experience; there are frequent exhortations to trust neither words nor the "reasoning power of the mind." We are considered to have higher mental or spiritual possibilities than ordinary logical thinking which is regarded as tied to, and on the same level as, the bodily senses. In ordinary life we live according to the perceptions of the senses and what we call rational thought; but the method of the Philokalia calls us to an inner turning towards a state of being not dependent on the external world. This special interior state is referred to as "prayer," "sobriety," "passionlessness," "silence," and so on. And in order to maintain this state in ourselves, we must wage a ceaseless and "unseen warfare" against "imagination," "thoughts," and the "aimless circling of the mind." The weapon with which we guard our inner state against the mind's endless distractions is attention.

The fathers distinguish several kinds of knowledge that correspond to the different aspects of the human being. There is "natural knowledge" or the state of knowing that relies on the evidence of the senses, but the hesychast is called to renounce natural knowledge and to submit himself to a series of disciplines that are contrary to his natural inclinations. Instead of gratifying the desires of the mind and the body, he must practice "fasting, prayer, alms, reading of the Divine Scriptures, virtuous life, struggle with passions and so on."[6] By these means he begins to collect "what is useful for the journey into true life"[7] and at the same time to acquire a "second degree of knowledge" sometimes known as "contranatural knowledge." The attainment of this new knowledge leads to "mastery over desires" or self-mastery, and also self-consciousness. There exists a third degree of knowledge called, in the Philokalia, "supranatural knowledge." This corresponds to what has been called elsewhere objective consciousness. It is "the degree of perfection ... a man becomes finer, acquires that which is of the spirit, and in his life comes to resemble the invisible powers, which perform their service not through sensory actions but through vigilance of mind."[8]

We call natural the knowledge the soul can receive by using natural methods and powers to investigate and examine the creation and the Cause of the creation, as far as this is possible, of course, for a soul tied to matter. For the energy of the mind is weakened by its closeness to and fusion with the body, as a result of which it cannot have direct contact with intelligible [spiritual] things but needs to form images for thinking of them. And the natural function of imagination is to create images, which have extension and volume. Thus, since the mind [mentation] is in the flesh, it requires corresponding images of things for forming judgments about them and understanding them. ...

But supranatural knowledge is knowledge which enters the mind by a way which transcends its natural means and powers, or in which the object of knowledge is transcendent in relation to the mind tied to the flesh, so that such knowledge is clearly the attribute of incorporeal mind. ...
—*The Blessed Theodore*[9]

Not only is it impossible that this spiritual knowledge should be received by natural knowledge, but it cannot even be experienced in feeling by a man who zealously exercises himself in natural knowledge. If any such wishes to approach this other, spiritual knowledge, he can come no nearer to it until he renounces natural knowledge, with all its subtle twistings and manifold methods. ... Until the mind is freed from the multitudes of thoughts and has achieved the single simplicity of purity, it cannot experience spiritual knowledge.
—*St. Isaac of Syria*[10]

The question arises, how can the mind be freed? How can natural knowledge be renounced? It is at this point that the candidate for hesychasm has to abandon "knowledge" and theoretical studies. The journey must begin in practice; the candidate must start acquiring that other kind of knowledge which only comes through the techniques of inner silence, contemplation, and non-attachment. "You will never learn the work of spiritual striving from words alone," says St. Abba Dorotheus.[11] Altogether new possibilities arise here that have little to do with words and ideas. But practical spiritual work must be carried out under the instruction of a teacher or superior. Again, it cannot be stressed too often, it is a matter of experience and not of theory. The instructor is one who has already traveled along the path and who, from practical knowledge, points out the way. In a literal sense this person is a guide:

> *Accept without fail words spoken from experience, even if the speaker is not learned in books. ... Confide your thoughts to a man who ... has studied the work in practice, rather than to a learned philosopher, who reasons on the basis of his speculations, with no practical knowledge.*
> —*St. Isaac of Syria*[12]

Just as the mystical path in ancient India was called the "Way of Self-Knowing," or the essence of Greek religious thought is summed up in the formula "Know Thyself," so does self-study play a central role in hesychasm. "Do you wish to know God? Learn first to know yourself," says Abba Evagrius.[13] Self-study is the basic precondition, and self-watching has to be precise:

> *Let us desire the renewal of our inner spiritual man ... let us wish at all hours to watch over ourselves.*
> —*St. Isaac of Syria*[14]

> *A man ... must observe his thoughts and notice on what they lay emphasis and what they let pass, which of them and in what circumstances is particularly active, which follows which, and which of them do not come together.*
> —*Abba Evagrius*[15]

Anyone engaged in the practice of watching over himself soon discovers the difficulties. It is soon apparent that we are not as we should be; as we are in our present state we are misfits not properly entitled to the name of human beings:

> *He alone can be called a man who is intelligent [true intelligence is that of the soul], or who has set about correcting himself. An uncorrected person should not be called a man ...*
> —*St. Antony the Great*[16]

Such is our condition. Caught between two worlds, that of the visible and the sensory, "the flesh," and that of the invisible, "the spirit," we fall between the two. We are not just animals, and are not yet properly humans. We have a "soul" which is in darkness and enslaved by our attachments to the material world. From the visible realm and the perceptivity of the senses come "thoughts" which crowd out our inner life with their agitation and noise so that inwardly we can have no peace; we can only stagger about in a confused and "drunken" state. The condition of mankind would be hopeless were it not for the fact that:

> *In creating man God implanted in him something Divine—a certain thought, like a spark, having both light and warmth, a thought which illumines the mind and shows what is good and what is bad. This is called conscience and it is a natural law ... but when through the fall, men covered up and trampled down conscience, there arose the need to ... rekindle this buried spark.*
> *—St. Abba Dorotheus[17]*

The tool for rekindling the spark is attention. It is by attention on ourselves that we can withdraw the powers of the mind from their state of dispersion among the senses and the multitude of thoughts they give rise to. Attention is the magic talisman that makes the proposals of hesychasm practical possibilities:

> *Attention is the appeal of the soul to itself, ... the beginning of contemplation, ... serenity of the mind, or rather its standing firmly planted and not wandering, ... cutting off thoughts, ... the treasure-house of the power to endure all that may come, ... the origin of faith, hope and love ...*
> *—Nicephorus the Solitary[18]*

> *Some of the fathers called this doing, silence of the heart; others called it attention; yet others—sobriety and opposition (to thoughts), while others called it examining thoughts and guarding the mind.*
> *—St. Simeon the New Theologian[19]*

Collect your mind from its customary circling and wandering outside, and quietly lead it into the heart by way of breathing.
—*The Monks Callistus and Ignatius*[20]

Wealth ... is brought to the soul from the daily practice of attention.
—*Hesychius of Jerusalem*[21]

The attention is needed to watch over thoughts that arise from the senses and to prevent them from disturbing inner silence:

If you wish ... to come to the knowledge of truth, always urge yourself to rise above sensory things. ... Thus compelling yourself to turn inwards, you will meet principalities and powers, which wage war against you by suggestions in thoughts.
—*St. Mark the Ascetic*[22]

It is impossible to subjugate these (external) senses to the authority of the soul without silence and withdrawal.
—*St. Isaac of Syria*[23]

Sensory perception, or the perception of sensory impressions, belongs to the man of action, *who labours over attaining the virtues. Non-perception by the senses, or being unmoved by sensory impressions, belongs to the* contemplative *who concentrates his mind on God.*
—*St. Maximus the Confessor*[24]

Many things in the Philokalia are said about "passions." This word has not quite the same meaning as it has in ordinary language, though it is related to emotional impulse. The passions that hesychasm speaks of are, for the most part, invisible movements of psychic energy between the mind and emotions related to the senses. Only one who is engaged in inner work can begin to throw light on this kind of activity taking place within oneself but beyond the sight of one's ordinary consciousness. Special attention is necessary to see what goes on beneath the surface, attention that itself has to be cultivated by long practice and exercises. Without it we cannot know ourselves psychologically, and descriptions we may come across will mean little to us unless we ourselves are interested in this path to self-knowledge.

What we like and dislike, our opinions, attitudes, and beliefs, are nearly always sustained by, as well as being the results of, that form of emotional identification that the hesychasts call passion. Our fixed, inner emotional attitudes are the bricks with which the walls of our spiritual prison are built; it is because of them that we are not free to move inwardly, to open to all the newness and richness of life and people around us.

Passions exist in the different components and subdivisions that constitute us. There are "passions of the excitable part; bodily passions; passions of speech and tongue; passions of mind; passions of thought."[25]

> *Passions ... are like dogs, accustomed to lick the blood in a butcher's shop; when they are not given their usual meal, they stand and bark ...*
> *—St. Isaac of Syria*[26]

> *An object is one thing, a representation another, passion yet another. An object is, for example, a man, a woman, gold and so forth; a representation—a simple memory of some such object; passion—either an irrational love or an undiscerning hatred of one of these things. It is against such passion that the monk wages war.*
> *—St. Maximus the Confessor*[27]

> *First comes* impact *(contact, action, when a thing thrown hits the thing at which it is thrown): then comes* coupling *(joining together; attention is fettered to the object so that there exist only the soul and the object which has impinged upon it and occupied it); next comes* merging together *(the object, which has impinged upon the soul and occupied the attention, has provoked desire—and the soul has consented to it—has merged with it); then comes* captivity *(the object has captivated the soul which desired it and is leading it to action like a fettered slave); finally comes* passion *(sickness of the soul) inculcated in the soul by frequent repetition (repeated gratification of the same desire) and by habit ...*
> *—Philotheus of Sinai*[28]

The state of "passionlessness" is not a passive silence but a highly active one maintained by all the powers of attention and spiritual vigilance.

> *St. Isaac writes: Passionlessness does not mean not feeling passions, but not accepting them.*
> —*The Monks Ignatius and Callistus*[29]

> *The best method [to resist passions] is to plunge deep into the inner man and remain there in seclusion, constantly tending to the vineyard of one's heart.*
> —*St. Isaac of Syria*[30]

Whoever seeks self-knowledge and enlightenment by means of hesychasm must also be constantly engaged in mental warfare. Without the discipline of attention the mind is in a disorganized and dispersed state, as the fathers never cease to remind us:

> *Thoughts change instantly from one to another … what gives them power over us is mostly our own carelessness.*
> —*St. Gregory of Sinai*[31]

> *We should strive to be empty even of thoughts which appear to come from the right, and in general of all thoughts, lest thieves are concealed behind them.*
> —*Hesychius of Jerusalem*[32]

> *Although our outward aspect is appropriate to prayer, for we kneel and appear to those who see us to be praying, in our thoughts we imagine something pleasant, graciously talk with friends, angrily abuse enemies, feast with guests, build houses for our relatives, plant trees, travel, trade, are forced against our will into priesthood, organise with great circumspection the affairs of the churches placed in our care, and go over most of it in our thoughts, consenting to any thought that comes along.*
> —*St. Nilus of Sinai*[33]

These last remarks, written in the early fifth century, are a direct piece of self-observation that lives on the page with the freshness of truth. It is by such examples that self-knowledge is a teacher.

An important idea in the Philokalia is the role of the body in spiritual work. As a general principle manual labor is considered always useful, not so much in itself, though that can have its value; but more important is the possibility provided by the conditions of the task for bringing attention to both the physical as well as the mental state in which the work is carried out.

> *A body labouring at some piece of work keeps the thought close by, since the task of thought, like that of the eyes, is to watch over what is being done and to help the body act faultlessly.*
> —St. Nilus of Sinai[34]

An aspect of the hesychast method is the exercise of repetition using the so-called Jesus Prayer. Without denying the importance of such an exercise, it should not be taken out of the context of the total teaching. The mere repetition of a phrase, unaccompanied by the right kind of inner attention as well as, in some cases, the right kind of work for the body, is in danger of becoming mechanical. There are no simple means that, in themselves, give a higher state of consciousness, nor are there any automatic methods.

It is also important in spiritual work that special care be taken when there sometimes appear, particularly to beginners, certain euphoric phenomena that can occasionally accompany inner work. While such states are not abnormal, they should not be mistaken for higher knowledge or higher energy just because they are new. They are a by-product and, though perhaps pleasant or fascinating, they should not be a distraction. The Philokalia contains frequent warnings against "beguilement," "mirages," or "beauty." Once again it is a question of the right guidance.

The main work of the hesychast is to acquire the blessing of attention. For this he must summon what natural gifts he has and develop them so that they serve his spiritual aim. In their undeveloped state they can only serve outer life. But for a higher aim, the intellect, the heart, and all the physical functioning must be tuned so finely that they work to their fullest capacity. Only then will they be fit for the role they were designed for: the preparation of a place within, where God may enter.

This great undertaking calls into play, within us, forces of the divine world which the powers of nature, also within us, seem to oppose. Our natural side, or what the fathers call "Adam" or the "old man," and which today we might understand as the egoistic and materialist side, lies in wait for the spiritual side to steal the attention, that special talisman that gives us power over the lower forces. This thief waits until "night" and lulls the hesychast into a state of "sleep" where he can steal his strength. As a result the hesychast is unaware of the danger of going alone and unprotected into battle against the forces of darkness without the miraculous intervention of higher powers coming to his aid.

Attention is our most precious gift; the secret charm that, as in the fairy stories, empowers its possessor to overcome insuperable obstacles. Without it we cannot know ourselves, we do not know where our thoughts go or with what we are inwardly occupied. Externally, we have a degree of attention for our material life. It is demanded of us and without it we make mistakes that may cost us dearly. But the call for inner attention is not easily heard for it is not sounded out there in life, but elsewhere, mysteriously.

Attention is the transforming force that carries us across the threshold from theory and reading into practice and personal experience. Like light, flowing down and penetrating the material world, it illuminates the lower and the dark in ourselves and transforms it. It enables the seeker to survey his thoughts, feelings, and actions impartially. He sees that he is not them, just as light is not the object it illumines. He knows attention as "I"; the inner God; Christ within. When such divinity is present, order and unity have come to reign over his inner world, and the act of creation is reflected in him.

Notes:

1   E. Kadloubovsky and G. E. H. Palmer, *Writings from the Philokalia on Prayer of the Heart* (referred to below as PH), (London: Faber and Faber, 1951), p. 5.

2   PH, p. 13.

3   Nicephorus the Solitary, PH, p. 22.

4   PH, p. 27.

5   See Maximus the Confessor, in Kadloubovsky and Palmer, *Early Fathers from the Philokalia* (referred to below as EFP), (London: Faber and Faber Limited, 1954), pp. 319, 372, 374.

6   EFP, p. 193.

7   EFP, p. 194.

8   EFP. p. 194.

9   EFP, pp. 389 ff.

10 EFP, p. 216.

11 EFP, p. 169.

12 EFP, pp. 197, 263.

13 EFP, p. 109.

14 EFP, p. 222.

15 EFP, p. 101.

16 EFP, p. 22.

17 EFP, p. 157.

18 PH, p. 32.

19 PH, p. 157.

20 PH, p. 195.

21 PH, p. 285.

22 EFP, p. 90.

23 EFP, p. 208.

24 EFP, p. 353.

25 For a full account of the different passions see St. Gregory of Sinai in PH, p. 51.

26 EFP, p. 209.

27 EFP, p. 323.

28 PH, p. 338.

29 PH, p. 253.

30 EFP, p. 221.

31 PH, p. 49.

32 PH, p. 299.

33 EFP, pp. 145–146.

34 EFP, p. 147.

Parabola
Volume: 7.4
Holy War

THE BATTLE FOR PERSON IN THE HEART

James and Myfanwy Moran

> *Fire is in all things, is spread everywhere, pervades all things without intermingling with them, shining by its very nature and yet hidden, and manifesting its presence only when it can find material on which to work, violent and invisible, having absolute rule over all things. ... It comprehends, but remains incomprehensible, never in need, mysteriously increasing itself and showing forth its majesty according to the nature of the substance receiving it, powerful and mighty and invisibly present in all things.*
> —St. Dionysus the Areopagite

When asked what a person should do to reach holiness, St. Anthony said, "Become what you are." According to Eastern Orthodox tradition, the aim of spiritual warfare in life is to achieve just such a becoming.

Eastern Orthodox Christianity believes that man is a being made to live in the great fire of the divine life and to participate in its energies, delights, and beauties. St. Peter speaks of human beings becoming "partakers" in the eternal life of God.

However, Orthodoxy believes that human personhood was not made to be in the divine life like a fish swimming in the sea, but to experience it more as God does. In the Holy Trinity, the divine life is conferred on and shared by the three persons only because they give it one to another out of love: divine life is a personal offering between them, given and received freely. Love never compels or seduces. It is humble. That is its beauty and its risk. Man's real greatness lies in the fact that his personhood was created to know this beauty and this risk. By receiving the divine life as a gift, and using its energies in his existence, man becomes God's intimate friend and co-worker in the creation.

Love, then, is no mere subjective emotion or feeling; no mere objective behavior or good deed. It is the very power, or driving force, of the human personhood. It is an energy with ontological reality and great creative force. It is nothing less than the spark of the divine fire which was meant to grow into a raging flame, provided that man uses it according to its true nature, to express the creativity and freedom of love. By "spending" this energy in that fashion, the personhood of a human being can grow from the image of God, or potentiality for divinization, into the likeness of God, or actuality of divinization. Each unique life would then express its fire differently, yet all lives would be drawn together into its communal feast and celebration. And the fire would dwell in spirit, soul, and body, and reach out to the rest of creation, releasing its potentiality to participate in the Kingdom. The Kingdom which begins in the Holy Trinity would extend, through man's free act of loving, to all that exists.

As a consequence of man's Fall, this active and sovereign love is almost, but not quite, dead. It is frozen. Thus the original image of God in man is put on ice; the growth toward the final likeness has been lost. The fallen personhood lacks fire: its spark is enslaved and burns only weakly.

A story from the Talmud tells of the son of a king who abandoned his inheritance and went far away. His father sent a messenger, asking him to come back. He answered, "I cannot." So the father sent another messenger, saying, "Come back as far as you can, and I will come to meet you there."

This story perfectly states how Orthodoxy sees the Incarnation. Christ is the Father's final messenger, His "only begotten Son," who comes to meet man where he is because man cannot come any further. And Christ comes not simply to justify us before the Father, but rather to restore us, heal us, rouse us. The Eastern Church Fathers said of this: "God became man so that man might become God."

This is the Orthodox meaning of redemption: Christ has rekindled in mankind the spark of divine energy, and thus made it possible for us to grow to completion by actively using this energy in our lives—to be aflame with it and united by it to the Holy Trinity and to all of mankind, and indeed to all creatures and things, in a single communion. St. Gregory Palamas said of this final transfiguration of the human personhood by divine fire that "God in all fullness comes to dwell in the complete being of those who are worthy of it." A statement of Christ preserved in the memory of the church declares: "He who is near me is near the fire."

But redemption is not magic. For it to be fulfilled in us, Orthodoxy believes, we have to be willing to co-operate with its gift of fire. Through the will, we bring our heart to God, with all its attributes, hungers, failings, to be changed by Him. This is what St. Gregory Palamas called "synergy" or "energy sharing." On the one hand, God's fire is necessary to re-kindle our spark, and so it makes a change in the heart we could not, by our own efforts, bring about. On the other hand, God cannot do it all, because our free will cannot be compelled, and our "yes" is shown by our willingness to make efforts in order to pursue the change God makes in us. In that sense, we complete it by furthering its work.

These efforts to co-operate with redemption initiate one into what the Orthodox tradition calls spiritual warfare. For when the individual starts to make these efforts, he soon finds that it is impossible to give the heart to God or to his fellow man, because he discovers that he has in himself something that follows the road of the fire of redemption and something else that resists it. Jewish mysticism calls the former the "heart of flesh" and the latter the "heart of stone." When one has truly seen the existence of these two hearts, the purpose of the entry into their hidden warfare is also seen: to consciously and willingly "fight" to strengthen the heart of flesh and resist the heart of stone. This struggle is necessary in order to be able to move from the position where we are half-hearted and divided in heart, with respect to the holy fire and our spark of it, to a situation where the division in us is healed and we can truly be whole-hearted.

In effect, man has to see into his heart and be willing to confront what is there and struggle with what is there. The spiritual warfare between the heart of flesh and the heart of stone is inevitable, raging in the depths, but man's task is to enter it and take sides. To be unconscious of the battle is, usually, to sit on the fence and allow the outcome to go by default, for in the fallen state and fallen world the heart of stone tends to suffocate the heart of flesh.

Does this mean man should be fighting to get rid of the heart of stone (the idealistic and puritanical solution)? Or to rise above it (the romantic and esoteric solution)? Or suppress and contain it (the humanistic and rational solution)?

These ways do not work: none of them in the least affects the power of the heart of stone to inhibit love, and all of them in different ways dangerously diminish the power of the heart of flesh to love. For they are all ways in which the heart of flesh hardens itself by dealing unlovingly with the refusal of the heart of stone. Thus by following them, the heart of flesh actually grows harder and more akin to the heart of stone. This is the great danger of the spiritual life.

Orthodoxy teaches that whole-heartedness, or healing of the heart, cannot be achieved by imagining that we can triumph over the heart of stone. It is fundamental Christian belief that the devil cannot create anything, that evil in us is actually a distortion of something originally good, and cannot be thrown away but must be redeemed: the good must be reclaimed from evil. If we throw away the deepest evil, we also throw out the deepest good, and live by a "good" of our own invention which is only a sublimated or inverted evil.

Hence the real heart of all our efforts in synergetic cooperation with God's redemption is actually our repentance: the acknowledgment that evil has distorted good, and the willingness to change, and to suffer for that change, so that the good will be freed from evil.

Repentance entails bearing the lesser heart in the greater heart, inwardly, like a cross. But from this comes the strength both to love more and to resist what inhibits love, to learn from it the virtues which are the strength of love: long-sufferance, patience, humility and courage. We become more merciful to other people without sentimentality, and more realistic without being judgmental. We learn to bear and forgive them. But by its bearing of the heart of stone, the heart of flesh also comes to see into and see through it, understanding its thoughts, images, and passions as they arise. Eventually, the heart of stone can be resisted not just outwardly, in behavior, but inwardly at its source. This bestows wisdom about the inner workings of the heart, and the ability to help others in their tangled web of flesh and stone.

What then is the good in us distorted by evil? In the Eastern Christian ascetic tradition, there are said to be three main expressions—which are both "faculties" and "energies"—of the spark of the fire of divinity in human beings. The Desert Fathers call these:

> Nous, *or the eye of the heart: "perception," or the intelligent aspect of the spark*
>
> Thymos, *or the vehement wrath of the heart for truth and against falsity, and the passion to act in and for the truth: "will," or the incensive aspect of the spark*
>
> Eros, *or the longing of the heart for ecstatic union with God and with all persons and creatures made by God (the East does not accept any distinction between* Eros *and* Agape, *for the former expresses only a more intense and ecstatic state of the latter): "desire," or the goal-directed aspect of the spark*

In their unfallen, or original state, one can speak of the clarity of the *Nous*, the strength of the *Thymos*, and the power of *Eros*.

The fallen state of *Nous*, *Thymos*, and *Eros* is, at root, simple. But it has effects at every level of personhood—spirit, soul (psychological and sociological), and body (biological and physiological). At root this fallen state is passivity rather than activity, bondage rather than sovereignty. Instead of being expressions of activity and freedom, the three fires become passions which possess us, and so scatter, dilute, and weaken authentic passion. In the Greek language, "sin" means "failure" or specifically "failure to hit the mark"; the three fires fail to achieve the *telios*, or final end, for which they have been created. This means, also, that they wander off the mark into illusion.

Fallen *Nous*, or spiritual delusion, includes the following: beguilement by demonic lies and illusions; loss of reality; self-enclosure and self-preoccupation; indifference or blindness to the other; abstraction and passivity; narcissistic states and schizoid madness; projection and introjection; idolatrous, rather than iconic, images of the psyche.

Fallen *Thymos*, or spiritual pride, includes: self-will, self-righteousness, self-justification, and self-glorification; personal aggrandizement through ownership (riches, status, property); domination, or power over the other; calculation and manipulation; coercion and seduction; violent power, hostility, resentment; rubbing out "the fine wirey line of creation" (Blake) in brutality or sentimentality; sado-masochistic states and obsessional-paranoid madness; reaction formation.

Fallen *Eros*, or spiritual hedonism, entails: theft of the gift from the giver, or loss of communion; self-preservation and self-indulgence; meanness and luxury; devouring, or power through the other; impulsiveness and inundation; sloppiness and inertia; unsteady power, vanity, and avarice; hysteric states, or manic-depressive madness; sublimation.

It would seem clear that these three faculties and energies are akin, in their fallen state, to what the Buddhists call the Three Fires of delusion, hating, and grasping. However, whereas purification in Buddhism aims at overcoming fallen attachment by non-attachment, purification in the Christian East aims at restoring it to its true standing. In this it shares that radical, total, unreserved attachment God has for the persons he has called into existence. It is the egoism of attachment, in its fallen state, which must be renounced and overcome in order to free its personalness.

Restoring fallen attachment to its true standing is accomplished through "putting on Christ's yoke." It is as if his *Nous* teaches our eye to be singular so it can see reality, his *Thymos* teaches our will to be emptied of itself so it can act in and for the truth, his *Eros* teaches our desire to be purged of its devouring so it can live by communion. Christ said: "I am the way, the truth, and the life."

The concrete practices employed within the church for putting on Christ's yoke in the *Nous*, the *Thymos*, and the *Eros*, purify them, and hence reclaim their true purpose from their fallen functioning.

These practices constitute, along with the repentance that is their context and precondition, the Christian Way as this is seen and walked in Eastern Orthodoxy. Repentance, stilling the heart, self-emptying, and togetherness are the Four Pillars of Orthodox life.

Hesychasm: The Lamp of the Way

"Blessed are the pure in heart, for they will see God."

"The light of the body is the eye: if therefore your eye is single, your whole body will be full of light. But if your eye is evil, your whole body will be full of darkness."

The *Nous* is not the discursive reason or the modern "intellect." St. Makarius of Egypt called it the "eye of the heart"; St. Diadochus, the "innermost aspect of the heart." St. Isaac the Syrian called it the "simple cognition" by which one apprehends divine truth in immediate experience. But since for Christianity the divinity is someone, not something, and indeed God in Trinity, the deepest perception is of the ultimate reality of personhood. Moreover, to see personhood is primarily to see God as its origin; to see the personhood of human beings is to see it in and through God. As St. Anthony wrote, "When you see your brother, you see God."

Seeing is the beginning of love: without it as the first and fundamental step, love is spiritual delusion or psychological fantasy—either a blotting out of the other, or an activity of imagining it in images that owe more to the psyche than to their reality. To bear the reality of the other is among the hardest of all spiritual disciplines.

Hesychasm is practiced through what is called the "Prayer of the Heart" (or the "Jesus Prayer"). This is prayer of the "hidden man of the heart," in St. Peter's words, or the prayer that should be "unceasing," in St. Paul's words. Clearly, the conscious mind cannot pray in this fashion. *Hesychasm* therefore demands that we "take the mind down into the heart" and "pray with the mind in the heart." This way of praying combines the deepest cry to God, like that made by David in the Psalms, with meditational concentration, mindfulness, and attentiveness. The heart has to be stilled of its agitation, anxiety, and clouded state to stand in the presence of God, face to face. *Hesychasm* has techniques both for breath control (to bring consciousness out of the mind down into the heart), and for emptying the mind of its attachment to, and domination by, images. Overcoming the domination of images—not eradicating them—is a major part of the work in *Hesychasm*. Images have to be discerned in terms of their origin. Thus they are regarded as arising from three different sources: (a) the celestial archetypes, or *logoi*, of the authentic imagination by which it both sees the divinity hidden in things, and creates "iconic" symbols of that divinity; (b) the thoughts and impulses which are suggested by demonic forces; and (c) the forms, pictures, and patterns that express the psyche's unconscious and conscious image-formation process. The Desert Fathers did not regard psychic fantasy as the same order of problem as spiritual delusion, except insofar as the latter often works through the former: fantasy is not to be indulged nor allowed to compulsively direct the attention, however. On the other hand, when the *Nous* is more "discerning of spirits," the psyche becomes more clear and its image-formation process more iconic and less idolatrous.

Two other practices much ignored in modern Christianity, East and West, but that are essential to *Hesychasm* are fasting and alms-giving. Fasting is to overcome bodily inertia, the automatic reaction in us whereby the most "natural" action is also the easiest and weakest. Alms-giving is not charity. It is the means to, and the fruit of, the deepest and truest enlightenment of the *Nous*: the apprehension of not only the reality but also the value of persons, and indeed of all things.

But prayer is fundamental and always comes first. Without it, we remain in the dark and do not know what we are doing; all other efforts come to nothing.

Kenosis: The Sword of Truth

"My judgment is true because I do the will of Him who sent me."

"Blessed are they who hunger and thirst after righteousness, for they will be filled."

The *Thymos* is the strength of the will to act decisively on what the *Nous* has seen. The *Thymos* is described by the Desert Fathers as "vehement for truth and against falsity," and shows this discrimination in all its action. Thus its action has an incisive, as well as decisive, quality, like the Zen swordsman's cut, or the Zen calligrapher's stroke. There is no room for brutality or blind force here, but equally neither for sentimentality or cowardly hesitancy. Thus the *Thymos* is the arousing power of the will, the root power of personhood. It is a power inspired by fidelity to truth, and therefore one ready to declare itself and suffer for truth. This has a very specific meaning. In a world that fears love, and indeed wants to kill it, acting in and for its truth may have a very high cost. Christ acted from *Thymos* when he flogged the money-changers and threw them out of the temple; when he denounced the Pharisees; and when he accepted Crucifixion.

Though loving is an action of the will, this action must be made first to God before it can be made with any discrimination and strength to human beings. Without giving the will to God first we become victims or victimizers in our action toward others. Our action is paralyzed at the core or becomes merely an attack of one kind or another: a manipulation, a display of power.

Kenosis—self-emptying—is not a moral, but an existential, act of will. By becoming empty of its own self-aggrandizement, the will becomes like that silence out of which true sound comes. Humility and poverty signify a state of emptiness in which God's will can act in man's will. Zen Buddhism calls this the "Great Death," and Chassidic Judaism the "Reduction to Nothing." In such self-emptying, one not only surrenders his misery and schemes and self-pity, but even the very best in himself, so that God can transform it from temporal riches into eternal gifts. This action of God is not like a spirit taking possession of a medium, for when the individual becomes self-emptied and filled with God, he becomes truly himself and in full possession of his true will. We come into the freedom of our royal personhood.

All of life can become an expression of *Kenosis*: it is political as well as mystical. The church has provided the sacrament of confession so that there is a means to be truthful with God, and ourselves, on the level where we really are. Both the spiritual zeal whereby we become egoistic bullies in the name of attacking evil in ourselves or others, and the spiritual despair—called *accidie*—whereby we give up on ourselves or others due to that evil, are manifestations of pride, and betoken a failure of *Kenosis*. The Beatitudes describe a growth in *Kenosis* through successive steps; St. John of the Ladder has written of these steps in detail.

Sobornost: The Cup of Life

"Greater love has no man than that he lay down his life for his friends."

"He who finds his life will lose it; and he who loses his life for my sake will find it."

The *Eros* is that power of desire, or longing, by which we are drawn out of ourselves toward God and other persons. *Eros* both recognizes the beauty of personhood, and yearns for communion with that personhood as the only fulfillment of its deep hunger. St. Dionysus says that this power of love to draw man out of himself and into communion is its ecstatic quality. "Love ... is ecstatic, making us go out of ourselves: it does not allow the lover to belong any more to himself, but he belongs only to the beloved." Does this mean ecstasy is a losing of oneself? No, it means that one ceases to be complete without the other. Life ceases to exist in self-preserved wholeness. Ecstasy also means that what *Eros* seeks is not a mere release of energy, but a meeting with the other, through contact with their energy. Ecstasy, in short, is the final fulfillment of synergy.

Since God is the source of personhood, our deepest desire is for communion with Him. But through God it becomes possible to give the heart to all persons, creatures, and things. Because God is the source of that community of life where communion is its very center and where all persons, creatures, and things together find their hunger fed, the kingdom is the place where all are brought together by the life that feeds them. Giving the heart is not a romantic, lonely action of our own, but rather the entry into a community which exists prior to us, and so does not stand or fall by us. It lives. We stand by it, and fall when we refuse to stand upon it, depend upon it, be fed by it. We can rely upon it. It has ontological reality. It is not invented by any good will on our part, but our will is used to enter it.

What prevents men from entering this community, and sharing its life, is what the Desert Fathers call spiritual hedonism. From God, we want rewards, experiences, higher knowledge, deliverance from pain and infirmity and death, but not God Himself. From people, we want sex and food without any gratitude toward, and solidarity with, those who offer those gifts. This creates a world not of ecstatic communion, but of rape and pillage and plunder. It makes of *Eros* a devouring hunger which sucks everything down into its black hole, and yet is unfeedable; or a miser who measures out love meanly, fretting over fair shares and his rights, spending nothing of himself or his possessions for love. Christ has said, in the parable of the talents, that if we are generous with the finite, we will be replenished by the infinite; but if we are mean with the little we have, we will lose even this. That is the Final Judgment in Christianity. The church is the early embodiment of the divine kingdom: literally its body. *Sobornost*, or the togetherness of persons in the communion created by God, is the rationale of the church. Without it, the church is merely an association of isolated individuals. By practicing *Sobornost*, the church becomes the physical altar and the physical cup which is the earthly home of the Holy Trinity.

The outward, or political, dimension of *Sobornost* means putting into practice the mystical communion of the kingdom in a concrete way. It becomes very radical if we have faith in, or experience of, the depth of *Sobornost*. All of the extreme, and seemingly foolish, injunctions of Christ are enactments on the surface of this depth: forgive seventy-times-seven; if your neighbor wants your coat, give him your cloak also; if he asks you to walk a mile with him, walk two; if you do it to the least of these, you do it to me. If *Sobornost* has reality, then it can be practiced radically. Not only does it mean taking others' sorrows and joys as one's own, but also that togetherness must stand firm even if those others reject the gifts or abuse them. Anyone can love those who make him feel good, or who are attractive to him, but *Sobornost* means loving to the very end as Christ did, even to His death on the cross.

The Desert Fathers took *Sobornost* so far as to say that one must "vindicate" one's brother. By this they meant, first of all, that since love is something that wins people, rather than compels them, we can redeem each other by bearing with and suffering for each other. We redeem others, and they us, by radical bearing one of another: "What is forgiven on earth is forgiven in Heaven." Secondly, the Fathers mean that we should repent when someone offends us as if the offense had been our own against them. No matter what our brother's offense against us might be, we must say to him and to God that the offense is not cause for his absence at the communion feast. For the final sanctity of *Eros* is shown in our inability to take joy in that feast if even one person is absent from it.

St. Isaac the Syrian describes this final *Sobornost* of *Eros* as the tenderness by which we weep for every person and creature, unable to bear their pain. These tears are the final fruit of Christian holiness, for they signify that love is "all in all" and has won us, totally. We live by love, no strings attached, no rewards, no stipulations, no reserves, no fears. We love and that love gives us life. It burns in us and is our ground, our wealth, our joy.

•

CHAPTER FOUR

ATTENTION AND REMEMBRANCE

And what I say to you I say to all: Watch.[1]

—Mark 13:37

Let us go forward with the heart completely attentive and the soul fully conscious. For if attentiveness and prayer are daily joined together, they become like Elias' fire-bearing chariot, raising us to heaven. What do I mean? A spiritual heaven, with sun, moon and stars, is formed in the blessed heart of one who has reached a state of watchfulness, or who strives to attain it.[2]

—Philotheus of Sinai

Parabola
Volume: 9.2
Theft

DEN OF THIEVES

D. M. Dooling

> *Even them will I bring to my holy mountain, and make*
> *them joyful in my house of prayer ... for mine house shall be*
> *called an house of prayer for all people.*
> *—Isaiah 56:7*

> *And Jesus went into the temple of God, and cast out all them*
> *that sold and bought in the temple, and overthrew the tables of*
> *the moneychangers, and the seats of them that sold doves, and*
> *said unto them, It is written, My house shall be called the house*
> *of prayer; but ye have made it a den of thieves.*
> *—Matthew 21:12–13*

This is one of the strangest, as well as most popular, of the stories in the New Testament about Jesus of
Nazareth. What did he mean by "a den of thieves"? No
doubt, the moneychangers charged their commission, as
they still do, but then as now with the approval of the
law; the merchants of livestock for sacrifice were selling
sought-after goods, and if the purchasers grumbled, as we
do, about prices, like us they paid them. Was the temple
being more seriously desecrated by these commercial
transactions than our churches nowadays, with their sale

of pamphlets and postcards, their bulletin boards of goods and good works for exchange? What was being stolen, by whom, and from whom? Do we really understand?

For this same man who so rudely cleansed the temple said other very strange things about it: "Destroy this temple and in three days I will raise it up"—a saying that was cast in his teeth as he hung upon the cross. "But he spake," his closest disciple added later, "of the temple of his body."[1] Or so his followers came to believe in the years that came after. "Know ye not that ye are the temple of God, and that the Spirit of God dwelleth in you? If any man defile the temple of God, him shall God destroy; for the temple of God is holy, which temple ye are."[2]

Is it true that there is an inner house that contains something precious, and if so, how can we be robbed of it? What is this "holy," this "prayer," that would link us with something higher? Did we lose it so long ago that we are not even aware of what it is, nor how it disappeared? Did we make some sort of deal with the thieves, or did they come silently, by night, and take us unaware, or were we deceived by promises to return the treasure with interest?

But what was taken? How can we complain of a loss, great or small, if we cannot report exactly what is missing?

"Prayer." "The Spirit of God." What are these, that we should contain them or even desire to do so? The Spirit of God moved on the face of the waters to create the world. It descended like a dove upon the baptized Jesus; it "came" suddenly upon Balaam and Saul and Azariah, so that for a moment they spoke with more authority, from a higher certainty, than other men. The power of knowledge, the power of understanding, the power to create: if there is in the human being a potential channel for this finer energy, what could open it? If "prayer" is the link, what is prayer?

Centuries after Jesus of Nazareth, centuries after John and Paul, a father of the Russian Church called Simeon the New Theologian wrote on "three methods of attention and prayer." "The mind should be in the heart," he says. "It should guard the heart while it prays, revolve, remaining always within. ... He who does not have attention in himself and does not guard his mind cannot become pure in heart and so cannot see God. ... Speaking generally, it is impossible to acquire virtue in any other way, except through this kind of attention. ... Keep your attention within yourself, not in your head but in your heart. Keep your mind there (in the heart), trying by every possible means to find the place where the heart is. ... Wrestling thus, the mind will find the place of the heart. This happens when grace produces sweetness and warmth in prayer. ... God demands only one thing from us—that our heart be purified by means of attention."[3]

"Trying by every possible means to find the place of the heart"—for where your treasure is, there will your heart be also.[4]

This attention—can we glimpse it? It is clearly far from that frowning mental effort of concentration by which we seek to nail down an understanding like a pinned butterfly. This attention does not close on anything; it is not a clamping shut, but an opening up to life in movement, an accompanying energy all the more intense because it is still, all the more still because it is continually, receptively alive to the flow of my life and being. This attention guards the feeling, and the feeling guards the attention; when they do not guard each other, both are stolen. The balance and energy of this relation are lost; the place of the heart is lost; the source and hearth of my consciousness, of my real being. I lose, in other words, *myself*.

Attention has never been defined. But it has been said: I am where my attention is; I *am* my attention. Unquestionably, my sense of myself—of where I am and who I am, as well as how and why I am—is bound up in what I am aware of at any given moment. At any given moment, its measure is my measure; its direction is the direction in which I am headed. That attention has value is conceded in the common phrase "to pay attention." At least one European language (Hungarian) acknowledges its active power by making it a verb instead of a noun. Certainly nothing can be done without it that could be called real doing rather than automatic reaction.

So it is my being and my doing that are at stake—my whole potential as a human being, with its possible development into knowledge and creativity—an upward evolving which "demands," as the author of *The Cloud of Unknowing* tells us, "that you persistently insist on bare consciousness of your own self."[5] Brother Lawrence wrote in one of his letters, "We must prevent our mind from wandering, no matter what the occasion may be, for we must make our heart a spiritual temple for him".[6]

The mystics, intent upon the upward, evolving direction, knew very well what attention is, and described it in all their writings, but in their own religious terms which have seemed irrelevant to our irreligious age. Perhaps we need to listen more carefully to the meaning behind those terms. It is a serious matter, evidently, in any age, to be in charge of one's own being and doing. What can I call myself if I am not in charge, if I do not *possess myself*? But do I? I have to see that I am not in command, that I am without access to the place in myself where the balance of energy exists, where I know myself and my surroundings with my feeling as well as my mind. My attention is taken by every circumstance, by every one of the pack of thieves which I also harbor within myself.

They are all there, every member of the brotherhood. There is the holdup man with his gun, threatening my life if I don't pay—"pay attention," give up all my interest, all my time and energy, to his demands. He wears a mask; but he speaks with such authority! Truly, it is my money or my life: my career, my family, are at stake; I am forced to give in. But if I took off his mask, whose face would I see?

They are all there, and some others are as bold as this armed bandit: the hijacker, who twists my journeys to his own ends and takes me where I had no intention of going. Others are less bold, but slyer: the cat burglar, who seems to have inside information about the times of my little indulgences and enters my room when I am sleeping the heavy sleep that follows them. Then I wake to find the drawers empty and the jewels gone. Or the safecracker, who also seems to know when the watchman is not there, and with a sudden small explosion in my unattended house—sometimes so skillfully muffled as to be almost inaudible—robs me of all my hoarded savings. Some, with even less respect, steal from me without my even knowing it, when I am pushing through a busy street with the sole intention of getting to my office in spite of all the hideous obstacles of crowds and traffic; the quick fingers picking my pocket feel no different from my own hand making sure the car keys are there—*but now, my God, where is my wallet? Have I dropped it somewhere?*

The shoplifter and the embezzler, the con man, the rip-off artist, the plagiarist and the bag snatcher—I could know them all if I chose to do so; even the phony beggar of self-pity, and his face beneath its makeup of unmerited disasters. But in order to admit their identity, I would have to give up "my own"—I would have to cease playing the role of the innocent victim, the philanthropist, the respectable, well-to-do citizen protesting against the violence of an ugly world. I would have to admit that my wealth was all in promissory notes, that all my gold was in the pockets of that grinning beggar and his confederates. I would have to give up my masks, my costumes, my lies, and my secret midnight revels with my companions, my other selves, the brotherhood of thieves. And this seems impossible to me, because I feel that I would have nothing left; I have forgotten what it is I have lost, I do not remember my treasure, I have lost the place of the heart; I no longer know what it is to love.

Yet in an unexpected, startling instant, when in spite of myself I recognize the robbery and know for my own the bandit's face, his voice, his way of moving, a strange feeling assails me that is very like the memory of love; for with the glimpse of what I am comes a longing for what I could be, a recollection and an acute valuing of what it is that I am losing. Then for that instant of compassion, I accept that I am both the robber and the robbed. I am the den of thieves; I am the house of prayers.

Notes:

1 John 2:19, 21.

2 I Corinthians 3:16–17.

3 *Writings from the Philokalia—On Prayer of the Heart*, tr. Kadloubovsky and Palmer (London: Faber & Faber Ltd., 1951).

4 Matthew 6:21.

5 *A Letter of Private Direction*, Spiritual Classics Series, ed. John Griffiths (New York: Crossroad Press, 1981).

6 *The Practice of the Presence of God*, tr. Sr. Mary David, SSND (New York: Paulist Press, 1978).

Parabola
Volume: 14.2
Tradition and
Transmission

THE GIFT OF LIFE

Cynthia Bourgeault

For an earliest generation of Christians, Jesus was not the Savior but the Life-giver. In the original Aramaic of Jesus and his followers, there was no word for salvation. Salvation was understood as bestowal of life, and to be saved was "to be made alive."[1]

This gift of life, moreover, was received in a clear rite of initiation, following the pattern of Jesus' own initiation. According to the ancient, Aramaic-derived traditions, Jesus' divine sonship began not in his sacrificial death on the cross, but in his spirit-filled baptism in the Jordan River. Entering the waters at the hand of John the Baptist, he emerged as the Life-giver (in Syriac, *Mahyana*), upon whom the Spirit "rested." He came forth also as *Ihidaya*, "the only one," or "the Unified One," and in this pattern his initiates became known also as *ihidaye*, "those who are one." This early Aramaic Christianity—scholars call it "Spirit Christology"—knew nothing of dying and rising with Christ, but only of a larger, more vivified and unified life made possible through the indwelling of the Spirit.

By the fourth century, however, Spirit Christology was already becoming a minority opinion. The day belonged to Paul, to the Greek language with its more intricate notions of "savior" and "salvation," and to a baptismal death-mysticism centering upon the cross. The emergent Christian Church erected its structure on the foundation of Paul, and the older tradition receded—but did not disappear. Handed down orally, often through baptismal ceremonies, it was written out in the fourth and fifth centuries in liturgical texts of the Syrian Christian and, through Syrian influence, also in Armenian Christian communities. The recovery of these texts has been an ongoing focus of the modern Syriac scholarship.

Only recently has the antiquity of these Syriac traditions come to be realized. Earlier, they were thought to represent mutant strains heavily influenced by later Syrian developments, in particular by Manichaeism. Now we are seeing that these later developments—including Manichaeism itself—may in fact represent parallel offshoots from an ancient, now archaic, stratum of Christian tradition, to which these texts bear the last remaining witness.[2] That recognition, with its renewed appreciation of oral transmission, is itself a radical corrective to our traditional understanding of Christian beginnings. But the picture of primitive Christianity that emerges from the ancient stratum is even more radical. In 1980 Jacob Needleman speculated on the shape and contents of a hypothetical "lost Christianity."[3] In the image of the *Ihidaya*, the Unified One, who calls us—impels us, empowers us—to become *ihidaye*, "unified ones," is there not at least the glimmer of that lost connecting link, that Needleman calls "intermediate Christianity"?

In the past, the term *ihidaya* has sometimes been translated simply as "monk," "hermit," or "solitary." And indeed, it is generally true that the most sustained exploration of the Christian spiritual path has been in monastic circles, particularly in that first great flourishing of monastic spirit in the deserts of Egypt and Syria during the fourth and fifth centuries. But it is important to recognize the direction of travel along this path. The monk's call to be "one"—in the sense of being solitary, or alone—derives from the prior call to be "one"—in the sense of being "single-minded" or "unified."

In the New Testament this call is frequently expressed as a summons to "be perfect," as in Matthew 19:21:

> *If thou wilt be perfect, go and sell that thou hast, and give to the poor, and thou shalt have treasure in heaven: and come follow me.*

This is not a call to be "faultless," or "sinless," as we might today hear it, through heavy Augustinian blinders. The Greek "telos" is better rendered as "to be *perfected*" — to be made whole, or one. (The *New English Bible* translates it as "If you wish to go the whole way. ...")

There are many such passages in the gospels, but this one is particularly important because it also marks the headwaters of Egyptian monasticism. In lower Egypt, toward the latter half of the third century, a wealthy young Christian named Antony heard these words read in church and was struck to the heart. Following the instructions literally, he immediately dissolved his worldly affairs and embarked on a life of asceticism and prayer. In the ensuing two centuries, tens of thousands of men and women would follow him into the desert, to create there the most vibrant response to the call to become *ihidaye* within the history of Christianity—and perhaps the closest thing to a "school" for spiritual development in the Christian West. Now that the desert tradition has been largely rescued from its earlier negative stereotype as a life-hating flight from the world, and reliable new translations of the teachings of the desert Christians have begun to appear,[4] there is much wisdom to be learned here—beginning with Antony himself.

Antony is often romanticized as the supreme spiritual individualist, fleeing into the desert for Promethean combat with the forces of evil, but *The Life of Saint Antony* paints a different picture. Antony does not head straight into the desert; instead he looks for a teacher:

> *Now, at that time there was in the next village an old man who had lived the ascetic life in solitude from his youth. When Antony saw him, he was zealous for that which is good; and he promptly began to stay in the vicinity of the town. Then, if he heard of a zealous soul anywhere, like a wise bee he left to search him out. ... He, in turn, subjected himself in all sincerity to the pious men whom he visited and made it his endeavor to learn for his own benefit just how each was superior to him in zeal and ascetic practice.*

Antony's spiritual journey, then, begins in the classic fashion, with a period of discipleship (the text calls it "the time of his initiation"). During this time he learns, among other things, the all-important quality of discernment, the ability to distinguish between a welter of conflicting inner impulses and demands (vividly portrayed in the text as a warfare with demons). Eventually he breaks with his teacher and withdraws into deeper solitude into the desert, but not before he has gained sufficient spiritual maturity to trust the validity of this call—and his own readiness to follow it.

Antony's experience, "writ large," will become the paradigm for the desert tradition. By the early fourth century the second great fountainhead of Egyptian monasticism appeared on the scene: Pachomius, founder of the *koinonia*—i.e., of cenobitic (communal) monasticism. Pachomius, too, begins his journey as a disciple—to an old hermit named Palamon—in a relationship so deeply transforming that it in fact furnishes the central motif of Pachomian monasticism. As de Vögué comments in his Foreword to *Pachomian Koinonia* (p. *xix*):

> *All of these [ascetic practices] Pachomius had learned from Palamon. And the simple fact of learning them from another provided the main lesson for him. From it he developed his idea of the role of the Father in the* Koinonia. *As a disciple of Palamon, Pachomius experienced with him the father-son relationship which he later lived out with innumerable monks in his monasteries. The humble and loving obedience which he had practiced for seven years with the old anchorite was to become a universal pattern for all that disciplined multitude. ...*

The wisdom of the desert is direct-line transmission; one-on-one, as father to son; not expounded but implanted. This, in turn, accounts for the central features of its teaching style.

Foremost among these is an economy of words. In striking contrast to the fathers of patristic tradition, the desert fathers shunned verbosity, preferring direct experience to theological speculation. Even the brilliant Evagrius, later to become one of the great teachers of the Christian spiritual life, learned his lesson the hard way when he arrived as Scetis, in lower Egypt, in 385 and made the mistake of trying to lecture his brothers. They let him hold forth, but then one of them said, "We know, Father, that if you had stayed in Alexandria, you would have been a great bishop." Evagrius, duly chastened, was afterwards more quiet.

Transformations intended to pierce the heart should not be pitched at the mind; the desert fathers understood this instinctively and confined their verbal teaching to brief *apophthegmata* (sayings), often reinforced by symbolic action. A monk who expresses pretensions to "live as an angel" is allowed to starve for a few days. Another monk is sent on a mission to a cemetery, first to throw stones at the dead, then to praise them; in such a way he learns the first lesson of detachment:

> *You know how you have insulted them and they do not reply and how you have praised them and they do not speak; so you too if you wish to be saved must do the same and become a dead man. Like the dead, take no account of either the scorn of the men or their praises, and you can be saved.*

Indeed, as Benedicta Ward notes in her introduction to the *Sayings of the Desert Christians* (p. *xx*), the real point is to get beyond words, to *word*:

> *The key phrase of the* Apophthegmata *is "Speak a word, Father." This occurs again and again, and the "word" that was sought out was not a theological explanation, nor was it "counseling," nor any kind of dialogue in which one argued a point; it was a word that was part of a relationship, a word which would give life to the disciple if it were received. The abbas were not spiritual directors in the later Western sense; they were fathers to the sons they begot in Christ.*

"The role of the 'abba', the spiritual father, was *vital*, literally, that is to say, "life-giving." Ward adds. "The abba was the one who, really knowing God in his own experience, could most truly intercede for his sons. He was the one who discerned reality and whose words, therefore, gave life."[5]

On the subject of asceticism, Ward writes:

> *Someone asked Abba Agathon, "Which is better, bodily asceticism or interior vigilance?" The old man replied, "Man is like a tree. Bodily asceticism is the foliage; interior vigilance is the fruit."*

By virtually unanimous testimony of the fathers, desert spirituality rests on the dual pillars of bodily asceticism and interior vigilance.

But Agathon's beautiful metaphor makes an important point about the relationship between the two, and about the nature of desert asceticism. Not only does he deftly avoid the question, he also reverses our normal thinking about cause and effect. Asceticism and vigilance are not bud and seed, bringing forth the tree; rather, they are manifestations of the tree: they derive from it and are the natural expressions of its health and vitality.

The distinction here is so crucial that it might almost be used as a litmus test for the health of a spiritual path. When the flow is in the "normal" direction (from bud to tree), asceticism quickly collapses into a means to an end: a rung-by-rung struggle up the "ladder of spiritual ascent." But in a deeper reading of the image of the tree, the movement is circular and interpenetrating: the tree gives rise to its fruit and foliage, but the fruit and foliage also sustain and nurture the tree. And so the spiritual life is seen in terms of an interpenetrating whole, and asceticism becomes the expression of that dynamic balance—almost, in fact, its lifeblood. Throughout the literature of the desert there is consistent evidence that this balance is understood and maintained. Asceticism is rigorous, but it is not cruel. Time and again monks are warned against an overzealous self-mortification which might leave them unable to carry out the rest of the work of God. When Pachomius is asked about extra fasting during Holy Week, he advises sticking to the Church's rule, which is to practice a total fast only during the last two days, "so that we might still have the strength to accomplish without fainting the things we are commanded to do, namely, unceasing prayer, vigils, reciting of God's law, and our manual labor, about which we have orders in the holy Scriptures and which ought to permit us to hold out our hands to the poor."

Antony makes the same point again, using his characteristically vivid teaching style:

> A hunter in the desert saw Abba Antony enjoying himself with the brethren and was shocked. Wanting to show him it was necessary sometimes to meet the needs of the brethren, the old man said to him, "Put an arrow in your bow and shoot it." So he did. The old man then said, "Shoot another," and he did so. Then the old man said, "Shoot yet again," and the hunter replied, "If I bend my bow so much I will break it." Then the old man said to him, "It is the same with

the work of God. If we stretch the brethren beyond measure they will soon break."

One reason for the cautiousness about overzealous asceticism was the recognition that it could easily become an inverted form of spiritual pride. Several days of rigorous fasting could be completely nullified if their result was a sense of superiority over one's brothers; in fact, Pachomius once specifically forbade a monk to fast because "he was doing so not for God but for vainglory." The best monks, in Pachomius' estimation, are those "who do not give themselves up to great practices and an excessive *ascesis*, but walk simply in the purity of their bodies … with obedience and obligingness."

"The desert fathers had a deep understanding of the connection between man's spiritual and natural life," writes Ward (p. *xxiii*), and she points out that the bulk of desert wisdom consists of homely, practical teachings on such matters as what to eat, where to sleep, and where to live. But on the other hand, it would be a mistake to miss the fiercer undercurrents at work through all this. Though it is never explicitly stated, there seems to be an intuitive awareness that in this new and vivified life, the usual metabolic balances of the world have been slightly shifted. What, then, *is* the connection between man's spiritual and natural life? Desert asceticism has an experimental streak to it; monks are constantly tinkering with the balances to discover the chemistry that works. How should one eat? (One small meal a day is the majority opinion.) What is the relationship between meditation and sleep? ("One hour's sleep a night is enough for a monk if he is a fighter. …") What of spiritual power? ("Obedience with abstinence gives men power over wild beasts. …")

And of course, there are demons, and there is fire, and that is the real point. This new life is not simply sweetness and light; there is a recognition that its currents run harder, deeper, more passionately than normal human life can bear. In one extraordinary story, Pachomius prays to God, somewhat naively: "Lord, may your fear descend on us forever so that we may not sin against you for all our life long." Two angels attempt to dissuade him, warning, "You cannot endure the fear of the Lord, as you request," but his response is an insistent, "Yes I can, by God's grace."

And at once the ray of fear, after the manner of the sun rising on the entire world, and without leaving its place, moved gradually forward toward him. That shining ray was very green and its sight wonderfully terrifying. When fear touched him, it pinched all his members, his heart, his marrow, and his whole body; and at once he fell to the ground and began to writhe like a living fish. His soul grew very sad and he fainted away toward death. The angels were watching him. ... They said to him, "Did we not tell you that you could not stand the full shock of the Lord?" He cried out, "Have mercy on me, my Lord Jesus Christ!"

Asceticism is not so much denial of the flesh as a honing of one's body to move at the faster, fierier tempos of spiritual life; to begin to bear that shock of the Lord. For in the end, as Abba Lot realizes, this new life is a quantum leap beyond anything that has gone before:

Abba Joseph came to Abba Lot and said to him: "Father, according to my strength I keep a moderate rule of prayer and fasting, quiet and meditation, and as far as I can I control my imagination; what more must I do?" And the old man rose and held his hands towards the sky so that his fingers became like flames of fire and he said: "If you will, you shall become all flame."

Much more elusive is this quality of interior vigilance. Over the range of desert literature it is applied to a variety of situations, from the struggle not to fall asleep during liturgy to the sophisticated discernment of demonic temptations. In general, it incorporates dimensions of wakefulness, attentiveness, discernment, and self-control.

Needleman has hypothesized that the missing piece in a "lost Christianity" is the development of a capacity for attention. Certainly, it is a long way from the early desert fathers to the elaborate psychology of attention developed by Simeon the New Theologian (d. 1022).[6] Yet it is indisputably clear that the early monks recognized this quality and knew its worth.

In a passage from *The Life of Saint Antony* we find the following description of Antony's spiritual formation:

*He did manual labor, for he had heard that he that is lazy, nei-
ther let him eat. … He prayed constantly, having learned that we
must pray in private without cease. Again, he was so attentive at the
reading of the Scripture lessons that nothing escaped him: he retained
everything and so his memory served him in place of books.*

It is easy to gloss over this passage as simply a testimony to Antony's
zeal. But it also describes a mental process at work—and in a spiritual
tradition carried forward largely by illiterate men and women, it provides a key piece of the puzzle: the importance of memorization and in
the focusing of attention. Some scholars have suggested that the typical
desert practice of reciting the psalms—all 150 of them—through the
course of a twenty-four-hour day was intended as a kind of mantra, a
means of quieting the mind. But there is evidence to suggest that it was
also, and even primarily, a way of focusing the mind. Says Evagrius: "It
is a great thing to pray without distraction, but to chant psalms without
distraction is even greater."

Or take the following, from Abba Alonius: "If only a man desired it
for a single day from morning to night, he would be able to come to the
measure of God." Is Alonius talking about desire, or the ability to remain
focused on that desire?

Antony also has words of wisdom here: "Just as fish die if they stay
too long out of water, so the monks who loiter outside their cells or pass
their time with men of the world lose the intensity of their inner peace."
"Intensity of inner peace" is a difficult term to define (it is virtually
meaningless if peace is perceived as an all-or-nothing proposition), but
it certainly implies a gathered concentration, which Antony recognizes
as having levels of intensity—levels which are easily dissipated by a too
casual relationship with the world. Only in that intensity of inner peace
can the possibility even begin to arise of desiring a single thing from
morning to night. And hence, the virtually unanimous refrain of the
desert fathers: "Sit in your cell, and it will teach you everything." The cell
is the place of fusion, from which will emerge—if it is ever to emerge at
all—the one who desires one thing only; *ihidaya*, the unified one.

For at least five centuries, then, Christianity carried at its heart the
knowledge of a spiritual path. Grounded in the image of Jesus the Life-

giver, its path was a middle way—not heroic individualism, or death-mysticism, or exaggerated asceticism, but an invitation to become unified ones, in dynamic communion with Jesus, the Unified One. Supporting this goal was an elementary psychology of the spiritual life giving clear recognition to values of physical preparedness ("bodily asceticism") and attention ("interior vigilance").

What became of that path? One prevalent hypothesis, popularized in Elaine Pagels' *The Gnostic Gospels* (1980), is that the consolidating Christian hierarchy in effect "amputated" its spiritual arm in order to gain tighter ecclesiastical control. But the heart of the matter is perhaps both simpler and more complex, taking us all the way back to that philological quibble with which we began. Jesus the Savior or Jesus the Life-giver?

In Jesus the Savior—the Rescuer—we have heroics, and an implicit negativity: one gets rescued out of something—in this case, out of sin and death. The dynamics of the imagery heavily favor a one-time intervention rather than a continuous renewal; already there is a gap in place. Over the next five centuries that gap would grow steadily wider. As the beginning of Jesus' divine sonship was pushed earlier and earlier—first to the conception and birth, and then, with John's gospel, to the beginning of time—as successive Church councils hyperbolized his divinity and postulated his "sending" the spirit, rather than, as in the earliest traditions, "receiving" it, the distance between Christ and humanity grew steadily wider and more unbridgeable, and the foundations of the spiritual path gradually eroded. In the fifth century occurred one of those watershed events in the history of religious thought. A monk named Palagius maintained, in what he took to be the traditional Christian position, that it was possible to live a sinless life—sinless as derived from the *ihidaya* line, that is, "capable of perfection, wholeness." His fate was to be damned as a heretic as the Augustinian doctrine of original sin came crashing down like a great iron curtain across the once flourishing desert path.

It is ironic that Christianity, so intent upon an orderly and orthodox transmission, should have come around in such short time to an almost polar opposite of its original self-understanding. When the original imperative toward *ihidaya*, unity or wholeness, was lost, and self-perfecting was seen no longer as a proper human task but as an arrogant denial of human sinfulness, one can legitimately speak of a "Lost Christianity."

Notes:

1   G. Winkler, "The Origins and Idiosyncrasies of the Earliest Form of Asceticism," in *The Continuing Quest for God: Monastic Spirituality in Tradition and Transition*, ed. William Skudlarek, O.S.B. (Collegeville, Minn.: Liturgical Press, 1981). Also, "Eine Analyse zur Geist-Christologie in Syrischen und Armenischen Quellen," *Le Muséon* 96 (1983) 267–326.

2   The discovery of the Manichaean Cologne Codex in 1970 established beyond all doubt that Mani emerged from a Judeo-Christian baptist group, the Elkesaites. For more than three centuries, arching from John the Baptist and Jesus to Mani, these groups were a powerful spiritual nurturing ground—or breeding ground. Winkler comments ("Origins of Asceticism," p. 12): "The inner force and far-reaching religious spirit that these Judeo-Christian communities imparted to their environment can hardly be overestimated."

3   Jacob Needleman, *Lost Christianity* (New York: Doubleday, 1980).

4   The sayings and teachings of the desert Christians cited in the text are taken from the following translations: *The Desert Christian: The Sayings of the Desert Fathers*, ed. Benedicta Ward, S.L.G., (New York: Macmillan, 1980); *Pachomian Koinonia*, Volume One, ed. Armand Veilleux (Kalamazoo, Mich.: Cistercian Publications, 1980); *St. Anthanasius: The Life of Saint Antony*, ed. Robert T. Meyer (New York: Paulist Press, 1950.)

5   Although the term "desert father" is commonly used, and the imagery is often in male terms, there were certainly "desert mothers" as well. Some of the sayings of these "ammas" are included in Ward's text.

6   "He who does not have attention in himself and does not guard his mind, cannot become pure in heart and so cannot see God." Simeon the New Theologian, in E. Kadloubovsky and G. E. H. Palmer, trans., *Writings from the Philokalia on Prayer of the Heart* (London: Faber & Faber, 1951), p. 158.

Parabola
Volume: 19.1
The Call

Ear of the Heart

Norvene Vest

"Listen, my child, ... with the ear of your heart. Hearken to my words if you would have life!" This is how St. Benedict began his *Rule* for the spiritual life. Writing in sixth-century Italy shortly after the fall of Rome, Benedict set forth this invitation in gathering around him a community of persons dedicated not only to God, but also to that human kindness which was to keep the hearth fires of civilization alive during the so-called Dark Ages of Western history.

Benedict's Prologue to the *Rule* is filled with images of calling, in which he employs the idea of call and response as a central metaphor for the spiritual life. The *Rule* consists of seventy-three brief chapters, many dealing with such daily routines as serving meals and caring for the sick. Throughout, Benedict emphasizes a concept of spiritual life based on call as invitation: to coax rather than to demand. The call is *into life* as it is meant to be lived, in relationship with the divine; it is a call to abundance, to a wholeness intended for and offered to every human being.

The invitation tendered by Benedict is an invitation to discipline, but not to rigidity. This discipline calls its initiates to listen attentively to life itself. Benedict urges aspirants to abandon the sloth of disobedience and take up "the strong and noble weapons of obedience." In Latin there is a connection between the words for obedience and listening: obedience comes through the "ear of the heart," and involves careful attention to both external circumstances and to inner response.

On occasion, argument or reproof is necessary to brush away accretions or hardness which prevent inner hearing. Sometimes we protect ourselves against the divine call, because we dare not risk the hope that such an invitation evokes. Each day Benedict directed the community not to "harden" the sensitive antennae of the listening heart:

> *Let us open our eyes to the light that comes from God, and our ears to the voice from heaven that every day calls out this charge: "If you hear (God's) voice today, do not harden your hearts."*
> —*Prologue to the* Rule *9–10*

Through this verse (Psalm 95:8), Benedict directed the seeker's attention to an event in the Exodus experience of the Hebrew scriptures.

Psalm 95 refers to the demands made upon Moses by the thirsty Hebrews in the Book of Exodus (17:1–7). The wandering people quarreled, asking, "Is God among us or not?" The Hebrews had forgotten that God had rescued them from slavery in Egypt, and instead lamented their present sense of loss in the desert. Only Moses was obedient; his heart was listening, so he was able to invoke the reality of God's presence and power.

This experience of scripture suggests a pattern which Benedict knew to be common on the spiritual journey. The *Rule* does not repress anxious inner doubts, but rather through daily remembrance of the Exodus experience, it encourages authentic questions, while remembering the tradition, and teaches the heart to listen attentively for God's call. Evidently the divine can be experienced even within situations of loss and need, when there is a sense that God's call is not so much a demand for perfection as it is an invitation to intimacy in the present moment.

For Benedict, call implies relationship. The movement is not primarily *from* something like sin, but rather toward something like lifelong intimacy with the divine. Call is not primarily to *do* something, but rather to be a faithful partner and friend. We are invited to discover our true nature, not out of fear of hell, but out of love for Christ and delight in virtue.

In developing his concept of call, Benedict emphasized the Judeo-Christian theme of relationship. In the Hebrew scriptures, God called Israel forth from Egypt and continued to address her in the metaphors of lifelong and faithful marriage. In the New Testament, Jesus called his disciples to come and be with him. In the Gospel of John (1:35–39), two of John's disciples have followed Jesus down the road, and when he turns and sees them, they stammer out, "Where are you staying?" He responds simply, "Come and see." When asked about their way of life, for centuries the response of Benedictines has been, "Come and see!" It is an offering of relationship, inviting personal response.

There is a significant contrast between the metaphor of call/response and that of sin/forgiveness. In the latter, there is a sense of chasm between the two parties; in the former there is intimacy. In the latter, the connection is formal; in the former, the experience is mutually delightful. In choosing to emphasize the metaphor of call and response in his *Rule*, Benedict called attention to the astonishing fact that it is the divine One who actually initiates intimacy. Such a concept of relationship clearly implies something more powerful than mere release *from* something, emphasizing mutuality, which helps the seeker move *toward* some radically new thing.

This "new thing" may not be something to do, but some*one* to be. It is a call not so much to demonstrate our worth as to be ourselves. We are not asked to make ourselves presentable, but only to be present with God.

Benedict urged his community to accept God's desire as the primary formative reality (Prologue 14–20). When God calls out, "Do you yearn for life?" it may seem that we are required to do something, as when young Isaiah felt himself in the presence of the Holy Spirit and cried out, "Here am I! Send me" (Isaiah 6:1–8). But Benedict's instinct leads instead to the experience of the older Isaiah, who finds *God addressing him*, and says "even before you ask me, I will say to you: Here I am!" (Isaiah 58:9). In our eagerness to do what is right, we may forget that the call of God carries with it the power of response. Our principal gift is ourselves, our willingness to be the focus of God's desire. It is not easy to accept this undeserved love, but that is the import of the divine call, which contains in itself the power enabling us to be who we really are.

Each of us hears God in a unique way, gradually becoming aware of the particular fullness intended for our personal lives.

The call makes us more whole by illuminating who we are in a way previously unknown. It is not like the ringing of a telephone, impersonal and demanding, but it is rather like a tuning fork creating an echoing response by the power of its own vibrations.

Benedict sketched a model of the abbot intending to show how God in Christ works with each person to draw forth a unique wholeness. The abbot

> ... serve(s) a variety of temperaments, coaxing, reproving and encouraging them as appropriate. He must so accommodate and adapt himself to each one's character and intelligence that he will not only keep the flock ... but will rejoice in its increase.
> —Rule 2:31–32

There is no more precious thing in the world than each individual soul, created by God and called forth into wholeness of being without which the universe is somehow diminished. In the rite of monastic profession, Benedict summarized this mystery of call to become something we cannot hide but also cannot quite name. He specified that the new member make this prayer, and be supported in its repetition by the whole community: "Receive me, Lord, as you have promised and I shall live. Do not disappoint me in my hope" (*Rule* 58:21; from Psalm 119:116). The seeker has heard the call to be received into God's very life and has accepted it is a promise. Based on a trust in this invitation to relationship, a hope arises for fullness of life. In that hope, a commitment is made.

Parabola
Volume: 24.2
Prayer and
Meditation

Going Out of Oneself

Bede Griffiths

If anyone asks me how I pray, my simple answer is that I pray the Jesus prayer. Anyone familiar with the story of a Russian pilgrim will know what I mean. It consists simply in repeating the words: "Lord Jesus Christ, Son of God, have mercy on me, a sinner." I have used this prayer for over forty years and it has become so familiar that it simply repeats itself. Whenever I am not otherwise occupied or thinking of something else, the prayer goes quietly on. Sometimes it is almost mechanical, just quietly repeating itself, and other times it gathers strength and can become extremely powerful.

I give it my own interpretation. When I say, "Lord Jesus Christ, Son of God," I think of Jesus as the Word of God, embracing heaven and earth and revealing himself in different ways and under different names and forms to all humanity. I consider that this word "enlightens everyone coming into the world," and though they may not recognize it, is present in every human being in the depths of their soul. Beyond words and thought, beyond all signs and symbols, this Word is being secretly spoken in every heart in every place and at every time. People may be utterly ignorant of it or may choose to ignore it, but whenever or wherever anyone responds to truth or love or kindness, to the demand for justice, concern for others, care of those in need, they are responding to the voice of the Word. So also when anyone seeks truth or beauty in science, philosophy, poetry or art, they are responding to the inspiration of the Word.

I believe that the Word took flesh in Jesus of Nazareth and in Him we can find a personal form of the Word to whom we can pray and relate in terms of love and intimacy, but I think that He also makes Himself known to others under different names and forms. What counts is not so much the name and form as the response in the heart to the hidden mystery, which is present in each one of us in one way or another and awaits our response in faith and hope and love.

When I say "have mercy on me, a sinner," I unite myself with all human beings from the beginning of the world who have experienced separation from God, or from the eternal truth. I realize that, as human beings, we are all separated from God, from the source of our being. We are wandering in a world of shadows, mistaking the outward appearance of people and things for reality. But at all times something is pressing us to reach out beyond the shadows, to face the reality, the truth, the inner meaning of our lives, and so to find God, or whatever name we give to the mystery which enfolds us.

So I say the Jesus prayer, asking to be set free from the illusions of this world, from the innumerable vanities and deceits with which I am surrounded. And I find in the name of Jesus the name which opens my heart and mind to reality. I believe that each one of us has an inner light, an inner guide, which will lead us through the shadows and illusions by which we are surrounded, and open our minds to the truth. It may come through poetry or art, or philosophy or science, or more commonly through the encounter with people and events, day by day. Personally, I find that meditation, morning and evening, every day, is the best and most direct method of getting in touch with reality. In meditation, I try to let go of everything of the outer world of the senses, of the inner world of thoughts, and listen to the inner voice, the voice of the Word, which comes in the silence, in the stillness when all activity of body and mind cease. Then, in the silence, I become aware of the presence of God, and I try to keep that awareness during the day. In a bus or a train or traveling by air, in work or study or talking and relating to others, I try to be aware of this presence in everyone and in everything. And the Jesus prayer is what keeps me aware of the presence.

So prayer for me is the practice of the presence of God in all situations, in the midst of noise and distractions of all sorts, of pain and suffering and death, as in times of peace and quiet, of joy and friendship, of prayer and silence, the presence is always there. For me, the Jesus prayer is just a way of keeping in the presence of God.

Meditation is naturally followed by prayer—*oratio*. Our understanding of the deeper meaning of the text depends on our spiritual insight and this comes from prayer. Prayer is opening the heart and mind to God; that is, it is going beyond all the limited processes of the rational mind and opening the mind to the transcendental reality to which all words and thoughts are pointing. This demands devotion—that is, self-surrender. As long as we remain on the level of the rational mind, we are governed by our ego, our independent, rational self. We can make use of all kinds of assistance, of commentaries and spiritual guides, but as long as the individual self remains in command, we are imprisoned in the rational mind with its concepts and judgments. Only when we surrender the ego, the separate self, and turn to God, the supreme spirit, we can receive the light which we need to understand the deeper meaning of the scriptures. This is passing from *ratio* to *intellectus*, from discursive thought to intuitive insight.

Contemplation is the goal of all life. It is knowledge by love. St. Paul often prays for his disciples that they may have knowledge (*gnosis*) and understanding (*epignosis*) in the mystery of Christ. The mystery of Christ is the ultimate truth, the reality towards which all human life aspires. And this mystery is known by love. Love is going out of oneself, surrendering the self, letting the reality, the truth take over. It is not limited to any earthly object or person. It reaches out to the infinite and the eternal. This is contemplation. It is not something which we achieve for ourselves; it is something that comes when we let go. We have to abandon everything, all words, thoughts, hopes, fears, all attachment to ourselves or to any earthly thing, and let the divine mystery take possession of our lives. It feels like death and is a sort of dying. It is encountering the darkness, the abyss, the void. It is facing nothingness or, as the English Benedictine mystic Augustine Baker said, it is the "union of the nothing with the Nothing."

Reprinted from *The Inner Directions Journal*, Summer 1996. Copyright © 1996 by the Inner Directions Foundation, www.InnerDirections.org. All rights reserved.

Parabola
Volume: 30.2
Restraint

On Not Speaking

Brother Paul Quenon

To speak of silence at all seems an infraction of silence. The less said, perhaps, the better. Not until silence is lost to a culture does description become useful, as if some stray being really beyond description had gone missing.

Monastic rules can trap silence in a cage and make it a mere restriction on speech. This shy, strange creature only approaches on its own, as it will, and is easily intimidated by a leash. Absence of noise is congenial to silence. But if my head is full of echoes of myself, its velvet passage will never brush my ankle. Silencing my mind then becomes the prescription. This in turn easily becomes such a huge project, it becomes another kind of noise. The harder I try, the further I get from the reality sought.

> *Never my silence,*
> *never my posture,*
> *my mind, quite perfect. Poor guy!*

Prayer is as easy as breathing. "Let it be brief and pure," says the Rule of St. Benedict. Silence is rarely other than pure and brief; it grips and releases the heart before its presence is even noticed. Better so. Better to breathe and just forget. Air will always be there for the next breath.

Strangely enough, it is rare to do the easiest thing in the world. I want something difficult. People suffer numberless breathing disorders. It has become a profitable business to cure them. Likewise there's a meditation market booming with anodynes and therapies. Even specialized resorts like monasteries to quiet down in.

All well and good, or in truth, useless and illusory for being a striving and a straining. The secret, rather, is right at hand. It is not-doing. It is not constructing some other moment. Be the moment as it comes. "Do what you are doing," said old Abba Anthony. Do-not other than not-doing. It's the easiest thing in the world. And the rarest.

> *Each one, each precious*
> *millisecond of silence*
> *a gem for the mind.*

Thomas Merton said of these moments: "It is not reached and coaxed forth from hiding by any process under the sun, including meditation. All that we can do with any spiritual discipline is produce within ourselves something of the silence, the humility, the detachment, the purity of heart, and the indifference which are required of the inner self to make some shy, unpredictable manifestation of his presence."

Words can usher in the guest, or at least open up a vestibule for the visitor: a psalm, a sutra, a remark of Jesus. Its arrival may be little more than a sound on the edge of silence.

> *Brief voice of a leaf*
> *clicking across the pavement*
> *this late dry season.*

Anything might do, for each moment brings its own drama, or the lack thereof:

> *Dribbles from a spout—*
> *sound enough for this dull hour,*
> *just leftover rain.*

To wait with high expectations, to expect a rich yield, will sink it. Forget greed. Silence likes what's poor.

Wind whispers secrets
to the firs. I listen hard
but don't understand.

There must be a slow process of conditioning, where one becomes this poverty, this empty field of manifestation. Lightness begins in accepting my own heaviness. What else do you expect?

The only gift truly mine is my poverty. I always have this to give to the universe, and that is how the universe comes to me:

Nothing to admire
but this featureless silence
in the windless night.

Christ comes as the poor stranger in numerous ways. And often leaves as little understood as when he came. He doesn't expect long sermons of me, and usually bids people touched to healing to keep it quiet.

The less said about silence the better. It offers no arguments, and hires no attorneys. Silence speaks for itself, all my effort otherwise risks perjury.

•

CHAPTER FIVE

A BODY OF BEAUTY AND LOVE

Our trance of selfishness must end, for we are all being organized by the one true life, in the one true body. Our Lord has need of each one in his great mystical body; and they must all be one in him, the Anointed. …

This life has been from eternity, uprising and blossoming! It is not of this earth, but substantial—the eternal life.

To all you who are in the process of birth these lines are written that each one may be strengthened, and bud in the life of God, and grow, and bear fruit in the Tree of paradise so that each branch and twig in this fair Tree may contribute, help, and shelter all the other branches and twigs, that this Tree may become a great Tree. Then shall we all rejoice, one with another, with "joy unspeakable and full of glory." Amen.[1]

—Jacob Boehme

Parabola
Volume: 3.2
Sacrifice and
Transformation

THE ENERGY OF LIFE

Sacrifice and Worship

Father Alexander Schmemann

There are many aspects of the idea of sacrifice, but I would like to begin with my chief interest, which is worship. This seems to me to be the very center of the whole idea of sacrifice, and the place where all its facets come together: renunciation, offering up, and transformation.

There was a controversy which developed in the West about the Eucharist as sacrifice. On the one hand, there was the concept that by accepting the sacrifice of Christ as unique and full, the sacrificial aspect of the Eucharist must be rejected; and on the other hand, there was the scholastic idea, which defined sacrifice only in terms of redemption and atonement—something bloody which satisfies divine anger or justice. From the Eastern Orthodox perspective I always felt the whole debate wrong, for that kind of theology and that kind of religion interpret sacrifice as a legal transaction: a satisfaction is required, a duty of the creation to the Creator, like an income tax: the oblation of the best animal or even of the child, to satisfy an objective necessity. This is the perspective which I think needs not only correction but a much more radical rethinking, starting with the very nature of sacrifice, which has been forgotten by the theologians and sometimes rediscovered in the study of religions.

I would like to point out that first of all, sacrifice is an ontology. It is not just a result of something, it is a major expression or a first revelation of life itself; it is life's spiritual content. Where there is no sacrifice there is no life. Sacrifice is rooted in the recognition of life as love: as giving up, not because I want more for myself, or to satisfy an objective justice, but because it is the only way of reaching the fullness that is possible for me.

So before sacrifice becomes expiation, reparation, or redemption, it is life's own natural movement. All this I find in the Eastern Eucharist, where before we come to the crucifixion, we speak of the sacrifice of praise, and of salvation as a return to the sacrificial way of life. Opposed to sacrifice is consumerism: the idea that everything belongs to me and I have to grab it—and we are restored from that only by the complex movement exemplified by the Eucharist where we offer ourselves and are accepted through Christ's offering of Himself.

So, contrary to some scholars and phenomenologists of religion, I would say that the origin of the sacrifice is not so much *fear* as the need for communion in the real sense: a communion as giving and sharing. One part of the animal which we eat is burned and offered up to God, which means that we are sharing food with God and so become con-substantial with Him. I think this is much more the primitive idea of sacrifice than any other idea. The authority of the sacrifice is in giving, because giving *is* life; it is a giving-and-receiving, and therefore this whole movement is central and reciprocal.

So much of the Western theological viewpoint has either fear behind it or else some kind of easy over-optimism; and that is a different spiritual climate for us of the Eastern Orthodoxy. It is very difficult to express the experience of the Eastern Church in these terms. Take the whole tradition of the sacrifice of the Mass: the broken body, the shed blood. We of the Eastern Orthodoxy see the bread and wine as symbolizing creation: the wine is a eucharistic gift not because it looks like blood, but because blood is life, and wine is something which makes the heart of man glad. Therefore when we raise to God the Offertory at the beginning of the Eucharistic observance, we haven't yet reached the Cross and the Passion, we are simply and joyfully restored to that situation in which we come to partake of life; the bread and wine is what is to become *my* body and *my* blood. This is the fundamental thing. The happiness is because in

Christ we have access to that sacrificial life. We not only give up but go up; there is no end to the possibility of going up.

It is not that there is no evil, as some people would have us think, including, I am afraid, Teilhard de Chardin; that is the weakness I find in him. Evil is very important, and sacrifice has something to do with that; but we have to establish the perspective in which the idea of sacrifice would not be reduced only to that of expiation and atonement for sin. We have to get rid of that narrow view, and on the other hand we have to get rid of an over-optimism that says all we have to do now is make every action a joyful offering. No, in this world Christ is crucified, as Pascal says; evil is a real presence, and the sacrificial idea is that most certainly joy cannot be reached without suffering; but suffering as exemplified in the Crucifixion is in itself a victory. The meaning of Christ's death is not that death is satisfied; it is a changing of the signs. But death is still death. We explain that by the doctrine of Christ's descent into Hades.

The whole perspective of sacrifice depends on the starting point. The beginning is before there is any sin or evil, with something that belongs to the real life. Then comes the second stage: evil, betrayal, suffering, death. Sacrifice remains there, but it acquires a new energy, and goes on finally to the third stage, the eschatological meaning: the end of all things, the fulfillment of all things in the perfect sacrifice, the perfect communion, the perfect unity. These are the three dimensions of sacrifice which it seems to me have to be restored for a balanced view and theology of the sacrifice. I think all these aspects are essential: thanksgiving, communion, giving up, sharing, transformation. They are all necessary to give this fuller view.

In the idea of communion, the question arises as to what is man's part; how does he fill his sacrificial role? Perhaps God also needs to be fed; and here, it seems to me, we could think of the place of food in the story of the creation and the fall. In the mythology of creation, the man is created a hungry being; that is why God made the world as his food. Man is dependent; and dependence is an objective slavery. But if God is the master and we are just slaves, what can He receive from a universe where everything depends on Him? This is where sacrifice enters, and priesthood. The priest is first and foremost the sacrificer—I am not speaking now of priesthood in the church's terms—and so he is the man who can freely transform that dependence: he is the man who can say *thank you.*

For the moment when the slave whom God has created can thank Him for his life and for his food, he is liberated; sacrifice, the thank-offering, is liberating. I have always understood the fall (or what is called "original sin") as the loss of man's desire to be a priest; or perhaps you might say the desire he has *not* to be a priest but a consumer, and then little by little he begins to consider that to eat and to live are his rights, which is a total enslavement, because there is no end to "rights." Dostoyevsky in *The Possessed* shows us the man who wants his final right, to be God; so he commits suicide, to prove that he is free, like God. But it is the offering, the thanksgiving and the praise that make us truly free. The mystery of the food is that it has no meaning unless it becomes life. The food I eat is dead, and its resurrection in me must be something more than calories and proteins; it must be truly the sacrament of sacrifice.

Perhaps we should touch on that extreme aspect of sacrifice which is martyrdom; which I think should be differentiated from heroism. We find the latter almost everywhere, even among animals. It is a very respectable virtue, of course, and I don't mean to denigrate it, but martyrdom is altogether different. The martyrs were witnesses: witnesses of the transformation of death. What Christ destroys is not physical death but spiritual death, which is the alienation we live in—alienation from one another, from the world, from nature, from God, from ourselves first of all. The first Christian martyr, Stephen, as he was dying, said: "I see heaven opening." He witnessed death becoming life. The "birthdays" of the martyrs are celebrated by the Church on their death days; on that day they were "born." The martyr does not think of his death as an increase in the capital of good deeds on which the Church can later draw checks, but as a sacrifice of love and praise; he is given the fantastic privilege of joining Christ in the death which is not an accident, but the culmination of a life filled to the brim.

But we don't have to go as far as martyrdom to find the real function of suffering. We all suffer, usually very passively; but there is another kind of suffering which I impose on myself when I "sacrifice" or "give up" something. This is the suffering of someone who returns from a fall. There was a Russian poet who said, "Give me, O Lord, the strength to face Thy *austere* Paradise." He used the word "austere"; this is different from the usual devotion to the pleasure principle, the notion that in the life eternal everything will be easy. The idea is rather that suffering is the very means of return, of discovery and of growth. That is the idea in Teilhard de Chardin, that it is the condition for growing; everything that grows, suffers. So there is a suffering which is chosen because there is no other way of reaching my real self. It is not that God has created suffering, I have created it myself by falling away from that life; and to return to it is painful. It requires a discipline.

That raises the whole question of today's approach to life, and to medicine. Of course there is a glorious growth of medical knowledge; on the other hand, I am afraid we are coming soon to a society in which suffering will be simply forbidden, by law. That is not a joke; it is very terrible. Already in church it is very difficult to preach anything that disturbs people; one must always preach some kind of happy ending to everything. I think the religious reaction should be a restoration of the real meaning of suffering, and I see that people, because they cannot face suffering any more, are falling into mental disease. The whole idea of the welfare state tends toward the belief that suffering is a crime against nature; you must not suffer.

Now I do not believe that God made suffering and death; He didn't create a world in which every love ends in separation, in which everything is exactly the opposite of what we wish; and to understand this, the liturgy is always taking us back to that moment when God, having created the world, "saw that it was very good." It is only when something very good is broken that you will pay almost any price to restore it. This is our participation: the sacrifice is not for our profit alone. It adds to that energy in the world which recreates life. Christ, using a massive weapon, makes death a servant of life; by making His death a sacrifice, by giving it with love, He makes even death into life. And it is of this the martyrs are the witnesses, and the participants.

There is a great depth of meaning in sacrifice, and a synthesis of its aspects which has broken down in our time needs to be remade. Maybe there is truth in almost every theory, if one brings them all together and starts with sacrifice as the very content of God-created life, because God Himself is sacrificial, a constant giving, a sharing with His creation; and ultimately what He needs in return, what will "feed" Him, is love.

It is strange that our concepts of sacrifice should be so poor, for the real meaning is in the very name: to make whole, or holy—it is the same word. The breaking down of that meaning is the essence of secularism and consumerism. Secularism is not, as some people think, the denial of

God; that kind of religion which offers health and therapy of all kinds is compatible with secularism: the idea that you need a pharmacy, you need a psychotherapist, and you need religion in order to be healthy. I have never considered the secular view simply atheistic, but a denial of the sacrifice: of the holy and the whole, of the priesthood as a way of life. The secular idea is that everybody needs religion because it helps to keep law and order, comforts us, and so on; it is that point of view which denies levels. But the whole terminology of the early Church is of ascension to another level: "He ascended into Heaven." Since He is man, we ascend in Him. Christianity begins to fall down as soon as the idea of our going up in Christ's ascension—the movement of sacrifice—begins to be replaced by His going down. And this is exactly where we are today: it is always a bringing Him down into ordinary life, and this we say will solve our social problems. The Church must go down to the ghettos, into the world in all its reality. But to save the world from social injustices, the need first of all is not so much to go down to its miseries, as to have a few witnesses in this world to the possible ascension.

Parabola
Volume: 10.1
Wholeness

IMAGE AND LIKENESS

Interview with Bishop Kallistos Ware

I am greeted at the door of his leaf-covered house on a quiet Oxford street by the man I know as Father Kallistos, who is now Bishop Kallistos of Diokleia. I have not seen him for a while, but he is one of those people who do not really change; he has become more himself. His welcome is friendly. We go into his study that acts as office and retreat—and probably tutorial room; he is Spalding Lecturer on Eastern Orthodox Studies at Oxford University. The room is full of books, some writ-ten by him: The Orthodox Church *(Pelican Books, 1983),* The Orthodox Way *(Mowbrays, 1979), and the translation (with Palmer and Sherard) of the complete* Philokalia *(Faber & Faber, 1981). By the wealth of books, one is made aware that had this man not converted to Orthodoxy, he would have fulfilled a more limited pattern of intellectual brilliance. The ikons in the room speak of a different light, and it is that light which has increased in the years I have known him. Now the intellect serves that light but does not usurp it.*

He is attached to the Greek Orthodox monastery of St. John the Divine on the Island of Patmos, where he spends the non-academic part of the year. His theme is that to be a whole person does not really mean "getting oneself together"; wholeness results from what we really do with our heart in our living of life: keep it, or offer it to God and the world.

—James Moran

James Moran: *The definition of the whole person that* Parabola *has suggested is: "one who has in his or her being, to a very high degree, freedom, consciousness, unity, and will." What do you think?*

Kallistos Ware: All four of these qualities are indeed very important for our understanding of the person. We are free, in the sense that we are capable of making moral choices in a way that the animals do not make moral choices. We are one, in the sense that we are a unity of body and soul. The whole person is not just the soul on its own, not just the body on its own, but the two considered as an integrated unit. Consciousness: this too is essential to personhood. We do not just act in the world, we understand that we are acting, and the greater our understanding, the more truly we are personal. Will: that surely is another aspect of freedom. But there are other things to be added to our definition of the whole person.

JM: *What would these be?*

KW: In particular, I would add two closely linked ideas: openness and love. The whole person is not just a self-contained, self-centered unity. The whole person is a person who is on the one side open to God, and on the other side open to other human persons. The human being without God is not truly human. We were created to enter into a relationship with God, to be in dialogue with Him, and if that relationship is not present something essential is lacking from our personhood. Equally, we are created to relate to other human persons. It has been said that there is no true man unless there are two men entering into communication with one another. The isolated individual is not a real person. A real person is one who lives in and for others. And the more personal relationships we form with others, the more truly we realize ourselves as persons. This idea of openness to God, openness to other persons, could be summed up under the word "love." We become truly personal by loving God and by loving other humans. By love, I don't mean merely an emotional feeling, but a fundamental attitude. In its deepest sense, love is the life, the energy, of God Himself in us.

JM: *The Greek word for personhood is "hypostasis." Could you tell us what this word means?*

KW: Literally, hypostasis means that which stands under, that which possesses independent existence and is in some sense complete in itself: something which possesses real existence, as opposed to that which merely changes, a transient appearance. If we say that a human person is a hypostasis, we mean that there is an element of continuity, an element of unity, behind all the passing experiences we have during our life. We also mean that the human person is a subject capable of making decisions, of initiating something new.

JM: *An agent.*

KW: Yes. The human person is that in which new beginnings are made. We do not just react, we act. But when we say that hypostasis means "that which is complete in itself, which possesses independent existence," we have to qualify, because we believe that the human person depends on God, and apart from God we are not truly human or truly person. There's another word in Greek used for person: that is the word "prosopon." Literally, it means "face." This second word for person helps us to understand what was said just now: that we are not truly personal as long as we are turned in on ourselves, isolated from others. We only become personal if we face other persons, relate to them.

JM: *Does hypostasis also say something about our uniqueness as persons, and the fact that a person called into existence by God is called eternally into existence?*

KW: When applied to humans, the term "hypostasis" has exactly that sense. We have a beginning as persons; we do not have an end. God calls us into being for all eternity.

JM: *Do you think the whole person is one who lives, as it were, in two worlds at once?*

KW: We can make a series of contrasts. We can say that the human person is both material and spiritual; that there is in the human person both something visible—the body—and something invisible—the soul. We might also make contrast between the natural and the supernatural. The human person has a natural existence in this world, but a more than natural life relating to God. I am not very happy about these contrasts, if they are made in a sharp manner, because the human person is a unity: the material and the spiritual are a single unity, not two parts making up a composite whole. These are two aspects of that which is, in reality, one and undivided. The same with the visible and the invisible: the body is not a component of the human person, part of the whole; the body is the whole person. It is a mode of existence for the total person, though the body does not exhaust the meaning of the person. Yet the body is the whole person acting, and looked at from a particular point of view. So it seems to me that the two worlds are in reality one world.

JM: *Is the whole person there, intact in everyone, or does it exist only in potential, as a seed which must grow?*

KW: I prefer, from a Christian point of view, to say that there is a seed of the fully whole being within each one of us. But it needs to grow. In the first chapter of the Book of Genesis, it is said that the human person is made in the image and likeness of God. In Hebrew, probably the words "image" and "likeness" meant the same. They were intended to be parallel. But many of the Greek Fathers saw a contrast between the image and the likeness. They understood the image to be the original qualities conferred on us from our first creation, which make us human, while the likeness represents the true use of those qualities, developed to the utmost. So image represents potentiality, likeness represents realization. Image represents innocence, likeness represents wholeness. Thus it could be said that as human persons we are on a journey from the image—that is our starting point—to the likeness, which is our final goal. We are not created perfect. We are created innocent and capable of perfection. So I prefer the image of a seed—the idea of a seed which needs to grow. To grow partly through our own efforts, but also through the grace of God.

When speaking of the image, there's another point to be added: we Christians believe that God is Trinity. God is One, but at the same time God is Three in One. God is not just one person dwelling alone in isolation, God is not just the monad; God is a triad of three Persons dwelling in one another by mutual love. There is a perpetual movement of love passing between the Father, the Son, and the Holy Spirit. God is not just Unity, He is also Communion. Now, if the human person is made in the image of God, that means in the image of God the Trinity, and that means we are intended to live in a movement of love with other human persons. We are intended to reproduce on earth the mystery of the Trinity in Heaven. We are to reproduce in our own human life the pattern of interpersonal relationships that exist also in God. So the image doctrine links up with what I said earlier: to be a person means to be open, in love, to other persons.

JM: *So human beings, as they are, are unfinished, would you say?*

KW: Many Christians would say, and I agree with them, that human beings are unfinished, in the sense that they have limitless possibilities. Other creatures in this world, in the animal world, have a specific nature, and they act by instinct within the limits of that nature. But man's distinctive character is that he is not limited by his nature, that he has free choice. Therefore, that he has limitless possibilities. We do not really know what it means to be a person. This is a mystery. We do not know what are the limits of personhood. We cannot say in words exactly what are the highest and fullest potentialities of being a person. In this way, for me, personhood means openness to the unexpected, to the new. Every achievement is only a step on a journey which then becomes the beginning of some fresh progress. Personhood as I understand it involves infinite progress. God is infinite; the human being made in God's image is made to have communion with God. We shall never learn all there is to know about God, so in our fellowship with God, we shall never cease to grow.

JM: *What is it that must be achieved for a person to be "whole"?*

KW: We have already used the words "love" and "wholeness." There's also another word that is important; in Greek, this is the word "theosis," which could be translated literally as "divinization." We are called to become like God. We spoke earlier of the likeness as being our final goal. We are called to share in God's life, in His Glory. We remain human, we remain created, but we are truly and fully united with God in His divine energies. And these energies transform us, so while we remain human we also share in the divine life. That is our final aim. Saint Basil says, "The human person is a creature that has received the commandment to become God."

JM: *You've already stated what it means to be open, but what does it mean to be free? In Orthodoxy sometimes the word "royalness" is used to speak of the freedom of the human agent. What do you feel about that?*

KW: Yes, indeed. In the Bible, already in the first chapter of Genesis, there is clearly the idea that the human being is the king of creation, the ruler. There is the idea that the human person in a special way represents God on earth. God has appointed us as persons to rule over the world. Other living creatures exist in the world; they alter their environment—ants construct ant heaps; beavers build dams—but only to a very limited degree. We humans have been given freedom; we have been given consciousness; and therefore we do not only exist in the world, we make choices and these choices alter the world in which we live. This is what is implied in the idea of our royal character. It places a very great responsibility upon us. We can achieve much for good, but equally much for evil. We can transfigure the material creation. We can make the material creation articulate in praise of God. We can give it new beauty and meaning. But we can also use the material creation for destruction. The making of an atom bomb, and our contemporary problem of the pollution of the environment—the deserts and dustbowls that we have produced in this twentieth century—all this shows how human persons can also use their freedom negatively. But that is our particular challenge. The greater our power for good, the greater also our potentiality for evil. Freedom means the possibility of great good, but also of tragic harm.

JM: *Would you say that freedom in a sense is the flaw in creation from the point of view of anyone who hopes for some kind of mechanical, guaranteed, assured road to holiness? That freedom means that there is something truly open-ended in life, and that in a sense a human being has the terrifying power to affect things differently? That there is a sense that the world, at least partly, is in our hands?*

KW: There is indeed a sense in which the world is partly in our hands. Speaking in metaphorical terms, we might put it this way: when God created the human person in his own image, and gave freedom to human beings, He took a risk; because God is love, and He wished love also to be the highest principle of His creation. And, as we have said, where there is love there needs also to be freedom. God could have created robots which would have automatically done always exactly what He wished. But the one thing a robot, acting mechanically, cannot do is love. God wished to have in His world not just mechanical forces, He wished to have free persons, made in His image: persons who would have freedom after the likeness of the Divine Freedom. His freedom is infinite and unconditioned; our freedom is created and limited, but nonetheless real. This was what God wanted: creatures who would freely love each other and freely respond to Him with love. In a sense, God had to take that risk. If He wanted there to be love, He had to give us freedom. And by giving us freedom, He gave us the possibility of rejecting His love. Freedom therefore implies the possibility of doing evil. The world was not created evil. But God took the risk because He wished there to be love. This is the true meaning of the Christian doctrine of Hell, which is so widely misunderstood. God does not condemn us to Hell; God wishes all humans to be saved. He will love us to all eternity but there will exist the possibility that we do not accept that love and do not respond to it. And the refusal to accept love, the refusal to respond to it, that precisely is the meaning of Hell. Hell is not a place where God puts us; it's a place where we put ourselves. The doors of Hell, insofar as they have locks, have locks on the inside.

JM: *What kind of effort is required to unlock those doors, and what prevents us? What gets in the way, and what helps?*

KW: We live in a fallen world. We drag each other down. Each of us from the moment of his or her birth exists in an environment in which it is easy to do evil and hard to do good, in which it is easy to hurt others and hard to win their trust. If I know somebody very well, in ten minutes, if I set my mind to it, I could perhaps say to them things so cruel, so destructive, that they would never forget them for the rest of their life. But could I in ten minutes say things so beautiful, so creative, that they would never forget them? It is easier to speak words of bitterness, of hatred, than to speak in a memorable way words of love. That is part of what is meant by saying we live in a fallen world. The world is fallen, but we still have freedom. The image in the human person has been clouded over, covered with dirt, but it's not been obliterated totally. But we are dragged down by the influence of sin. Our own past sins, and also all the other wrongdoing that has happened in the world over many generations.

What helps us? The Grace of God: which means the Love of God in action. Everywhere in the world there are present the Divine Energies. God is not distant. Though He is above and beyond all things, He is also within all things and within all persons, and this active, fiery, creative Love of God is present everywhere. That is what we mean by grace. That is our fullest support. This grace works with our human freedom. With God's help, we can then become whole persons. We can not become whole persons by ourselves. We need help. Though God expects us, with our freedom, to play a part.

JM: *So the effort involves both cooperation with God and making efforts that show that we actually do rely upon this help.*

KW: Yes. It is the convergence of God's initiative and our response. Divine grace and human freedom. What God does is incomparably more important than what we do. But what we do is also essential. The will of man is an essential precondition, for without it God does nothing.

JM: *There's an image of Christ in Revelation, in the Apocalypse, in which He speaks of conquering and overcoming the world, and implies that we have to do that, and that we also have to conquer and overcome ourselves in order to do that. What is the Christian meaning of conquering or overcoming the world?*

KW: The term "the world" is used in two different ways in scripture. On the one side, by "world" we mean that which God has created: the real world. And this is good. As it says in the Bible, "God saw everything that He had made, and behold, it was very good." In this sense, we are not called to conquer God's world, we are called to live in it and to realize its potentialities. But on other occasions the term "world" is used to mean the fallen world, the world turned away from God. And in this sense of "world," we are called to conquer the world. The term "self" also has a double meaning. It can mean the real person created in the image of God, but it can also mean our fallen self, what with our limited understanding and our sinful outlook we imagine to be our true self but which is not our true self at all. So in this second sense we are called to conquer or overcome ourselves. But properly understood, the self is good. Christ told us to love our neighbor as ourselves. This means we are not to hate ourselves. The true self has been created by God and we are not to hate what God has created. But we are to see that the true self which is within me, that God has created, exists also in others. And we are to love them, therefore, as we love and honor the Divine Image in ourselves. The desert Fathers sometimes said, "Know yourself and forget yourself."

JM: *Is "conquering and overcoming ourselves" a process of purification or of transformation? Must lower energies be eliminated, or changed?*

KW: Properly understood, purification means the same as transformation, though there is a slight difference of emphasis. When you speak of purifying something you mean removing that which disfigures it, so that it becomes truly itself. If you speak of transforming it, you see the nature of that thing as something dynamic, capable of growth. Certainly I do not understand purification in the sense of removing something. When you remove something you don't purify it, you abolish it.

The human person is to be seen as a diversity in unity, an integrated whole with many aspects, with all these aspects interconnected. Therefore nothing in ourselves is to be abolished, or mortified in the sense of being destroyed. But it is to be purified, to be transformed or transfigured. For example: we have in our nature a desire for food and drink. If this is misused, then we suffer from gluttony and from alcoholism. But the desire is not to be abolished. God has given us food and drink, and we are to enjoy these things, although not to be dominated by them. The same can be applied to the question of our sexual energies. These are implanted in us by God. They can be misused, and then they take the form of lust. The essence of lust is the loss of personal relationship. But the sexual energies are not in themselves evil. And they are capable of being transfigured. Even those who have chosen the life of celibacy or of virginity are not called to deny their sexual energies—if they do, they may find themselves in great difficulties—but they are called to transform and purify those energies, to direct them towards God. Eros, understood as physical, sexual love, is an important aspect of Christian love. We shouldn't make a sharp contrast between eros, meaning sexual love, and agape, meaning Christian love. Eros and agape are two aspects of a single reality.

JM: *What is the right attitude toward suffering? Can we learn to suffer creatively—and how?*

KW: Suffering remains a mystery. We cannot fully understand why it is that in a world created by a God of love there is suffering. Insofar as suffering can be relieved, it should be relieved. That applies to others as well as to myself. If I have a toothache, then I should go see the dentist and have it put right. Unnecessary suffering is not good. What are we to do, however, with unavoidable suffering? Suffering itself is an evil. God did not create us to suffer. God does not want us to suffer; He may permit it, but He does not want it. Suffering, however, is something that can be used. The vital point is: what is your attitude towards suffering? You can be destroyed by it, embittered, called to darkness and despair. Or you perhaps can be transformed by it. Perhaps through suffering you can become a whole person in a far deeper sense than you would have been able to do if you had never suffered.

How can we learn to suffer creatively? There is no easy answer, but one way in is this: we can relate our sufferings to the sufferings of others, first of all to the sufferings of Christ Himself on the Cross. If we suffer, then Christ, who is God, has suffered before us, and He is suffering with us. Our suffering is united with His. Also, we can see our suffering as joined to the suffering of all other humans. So the way forward is through solidarity. If I can offer up my sufferings on behalf of others, in unity with Christ, they can be creative and not destructive.

JM: *What do you think is the major difference between someone who really wishes for wholeness and has begun to look for it, and one who ignores the possibility?*

KW: In the Orthodox spiritual tradition, one word that occurs very frequently is "nepsis." This means sobriety, wakefulness, vigilance; the opposite to the state of one who is in a drunken stupor. One who ignores the possibility of starting on the journey towards wholeness is, as it were, asleep. One who has started on the journey is awake. Perhaps the first thing to say to people is "Wake up! Look, listen, open your outer eyes, open your inner eyes." That is said not only in Christianity, but in perhaps all the great spiritual traditions.

JM: *Can there be a waking up and a growth of being without a religious practice?*

KW: For me, as an Orthodox Christian, the journey towards wholeness involves prayer, in the sense of personal, private prayer, standing in silence before God; but also in the sense of communal prayer, sharing in the services of the Church, sharing in the Sacraments. It involves, beyond prayer, joining in all the other practices of the Church: in fasting, in the reading of Holy Scripture. Is it possible to grow without these things? God is very generous. Many people who have no religious practice do grow in self-understanding, do show creative love towards others. They are open to their fellow humans. And there are many people who are open towards God who do not belong to any particular church. I do not wish to judge them. I accept the authenticity and integrity of their inner life. Yet, I believe that in its fullness, the growth of the human person towards wholeness is intended by God to take place within a church life.

JM: *There are so many religious traditions being taught in the world today, that a lot of people find it confusing and take bits from here and there in a sort of patchwork combination. What do you think about that?*

KW: Let me use here a familiar image: the image of climbing a mountain. A mountain has only one top, though there may be many paths up towards the top of the mountain. As a Christian, I believe the fullness of the truth exists only in Christianity, only in faith in Jesus Christ. But I believe that God speaks in the hearts of all humankind, and therefore I believe that there is a true revelation of God, incomplete but genuine, in the other great religions. So I believe that they too are following a path that will lead them to the top of the mountain. And since the mountain has only one top, we shall all meet there if we are faithful to our vocation, if we respond to the light that is given to us. What is dangerous is exactly what is mentioned in this question: if instead of following one path with integrity, we try to combine a number of different paths. If you try to hop from one path to another, you will make no progress at all. You will fall into thorn bushes and disagreeable ravines. So my counsel is: follow the way on which you are, with integrity.

JM: *What other counsel would you give to someone who is beginning to look for a way?*

KW: I would give one particular piece of advice: try to find a guide, a spiritual father or spiritual mother, a person endowed with discernment and love who can help you on the way. If you are going up a mountain for the first time, you need to have someone with you who knows the way. We can learn many things from books, and many things from the inner light of our own conscience, but it is easy to misunderstand what is written in books—perhaps it is true but it is not written for us, or not for us at this moment—and it is easy to confuse the advice of the conscience with our own wishful thinking. If we have an experienced guide, an elder, that is an enormous assistance on the way. The truth is not so much taught as caught; caught through personal contact. Things can be learned through living with another person which can never be learned just from verbal statement. The truth is caught and the spiritual father or mother is the infectious person. In the Christian tradition very often the spiritual father is a priest-monk. But he needn't necessarily be a priest, he needn't necessarily be a monk, he needn't necessarily be a man. Any human may be given this gift. The same person cannot act as guide to everybody. It is a personal relationship. But if we look around us, perhaps in the persons whom we meet we can discover one who is able to give us the help we need.

JM: *Today there are many gurus around who are selling themselves as spiritual fathers and mothers, and some of them seem to be bogus, dangerous. Are there any criteria in religious tradition to help people look out for those who might have gifts and powers, but who are in fact Satanic in their use of these gifts and powers?*

KW: The problem you mention is a real one. There are many false guides. There is no automatic way of discovering a true guide, but there are certain criteria. First, the spiritual father, if genuine, does not usually impose himself. He doesn't necessarily hide, but he waits for the others to come. The true spiritual father helps us to develop our own freedom. He does not impose his way on us, but helps us to discover our own way. The true spiritual guide does not promise instant success. In the spiritual life there are occasionally shortcuts, but ones provided by God. In general, what is asked of us is fidelity and the willingness to go deep. Those spiritual teachers who claim to offer us the higher gifts of contemplation through a few simple exercises should be treated with great caution.

JM: *We speak of the "whole person," but doesn't that imply a relationship of his parts—a relationship of knowledge to feeling, and also the part the body plays?*

KW: In the Orthodox spiritual tradition we often use the word "heart." By heart we mean not just the emotions or feelings but the deep center, the true self. Our aim is to discover the place of the heart, to unite the brain with its knowledge to the heart; and in the heart also feeling is found. Our aim, then, is to integrate them on the level of the deep heart. And the body is also involved in this, because the body is not a piece of clothing but our integral self. The body plays its part through ascetic effort, by which I don't mean just self-denial, but self-control. It plays its part through symbolic actions. There are ways also in which the rhythms of the body, the rhythm of the breathing, for example, can be used in prayer and meditation. The body is not just a piece of matter to be ignored, and still less something evil to be hated. The body is an aspect of ourself which we are to live to the full.

In the Greek Christian tradition, the person is often described as being at the center of creation, at the crossroads. The human person is seen as a microcosm reflecting the whole creation, both material and spiritual. In this way, the human person is the bond of creation, the bridge—the marriage song of creation. The human person is called to be the mediator. We are called to unite. We are called to take material things and make them spiritual. Though they still remain material, we raise them to a higher level. And because we are made in the Image of God, it is the task of each one of us to be the priest of creation, to take the creation and to offer it back to God.

Parabola
Volume: 23.2
Ecstasy

The Door to Joy

Irma Zaleski

> *A man once asked Mother Macrina how he could acquire joy. "You cannot acquire joy," Mother Macrina told him, "you must find it."*
> *"But how I can find it?" he asked.*
> *"Oh, that is simple," she replied. "There is only one way. To find joy you must lose your self."*
> —*Stories of Mother Macrina*

In the language of religion, joy is not a merely human emotion but a spiritual experience. It is a "fruit of the Holy Spirit," a *grace*. Joy comes to us from a place outside of ourselves, or from so deep inside that we cannot reach it at will. This is why we are always, as C. S. Lewis has said, "surprised by joy." It may burst upon us in moments of great happiness, in a world flooded with beauty, in an ecstasy of love. We hear it, perhaps, in the sound of our children's voices playing outside, or the song of birds, or the night rumor of the sea. We recognize it in a great work of art. But joy may also come to us in the midst of unbearable suffering, at the end of our endurance, in the face of death. It breaks into the prison of our misery and pain and, for a moment *we forget* ourselves and are free. True joy is a form of ecstasy, a state of being *out of our ordinary minds*. In the words of St. Augustine (*On Psalm 99*, 3ff.) joy is a "song of the soul," a spontaneous response of the human spirit when it is able to step away beyond the confines of its own ego and find itself in the presence of God.

God is not a concept or an "article of faith." Although we give him many names, he is not a creation of the mind. We may not even believe in him, yet, he is real. Children see God quite often, I think. They see him in the essential *mysteriousness* of things, they experience him in wild joy which seems at times to possess them, in laughter and play. They also meet him, perhaps, in an abandonment to grief, in a flood of uninhibited tears. When we begin to grow up, however, we quickly lose our ability to encounter God in such direct, simple ways. Our minds are too restless, too noisy to hear the sound of his coming. We cannot believe what our hearts experience, we cannot find him among the evils which seem to rule the world. We think and worry too much and try to create our own safe gods. This is why we must relearn to see the signs of the Divine Presence and to open ourselves to it. We must find our way back to joy.

Because joy is an inner experience of the presence of God—a relationship—it is impossible to categorize it or define it in words. It cannot be taught. Each human being must find his or her own path which leads to its door. For some it is a "high road" of contemplation, of ecstasy and bliss. To most of us, however, joy comes in small doses, in little "whispers" of God's passing, in sudden, unexpected glimpses of mystery in the midst of our ordinary lives. But whatever way it comes, it is always an experience of "losing ourselves," of being emptied of self and opened to what is *beyond*: of being in *love*. The true source of joy is love—love of God, love of beauty, love of wisdom, love of another human being, it does not matter which. It is all one love: a joyful awareness of dissolving boundaries of our ordinary narrow self, of being one with the reality beyond, of being made whole.

When I was little, in Poland before the War, we used to spend nearly every summer at my grandmother's house in the mountains. She lived alone, in a house built by local craftsmen on the edge of a torrent. The noise of its rushing waters was the background of every moment of our holidays, and the first sound of eternity which I learned to hear. My grandmother was the kind of grandmother that everybody should have. She was brilliant and wise, although a little bitter at times. She had lived through wars, revolutions, a bad marriage, and the death of two children. What had saved her sanity, I believe, was her love of beauty and a passionate interest in all the things of the mind. She loved literature and art, she was fascinated by science. Above all else, she loved the beauty of the mountains among which she lived and among which she eventually died.

I must have been five or six at the time. One night, I was awakened by my grandmother leaning over my bed. There was a noise of a great storm outside. Grandmother picked me up and carried me out onto a big veranda which ran all along the front of the house. "Look!" she said, and turned my face toward the mountains, "Look, this is too beautiful to sleep through." I saw black sky, torn apart every few seconds by lightning, mountains emerging out of darkness, immense, powerful, and so *real*. Thunder rolled among the peaks. I was not frightened—how could I be?—I was awed. I looked up at my grandmother's face and, in a flash of light, I saw it flooded with wonder and joy. I did not realize it then, of course, but now I do, that what I saw was ecstasy. My grandmother was the first to point out to me a *door to joy*.

The war years in occupied Poland were not conducive to joy. Like millions of other people, we lived on the edge of disaster, surrounded by horror and fear. There was very little beauty in our lives. We did not go to the mountains, we heard very little music (orchestras were disbanded and the radios forbidden), theaters and even schools were closed. It was hard, often impossible, to get away from the city. We dwelled in a bleak, inhuman world, in small rooms filled with all the belongings we had managed to save, always aware of the evil outside.

And yet, even during the darkest years, there were times when joy would suddenly burst out of darkness like lightning and, for a moment, all was well. It could have been on a summer night, when tossing and turning on the bed I shared with my mother, I would hear a song of a nightingale in the jasmine bushes outside, and the beauty of it would be nearly impossible to bear. Or, on an autumn evening, as I was hurrying along a grey, empty street, anxious to be home before the curfew, I would look up and see the flaming glory of the setting sun and, for a split second perhaps, there would be no more darkness or war. A door would fly open at the center of my being and I would walk through it unafraid. The darkness, of course, would soon return and I would run home, fearful again of the curfew police.

The war finally ended, although not in the way we had hoped. In September of 1946, we—my mother, my brother, and I—escaped from communist Poland, and eventually joined my father who had spent the war years with the Polish Army in the West. Upon our arrival in Britain, my parents decided that, in order to learn English as quickly as possible, I was to be sent to a boarding school in Scotland, run by Catholic nuns. I loathed it at first and made myself a nuisance, I am afraid. I was angry, rebellious, and scared. But the nuns won me over in the end. In spite of myself, I was moved by the beauty and peace of the life they had embraced, by their kindness, by the way they prayed and sang in church. I began to appreciate the beauty and the sacred order of their religious celebrations and liturgies. Sometimes, as I knelt with the other girls at evening prayers in the dimly lighted church, a faint scent of incense lingering in the air and the flickering flame of a vigil light throwing immense shadows on the high ceiling above, the horror and the chaos I had lived through receded and I would find myself relaxing into silence and peace. Without realizing it, I think, I had begun to pray.

I also learned to love the hills among which the Convent stood, the tall, dark trees which surrounded it, the pale Scottish sky and, above all else, the walled-in garden where I often escaped to be alone. It was in that garden, when I was about fifteen, that I wrote this poem, the first one I had ever written and which, miraculously, I have kept:

> *God struck a chord of purple and gold,*
> *behind the pine trees on the*
> *lawn,*

> *and as he was very near, I said softly so that*
> *only he could hear,*
> *that it was good.*

> *God smiled, the wind gently sighed and*
> *smoothed the dark heads of*
> *the trees.*

> *God came where I stood and said it was very*
> *good*
> *then began to light the stars.*

It was not a great poem, of course, but it expressed, however naively, a beginning of an insight which was to become the root of my spiritual life: that God was very beautiful and that all created beauty was a sign of his presence. I began to realize that to be touched by beauty, to search for it in all things and *rejoice* in it, even amid the ugliness and sorrow of life, was to be for me a path of prayer and the way to God.

Such moments of insight are very rare, they pass and one forgets. It has been so in my life at least. But I have never ceased to search for God, however childish and superficial some of the ways I looked for him were. I studied different religions and read books. I talked to priests, Zen Masters, Buddhist monks. I joined meditation groups and investigated every spiritual path I came across. But still, I was never satisfied, never at peace. A friend who knew me well used to become exasperated with what he called my "running into caves." "For heaven's sake, woman," he would shout, "do you think God is a pussy-cat that you can play with? God is a tiger! You'd better watch out if you ever succeed in falling into his cave."

"You might be right, Dante," I answered, "but I *want* God!"

"Well, you will not find him in books, or running after gurus," he said.

"How shall I find him, then?" I asked.

"By standing still!" he replied.

Dante was an artist, a husband of a life-long friend. Even after I had left England for Canada, I used to see them in London every few years. It became an established custom during those visits that Dante and I would go to museums and art galleries together. Or, it would be better to say, Dante took me to see what he felt I should learn to see. At first, we used to talk a good deal and I would ask many questions, but, during later visits, we often stood silent before a painting, a sculpture or a vase, and then we would just smile at each other and leave.

It was during one of those visits that I experienced a moment of the purest joy, and, I think, came closer to ecstasy than ever before or since. We were in the British Museum, in front of a three thousand-year-old Egyptian sculpture which Dante particularly loved. He thought it was the work of a great spiritual master and contained deep wisdom which one needed to absorb. We had visited it many times in the past, and it had become very familiar to me. But now, suddenly, I realized that I had never really seen it before. For a moment, I don't know how long, it became alive, perfect, full of beauty and wisdom, radiating compassion and peace. For the first time in my life, I felt totally focused and still. At that instant I knew what it meant to "find God" and that he was indeed a "tiger." In that one single moment out of time, I had been given a glimpse of a reality which could never *not be*, a pledge of eternity at the core of all being.

But we do not live out of time. Moments of ecstasy, however significant and profound they may be, must pass, and their memory alone cannot sustain our everyday spiritual lives. We must find a way of living eternity within the dimension of time. For most of us this means a very great struggle. It means the breaking down of protective walls we have built around our time-bound egos and opening them to what is beyond: not only in moments of ecstasy but every moment of our lives. In other words, it means the painful process of *learning to love*. Truth, beauty, joy—the presence of God—can only be found in a living encounter with another, in a relationship of love.

Christian tradition has been for me the most real and the most *natural* path to that relationship. Not because I believe it offers a "final solution" to the mystery of being, or is the only path to God, but because, at its very core, it is a *religion of love*. It is true that Christianity is a narrow path and anyone who walks on it faces the danger of falling into exclusiveness and pride. No religious path, perhaps, is free from that danger. But, as I tried to follow in the footsteps of him in whose face I recognized the fullness of the divine presence, that danger receded and I became, I hope, more open to truth and beauty, wherever they could be found, not less. I was led to see ever more clearly that at the *heart* of all true religion is "good news," a call to the joy of Bethlehem, a proclamation that God—the infinite, unknowable reality—makes himself present in the world and summons all of us to that same encounter and that same relationship of love with himself and all of his creation.

For God never comes to us alone, but brings with him the whole universe. He opens our eyes to the beauty of everything that is. He brings with him every human being who has ever lived. He breaks our hearts open to what is *not self*. He shares with us his own joy and his own total, all-embracing love poured out on us in Christ (Jn. 15:11–12.) This is why the great Christian teacher and saint, Seraphim of Sarov, having spent thirty years alone in the silence of his cell, used to run out to meet every person coming toward him, bow down to the ground, and say, "My brother, my sister, my joy!" This is why all true saints have always loved every creature which came from the hand of God. Love does not discriminate or categorize; it does not insist on being right. Love embraces all things in that great, empty silence beyond words or thought, which is the wide-open door to ecstasy and to unending joy.

Parabola
Volume: 10.3
The Body

Washing the Feet

Christopher Bamford

> *There is one body, and one Spirit, even as ye are called in*
> *one hope of your calling; one Lord, one faith, one baptism, one*
> *God and Father of all, who is above all, and through all, and*
> *in you all. …*
>
> —*Ephesians 4:1–6*

The fundamental relation of humanity to the ground of its being is paradoxical; it is a relationship which presents two faces. One is built upon the premise that each living, individual human being is potentially in contact with the eternal and uncreated ground of all being. This is the divine spark in each person to which Meister Eckhart refers when he writes, "There is something in the soul which is uncreated and uncreatable; if the whole soul were this it would be uncreated and uncreatable; and this is the intellect." Intellect here is the Latin *intellectus*, synonyms for which are *spiritus*, spirit and *animus*, mind. There exists a spiritual ferment in the soul, says Eckhart, which, under certain conditions, can transform and spiritualize it. "In this power, God is fully verdant and flowering, in all the joy and honor that he is himself." That is to say, each particular has potentially a unique connection to the universal; but the connection must be made.

Such is the relation of the individual to God: alone before the alone. But the uncreated ground present in each also has a relationship to all other human beings—indeed to all of creation. This is the second face of the paradox. Both relationships are religious in the sense of "binding together" in order to re-form the whole, religion and reformation being one. Today there is a tendency to emphasize the mystical spirit immanent in each human being and to ignore the aspect of humanity itself as a mystical body. And yet these two aspects cannot be separated, any more than the many can be separated from the one, or the body from the spirit. All things in the universe are essentially two—uncreated and created, creator and creation—and these two must be made one or, at least, not-two: that is the paradoxical work of creation. In the phrase of Maximus the Confessor: "... always and in all his Word God wills the mystery of his embodiment."

A precursor of Meister Eckhart, the ninth-century "Holy Sage" John Scotus Erigena, is of help in two ways. He tells us that the virtue of the soul is faith, while that of the intellect or spirit is knowledge. Secondly, in his interpretation of the Johannine story of the encounter of Christ with the woman of Samaria at Jacob's Well, he makes the logic of their relation quite clear: the soul must summon her spouse, the intellect, in order for them both to receive the inexhaustible gift of the Holy Spirit, the invisible divinity that can act in man to guide him to all truth. Everything hangs, therefore, upon the soul, the *anima*.

Contrary to what one might expect, this soul or *anima* is traditionally taken to be the individualized and individualizing aspect of the human being, the separative, discursive faculty which establishes the line between this and that, past and present, self and not-self, I and other. By means of such distinctions human beings begin to feel themselves at first distinct; later, isolated; and finally, opposed to each other in fear, greed, envy, lust, etc. Faith, according to tradition, is the hidden virtue and cure of this. It is the eye, the opening of the soul, by which she first sees and gives birth. For this reason, in Christianity, the exemplar of faith in its purest form is the Virgin Mary, the "handmaid of the Lord," whose perfect surrender, epitomized in the phrase, "Be it unto me according to thy Word," echoes down the centuries to instruct us still.

"Virgin," according to Meister Eckhart, "designates a human being who is devoid of all foreign images, and who is as void as he was when he was not yet." "Listen closely to the instruction that I am going to give you," he continues.

> *I could have so vast an intelligence that all the images that all human beings have ever received and those that are in God himself were comprehended in my intelligence; however, if I were in no way attached to them, to the point that in everything I do or fail to do I did not cling to them with attachment—with its before and after—but if in this present now I kept myself unceasingly free and void for the beloved will of God and its fulfillment, then I should be a virgin, without the ties of all images, as truly as I was when I was not yet.*

By images Eckhart means the contents of consciousness: the finished, fixed forms—past thoughts and memories—which we take to be the world, but which in fact are not the world in its immediacy and presentness, but only our own past, our own habits and fixed tendencies. Immured within these images, we feed upon ourselves and take our self-feeling for the world. These images interpose themselves between us and the world, breaking the continuum of being, and making any true meeting or true knowledge impossible. The antidote to the attachment to these, which is the normal condition of human consciousness, Eckhart calls *Gelassenheit*, releasement or detachment. Attachment imprisons us in the past, dismembers and fragments us. Detachment releases us for and to the present. Surrendering what is dead, materialized, and arrested in us—our mineral body—we become open to the genuinely new, a new body. Such detachment and openness is faith, the body of faith. Voidness is its activity; dematerialization, spiritualization is its effect. "Faith cometh by hearing and hearing by the Word of God." Now, hearing is listening, attending. It requires silence and patience; for if you are talking or in a hurry you cannot listen. Faith is inner silence. Listening in silence, renouncing and dissolving the categories of thought which rule us, relinquishing our ego's claim to be self-constituted and autonomous, we become open to the true awareness of things as they are. We hear the word spoken in silence, hear the word that silence speaks. In this way, as Eckhart says, the Virgin becomes a wife, a mother.

In the words of St. James: "Faith, if it hath not works, is dead, being alone. ... For, as the body without the spirit is dead, so faith without works

172 WASHING THE FEET

is dead." What this might mean is suggested by the fact that Eckhart's "Hymn to Detachment," quoted above, explicitly echoes St. Paul's "Hymn to Love," with its refrain that whatever gifts I may have "and have not love" I am nothing, a sounding brass or a tinkling cymbal:

> Love is patient; love is kind and envies no one. Love is never boastful, nor conceited, nor rude; never selfish, not quick to take offence. Love keeps no scores of wrongs; does not gloat over other men's sins, but delights in the truth. There is nothing love cannot face; there is no limit to its faith, its hope and its endurance.

Love in this tradition is the *fruit* of faith. "For the beginning is faith and the end is love and when the two are joined together in unity it is God" (Ignatius). Faith is "freedom from the known" (in Krishnamurti's phrase); the *sine qua non* of unmediated knowing. The openness of faith or active release dissolves the carapace of habitual images and fixed circuits which we took to be the boundaries of the self. The objectified, materialized self opens into an experience of a provisional, contextual, "empty" self. Who we are becomes immanent in the network of relations we are engaged in. For a moment, indeed, we seem to be constituted by those relations, determined wholly by our recognition of an "other." Who we are becomes who we are *with*, as the Word is with God. In that space of our relations we first come to be, and awaken.

But perhaps that is to move too fast. To truly meet another one, as we are one, to feel something or someone in our inmost being as truly *real*, is very rare. We do not have *gelassenheit*, and for the most part feel ourselves as more real than what surrounds us. We are the center of our attention. Indeed, if we are honest, we rarely attend to anything else. Love, *agape*, as St. Paul means it, begins with the terrifying recognition of the reality of something, someone, truly "other." In this sense, love and beauty are closely allied—beauty which, in Rilke's words "is the beginning of a terror we can hardly bear": the sudden, overwhelming presence of a reality that seems greater than we are. Love recognizes the unconditional significance of something other than ourselves. We have a dense and carefully cultivated sense of our own importance—which we forever shore up and reinforce by projecting the world in our own image and then acting in it like a god. Then, suddenly, standing before a great work of art, a beautiful landscape, a person, something happens: we lay down this objectified self in recognition of something larger that, momentarily, takes possession of us and makes us feel more fluid and less bounded than we felt before. This is all well known. Lovers, like mystics, feel themselves "melt" into their surroundings. We have all felt it. Truly, our subject is one of the most ordinary. Of all the miracles of the everyday, it is perhaps the most clearly available—each time we meet. "When two or three are gathered together in my name I am there." The mystery is, if this is so, what *body* shall he have, shall I have?

St. Paul can best guide us here, for he makes the right distinctions, separating flesh (*sarx*) and body (*soma*). Flesh he uses above all to refer to the outward, visible, mortal condition—to creation in the solidarity of its dismemberment, pain, and solitude. Flesh is the letter, the law, idolatry, by virtue of which sin (which is unfreedom, ignorance, suffering) comes to be. "Flesh" thus connotes the human being in his distance and difference, his isolation. It is "sin" because, denying the consubstantiality of humanity, creation, and God, it distorts the fundamental relationship of the universe, which is harmony, wholeness, and unity. Only by virtue of the spirit are humanity and human beings open to and together with the whole. Walking "after the spirit" is therefore contrasted by St. Paul with walking "after the flesh"; and "carnal-mindedness," which is death, division, strife, and envy, is contrasted with "spiritual-mindedness," which is life and peace.

St. Paul, however, also uses the word "body" to refer to the external man, but this time with the connotation of wholeness or unity. Wholeness indeed is of the essence of what a body is, and therefore body comes to mean what is essentially whole or has become so. It is the body, not the flesh, which is the Temple of the Holy Ghost, the place of God's manifestation or glorification, where his Word is magnified.

We come closer to the mystery we are approaching when we notice that St. Paul uses the term "body" collectively as well as individually. Indeed, he moves freely from the one to the other, speaking now of the "individual" body, now of "the redemption of *our* body," of Christ reforming "the body of *our* humiliation." By this usage, body comes to connote what human beings have in common, irrespective of what appear to be individual differences. Mystically, we may take this consubstantiality to refer to human nature as a whole. This "body" is what connects human beings to each other and the universe. While "flesh" establishes human solitude and otherness, "body," joining human beings together, is the bearer of the resurrection. There is a body of sin, death, and humiliation, but there is also an immortal, resurrection body. In this sense, there is no resurrection of the flesh. It is the body that is for the Lord and the Lord that is for the body.

Looking more closely at this body, which from another point of view is the bride whose disunity is fragmentation and exile, we find that it is made up of beauty and love: it is, finally, a body of beauty and love. Call it Shekhina or Sophia. Love binds together what is separated, overcomes what separates, brings parts together into a whole, a body. Love makes the body. But this love is not *eros*; it is *agape*. Platonic *eros*, though beginning with the soul movement inspired by the beauty of sensible things, leads the Platonist out of this world, intensifying desire into a single-pointed heavenly desire, whereby what is human is raised up. Platonic love, unlike Christian, proposes as its end not identity-in-difference (i.e. relation) but identity-in-union. Its last term is death. But for *agape* or *caritas* (charity) death is the beginning. Love, which was death, becomes life, particularity. As God's love is particular—"He first loved us"—human love too must be particular, specific, from moment to moment.

"A new commandment I give you, that you love one another as I have loved you." There were two old commandments—to love God with all one's heart and all one's mind, and to love one's neighbor as oneself. These are human loves; they derive from the human point of view and indicate the path from the human to the divine. Such is the activity of *eros* by which all things yearn for unity. The new commandment, fulfilling but not eliminating the old, proposes an inversion: that one love, not from a limited, human perspective, but from an absolute, universal, limitless point of view. This inversion is profound; by it "human" love is "divine presence." To love one's neighbor as oneself means to love one's neighbor *as if* he were oneself. The new commandment inverts this. It enjoins one to love for the sake of the other alone, to give oneself unconditionally, to empty oneself utterly: to go beyond oneself, out of oneself, so that one becomes, as it were, "nothing." It is to act as God acts, to love as God loves.

Such action, or love, which does not imitate but makes present, has been called (by J. Edgar Bruns) "the Christian Buddhism of St. John," who is the greater teacher here. According to this, it is what humans *do* that reveals God's presence, and is God's presence, just as for the Mahayanist it is his understanding that is the Buddha-nature—not conversely. "No one has seen God," but the Son has "acted him out." Similarly, "No man hath seen God; if we love one another, God abides in us"—because, for St. John, God *is* love. God is not some thing; he does not do anything: he is the doing. God cannot be identified with any faculty or any entity: in our activity we reveal him, he is there. Consequently, to be born of God means to bear God—in both senses of giving birth to and carrying. If we "love" we make "God" present, because "God" is "love." "God is love, and whoever abides in love, abides in God, and God abides in him." If we abide in love, remain in and one with it—if it becomes our body—our activity becomes what is divine. There is no dualism here—no difference between the love that is our body and our spiritual unity with God, because God, Spirit, True Self, is simply another name for the love which is our body. What is most important in this is that the activity of love, which allows for such presence and realization, requires the recognition, the presence, of another. The making of God present is an interhuman, relational activity. It is not achieved on the mountain-top. St. Basil had something of this kind in mind when, after a trip to the eremitical settlements of the Egyptian desert, he remarked, "That is all very well, but whose feet will they wash?"

To wash the feet, as an activity paradigmatic of love, means the laying down of our own sense of unconditional value in recognition of the unconditional value of another. By this we shift the center of our lives away from ourselves as objects of our own attention; we change the direction of our attention and we become other. Forced to acknowledge the reality of another, we are forced to relinquish the sense we have of ourselves as isolated, atomic, egoic beings, to abandon the selves that we have constituted by materializing past memories, thoughts, and desires into the complex artifacts with which we are identified. As the Russian philosopher Solovyov puts it, "The meaning of human love, speaking generally, is the justification and deliverance of individuality through the sacrifice of egoism." Otherwise stated: "The truth, as a living force, taking possession of the inward essence of man, and effectively rescuing him from false self-assertion, is termed love." As to the difference between true individuality and the false individuality which is egoism, Solovyov is very clear. The fundamental illusion of egoism lies not in the absolute self-assertion and self-estimation of the subject; rather, that while rating himself in accordance with what is due to unconditional significance, the subject denies that significance to others, relegating them to the circumference of his being and giving them only an external and relative value.

Washing of the feet, in this sense, is more than simple humility or ordinary selflessness. By its active identification with the other, the love it manifests at the same time overcomes "materiality" and affirms the consubstantiality of creation, the body of the whole. "Materiality," material existence, which from this point of view stands opposed to the consubstantial unity of the world, presents us with a twofold impenetrability; in the words of Solovyov:

> *1. Impenetrability in* Time, *in virtue of which every successive moment of existence does not preserve the preceding one within itself, but excludes it or, by itself, dislodges it from existence, so that each new thing in the sphere of matter originates at the expense of, or to the detriment of, what preceded it.*
>
> *2. Impenetrability in* Space, *in virtue of which two parts of matter (two bodies) cannot at the same time occupy one and the same place, i.e. one and the same part of space, but of necessity dislodge one another.*

By this we define our selves, our bodies, and thereby irrevocably make the world a place of dismemberment and conflict. Unmaking this view, transforming ourselves by love as spoken of above, we become consubstantial with one another. We become many persons in one body.

What is this body? According to one view it is *Sophia* or Divine Wisdom. Florensky speaks of Sophia as "the great root of the created world in its wholeness and unity," and "the original substance of creatures, the creative Love of God in them." Sophia is at once the ideal substance of the created world, its truth or meaning, and its spirituality—its holiness, purity, sinlessness, beauty. At the same time, she is the beginning and center of the redeemed creation, the Body of the Lord. In Christian terms, she is the Virgin, Mary, the purified human soul. But there is a mystery here, that Boehme brings out, but that the Russian Sophilogists (Solovyov, Florensky, Bulgakov) also knew; there is an uncreated Sophia, a sense in which Sophia is "God's revelation and the Holy Spirit's corporeality, the body of the Holy Trinity." That is to say, as on earth Sophia is the unity of creation, so in heaven she is the Godhead's unity.

This unity of the Godhead, of the Persons, brings us closer to understanding the unity or body that human beings have and are—and that allows them to become true persons likewise. For the self or intellect to manifest, said Erigena, the soul, whose virtue is faith and whose vice is egoity, must summon it. By faith it must, in Eckhart's words, overcome egoity and become virgin, imageless, a perfect mirror. Considering the Virgin in her activity, we find her the exemplar of the human virtues of chastity, poverty, and obedience. Such must we be also. She lays down her will in order to live from moment to moment the will of the divine. According to Christian story, by that activity of perfect love and surrender, the Virgin was able to form a body for the Logos, God's Word: become his mother and his bride. Generalizing on this, Christian tradition takes her for the true type of the church or mystical body—which is the universal body redeemed at once from below and from above. From below, by the human activity of the renunciation of egoity, from above by the descent of the holy spirit. But these two activities are one, as body and spirit, soul and spirit are one. The place of their meeting is who we are.

Have I dissolved the body by some metaphysical sleight-of-hand? Have I denied the unique relationship each one of us enjoys with the unfathomable ground of being? I hardly think so. There is no body outside the body we cognize, perceive, think about—and that body is the projecting of the self we think we are: we only see ourselves. All the great traditions teach us to become other—thereby, too, our body must become other. We are our body, but not the body we think we are. Realizing our true self through the laying down of our egoic selves, we become one with each other, we realize the single body of all humanity and become truly one for the first time. He who would find his life must lose it.

Parabola
Volume: 12.3
Forgiveness

Living in Communion

Interview with Father Thomas Hopko

Father Thomas Hopko is a priest of the Orthodox Church in America and a teacher of theology and spirituality at Saint Vladimir's Seminary in Crestwood, New York.

When we asked Father Hopko to speak to Parabola *about the theme of "Forgiveness," his response was immediate and enthusiastic. It is a question that has long been of concern to him and one that he places at the center of the Christian way. Father Hopko's intensity is deeply informed by his devotion to the traditions of his Church. He is a committed man, and speaks with a force that brings his words about the process of forgiveness to a vivid and compelling life.*
—Lorraine Kisly

Parabola: *I think that many people today approach forgiveness from a secular viewpoint. They recognize that there is a value in forgiving and being forgiven, but see it on the human level only. Without a theological dimension, or a higher level, there is no context for forgiveness. Wouldn't you say that forgiveness is a divine act?*

Father Thomas Hopko: If a person is inspired by the spirit of God, he or she can forgive, certainly. People can forgive. But I'm not so sure you can say that in general there is the feeling that forgiveness is of value. I was a parish priest for twenty years, and I encountered people who would say, "I don't care. I can go on and live my life—it really doesn't matter to me. If I'm not bothering you and you aren't bothering me, why be reconciled?" This is plain indifference.

Another reason why people don't value forgiveness is that they consider it to be collusion with evil. They feel that if a person has done something really terrible, he or she should be reminded of it until death, and further, that the evil should be avenged. And of course, most of us feel that any offense committed against us is irreparable. Nothing that the other person does can ever cancel it. If you kill my child, for example, there is nothing you can do in reparation, and for me to forgive would simply be to condone the evil. So I'm not sure that most people value forgiveness.

When you look at it from the point of view of justice, there is no reason for forgiveness. Only if God exists and we realize that there is either a world with evil or no world at all, only then can we understand that we are going to have to undergo the trial of evil. But if that is not there, I don't know why anyone would forgive. Or want to. But I do think that people who are not believers in God, by the fact they are made in God's image, can have the sense that reconciliation is better than allowing the evil to go on. By definition, forgiveness is breaking the chain of evil, beginning by recognizing that evil really has been done. People tend to think forgiveness means something really bad was not really done—that a person didn't understand the consequences, or whatever. If that were the case, there would be no need for forgiveness; it could be seen simply as a mistake. Forgiveness has to admit, and rage over, and weep over a real evil, and then say, however, "We are going to live in communion one with another. We are going to carry on." Never forgetting—you can't, at any rate—but carrying on in a spirit of love without letting the evil poison the future relationship. And certainly, from our perspective, that is what happens theologically. The striking thing in the Gospel is that God refuses to let evil destroy the relationship. Even if we kill *him*, he will say, "Forgive them."

P: *Implied in what you say is that the relationship is the highest aim, and that an obstacle to relationship is what calls the need for forgiveness.*

TH: Yes. I would prefer the word *communion* to *relationship*, but yes. The Orthodox approach is that we are made in the image and likeness of God, and that God is a Trinity of persons in absolute identity of being and of life in perfect communion. Therefore, communion is the given. Anything that breaks that communion destroys the very roots of our existence. That's why forgiveness is essential if there is going to be human life in the image of God. We are all sinners, living with other sinners, and so "seventy-times-seven" times a day we must reestablish the communion—and *want* to do so. The desire is the main thing, and the feeling that it is of value.

The obsession with relationship—the individual in search of relationships—in the modern world shows that there is an ontological crack in our being. There is no such thing as an individual—he was created, probably, in a Western European university. We don't recognize our essential communion. I don't look at you and say, "You are my life."

Contemporary interpretations of the commandment in the Torah reflect this individualistic attitude. The first commandment in the Torah is that you love God with all your mind, with all your soul, and with all your strength, and the second is that you love your neighbor as yourself. The only way you can prove you love God is by loving your neighbor, and the only way you can love your neighbor in *this* life is by endless forgiveness. So, "love your neighbor as yourself." However, in certain modern editions of the Bible, I have seen this translated as, "you shall love your neighbor as you love yourself." But that's not what it says."

I once had a discussion with someone on a Sunday-morning television program about this. We were asked what we thought was most important in Christianity, and part of what I said was that the only way we can find ourselves is to deny ourselves. That's Christ's teaching. If you try to cling to yourself, you will lose yourself. And of course, the unwillingness to forgive is the ultimate act of not wanting to let yourself go. You want to defend yourself, assert yourself, protect yourself, and so on. There is a consistent line through the Gospel—if you want to be the first you must will to be the last, and so on. And the other fellow, who taught the psychology of religion at one of the Protestant seminaries, said, "What you are saying is the source of the neuroses of Western society. What we need is healthy self-love and healthy self-esteem." And then he quoted that line, "you shall love your neighbor as *you love* yourself." He insisted that you must love yourself first and have a sense of dignity. If one has that, however, forgiveness is then either out of the question or an act of condescension toward the poor sinner. It is no longer an identification with the other as a sinner, too. I said that of course if we are made in the image of God it's quite self-affirming, and self-hatred is an evil. But my main point is that there is no self there to be defended except the one that comes into existence by the act of love and self-emptying. It's only by loving the other that myself actually emerges. And forgiveness is at the heart of that.

As we were leaving we saw a very old, venerable rabbi with a shining face. He called us over and asked if he could say something to us. "That line, you know, comes from the Torah, from *Leviticus*," he said, "and it cannot possibly be translated 'love your neighbor as you love yourself.' What it says is 'you shall love your neighbor as *being* your own self.'" Your neighbor *is* your true self. You have no self in yourself.

After I heard this I started reading the Church Fathers in this light, and that's what they all say. They say, "Your brother is your life." I have no self in myself except the one that is fulfilled by loving the other. The Trinitarian character of God is a metaphysical absolute here, so to speak. God's own self is another—his Son, to use Christian evangelical terms. The same thing happens on the human level; so the minute I don't feel deeply that my real self is the other, then I'll have no reason to forgive anyone. But if that is my reality, and my own real self is the other, and my own identity and fulfillment emerges only in the act of loving the other, that gives substance to the idea that we are all potentially God-like beings. Now, if you add to that that we are all to some degree faulty, weak, and so on, that act of love will always be an act of forgiveness. That's how I find and fulfill myself as a human being made in God's image. Otherwise, I cannot. So the act of forgiveness is the very act by which our humanity is constituted. Deny that, and we kill ourselves. It's a metaphysical suicide.

P: *You are making a very definite distinction here between the individual and the person.*

TH: Well, we would say the individual is the person that refuses to love. When a person refuses to identify in being and value with "the least," even with "the enemy," then the person becomes an individual. He or she becomes a self-enclosed being trying to have proper relationships—usually on his or her own terms. But again, we would say that the person only comes into existence by going out of oneself into communion with the other. So my task is not to decide whether or not I will be in relationship with you but to realize that I *am* in communion with you: my life is yours, and your life is mine. Without this, there is no way that we are going to be able to carry on.

P: *Forgiveness is not an achievement, an act, so much as the development of an understanding of reality?*

TH: It is a decision in the sense that you have to will it. You have to choose life. A person can choose death by not forgiving. So there is a sense in which you can destroy yourself by not saying "yes" to the reality that actually exists. That's the choice: "yes" or "no" to what truly exists. Forgiveness is the great "yes." So there is a choice. In the Greek patristic tradition, the more a person is a person, the more we realize and will our communion with others in the act of love, the less we choose. So the freer we are, the less choice we have.

That's almost opposite to the post-Enlightenment, secular Western thought. We tend to think the freer we are, the more choice we have. For example, if you would sin against me and I want to love with the love of God, then I do not have a choice whether or not I should forgive you, I only have a choice of whether or not I *will*. And I must, if I want to be alive. If I were truly holy, I wouldn't even choose—it would be a spontaneous act.

P: *As an individual in the sense you were speaking of earlier, if someone insults me or offends me or betrays me, it is impossible to forgive them, lacking this understanding of the reality of our interconnectedness. So this understanding is needed.*

TH: Otherwise there is no reason to forgive.

P: *There is a reason, because one suffers from not being able to forgive.*

TH: Yes, but within the categories of what we would call "the fallen world," there is no reason. Unless communion enters into the picture.

I think that in our culture the willingness to admit that there is real evil is difficult for us—it is such a violent and awesome position towards life. Of course, people in tremendous pain—rape victims, incest victims, etc.—have to forgive if they are going to go on living. But the main forgiving that needs doing in everybody's life, the central act of forgiveness and one that indicates spiritual maturity in every case without exception, is the forgiveness of the parents. We tend to either blame parents or idealize them—both of which cripple life. In order to forgive them, one must first admit the offense, and that may mean enduring incredible pain. Rage and sadness have to be faced in order to forgive. The reason that we can't forgive is because we don't want to face the pain and rage, to admit what really happened.

So people try to live without facing all this. Or when that becomes impossible (because if there is a shred of honesty left, it does become impossible), it can mean trying to lose oneself in a cult or other form of collective. You sell your soul so that you don't have to choose anymore. This wish to escape is what fueled a great deal of what happened in the 60s and since. People wanted to lose themselves; they couldn't handle the individual freedoms, because they weren't on a deep enough level. So there was a flight. I think the feminist movement is a response to this. For example, Karl Stern's book *The Flight From Woman* examines the writings of Descartes, Tolstoy, Kierkegaard, and others to show that in Western culture there has been an almost pathological flight from the feminine, from woman, which means a flight from communion, a flight from the other. The individualistic, radical, fallen, male values became the values for the culture as a whole, and *that's* the cause of the Western neuroses.

The burden of freedom is cruel—"how cruel is the love of God." But that's what we are called for. The individualistic or the collectivistic solutions will not work. We are persons made for the free and voluntary communion in love and truth in reality with other persons. This means that in the way we experience life, mercy and forgiveness are at the heart of it, beginning in one's own family. That's where it's so, so painful.

Of course, my feeling, being a radical Orthodox Christian, is that God is not removed from the world but rather one who enters into the world and gets nailed to a cross. And unless we accept Christ crucified, which is a scandal to those who want God to be some kind of power figure and total foolishness to those who want it all to fall into place intellectually, within our terms, there's no Gospel. But if Christ crucified is at the heart of the matter, then evil is real and forgiveness is real and freedom is real, and there's no other way to deify life but through an act of mercy.

P: *There are some who feel that to understand all is to forgive all. If we could see the entire chain of causality, there would be no reason to forgive, because we would understand.*

TH: I wouldn't agree with that at all. Not at all. Actually, when you see things clearly, you can see that certainly we are victimized. Let's take as an example a woman I'm thinking of, a woman who must forgive her father and her uncle for raping her over a period of years when she was a child. Once she begins to see things, she can admit that her father was also a victim, that in very many ways he was conditioned—that's what the Bible means when it says sins visited to the fourth generation. There is such a thing as a tradition of evil. That's why I like to use the expression that forgiveness is breaking the chain of evil. But everyone is given that possibility to break that chain. We are victimized but always somehow willingly victimized. As long as I'm understanding, justifying, explaining, I become just one more link in the chain of evil.

P: *Could you please explain what you mean by evil?*

TH: Well, in Orthodox theology, we always speak about evil, or sin, as either voluntary or involuntary—conscious or unconscious. We would not define sin as the cold-blooded, freely sovereign and intellectual act whereby I perpetrate evil of some sort—destroy someone's life, for example. It's much more complicated than that. One of the points of the Adam story is that we are not born in Paradise. It is anything but Paradise. A child of a hysterical, drug-addicted parent is going to be born drug-addicted as well. There is a tendency toward "evil" in us, biologically, psychologically, genetically. Father Alexander Schmemann used to say that the spiritual life consists in how you deal with what you have been dealt. We've all been dealt something. Our theological claim is that where you have a good measure of faith, and love, and forgiveness, you can restore human nature. You can pass on a more healthy, integrated, peaceful, joyful humanity to your progeny. You can be a presence of forgiveness and mercy, but you can also be a presence of the opposite. In order to be a presence of mercy, you must admit tragedy, you can't just explain it away in terms of genetics, or economics.

There is a freedom: what you do with what you have. It's not a sovereign freedom as though I were just emerging as a pristine pure angel. No. But the point is—and this is where I disagree with your statement—if you could see the causes and influences, you would come to the conclusion that there is a great deal of victimization, but at the same time, there are opportunities for people to break the chain of evil, to forgive and not allow it to go on. Sartre says you make a choice every second. A choice about what? A choice about what you are going to do about where you are. At the very heart of that choice is always going to be an act of forgiveness.

You know Karl Stern, whom I mentioned earlier, wrote another book called *The Pillar of Fire*, and what he says there is that what the modern human being cannot accept is forgiveness and grace. We would rather take our punishment, as it were. And the Christian God says, "No. I forgive you whether you like it or not." That's the only fire of hell—this loving forgiveness of God. That's why Jesus says there is only one unforgivable sin—the blasphemy of the Holy Spirit. And what is that? It is the unwillingness to be forgiven and to forgive. The proud cannot accept grace.

P: *There is a great deal written today about the need to forgive oneself. Does that make any sense in Christian terms?*

TH: Oh, of course. Forgiving oneself means accepting forgiveness from God—and from other people. Evagrios of Pontus, a fourth-century writer, wrote about this. He said that there are in us many selves, really, but at base there are two: the real self, which is the Christ-self, and a legion of other selves, which are the Adamic selves. What happens when we hear the word of grace is that we are split down the middle. We don't want grace because of the pain we have to face, the fears and so on.

But one of the things that happens—one of the lies of the Devil, so to speak—is the conviction that we are not worth it. It is not for us. We are too bad, worthless. Then there comes a point, as Evagrios said, when the Christ-self needs to be convinced that "yes, I exist, and I am acceptable," and so to have pity and mercy on those other selves.

P: *Do you see a difference between evil or sinful acts and a larger attitude that chooses darkness rather than light? Evil is not outside of us, isn't that so?*

TH: For many people evil resides in someone else. But I think your distinction is very good, because our understanding of the Christian view is that we will sin until we die. Even baptism is for the forgiveness of sins "all the days of our life." Baptism puts us in the context of forgiveness and mercy, which then allows what is called the invisible warfare, the unseen struggle, to go on. You are going to be sinful—that's why Jesus says "seventy-times-seven"—it is inherent in human life. The sin is to be expected, but the loving of the darkness is not.

P: *In the Christian view, we are reconciled, we are forgiven. Paul Tillich, in his sermon on the parable of the sinful woman and the Pharisee, points out that repentance comes after being forgiven. It is not a payment in order to be forgiven.*

TH: Well, it's both. However, it's important from our perspective what the woman in the parable then does. She certainly does not live happily ever after. What she enters into is a life of tremendous struggle.

Chrysostom says you are baptized in order to struggle. Take Mary of Egypt, the classic example of the forgiven harlot: she went into the desert and wept the rest of her life, not to win God by her tears, or to earn forgiveness; not to make reparation; but out of love of God for being liberated and for the sense of what sin really is and the desire not to fall into it again. I think one problem in both the liberal and the fundamentalist forms of Christianity is the absence of an ongoing ascetic dimension. If you don't have to pay for your sins because Jesus has, this can open the door to a life of profligacy without that ascetic dimension. The more liberal line is: this is the way I am; this is the way God made me. God loves me, God forgives me, and so there's nothing for me to do but carry on with my life.

P: *What do you mean by the ascetic dimension?*

TH: It is making nothing an end in itself except God, that is, ordering the natural passions to their proper end, which is God himself, and love itself. The passions are part of our nature—desire, anger, zeal—but they must be directed in the service of love, love meaning the good of the other, the affirmation of the other. This nature must affirm the truth, that is, the reality of things the way they are. The metaphysical base is a communion of love and being and truth for which we have been created. To say "yes" to that is the deified life. But to say "yes" to that, in the fallen world, means that you must, as Saint Paul says, crucify the flesh with its passions and desires. You must kill the ego. The "old Adam" has to die, and he always dies kicking and screaming. The multiplicity of these false selves must be exposed, and that is not easy. The evil of other people has to be named and forgiven, which is also not easy.

This is what you find in the wonderful short stories of Flannery O'Connor. The moment of grace is usually a violent moment, as, for example, in the story of the old lady in "A Good Man Is Hard to Find." After he shoots her, the killer comments, "She would of been a good woman if it had been somebody there to shoot her every minute of her life." To see things clearly, to realize, as O'Connor says, that even the virtues will be burnt up, very often requires an incredibly violent act. We often need to be shaken into that realization. It seems to me that that's the meaning in the scriptures of the trials and sufferings and afflictions and so on—to have people realize what and who they are, really. That's the ascetic dimension, because the minute a person says, "I will work to show mercy," every devil in hell will work to try to stop him.

P: *You spoke of the division in us between the Christ-self and the legion of other selves—so there are really two natures at war within us. Is it that one nature has ultimately to be transformed? You spoke earlier about a person who is free and yet has no choice—this is a totally transformed being, isn't it? All the energies of the passions, all of the forces of the other nature, have been somehow changed?*

TH: We would say there's a human nature that when it is truly itself is full of the grace of God and in communion with God and is, therefore, deified and becomes one with the divine nature. On the other hand, there is the human nature that is broken, fragmented, estranged from its real foundation and in need of salvation, of some transforming power. The transforming power of grace is there. But in a sense, it takes all of time to be deified. There are no miracles on this level. The degree of suffering that has to take place is very great.

P: *It's an incarnated struggle on this level.*

TH: Yes, and I believe it can't be done alone. You need a community.

P: *Our culture today places a great emphasis on improving oneself. There is a difference between improving yourself and being made whole, being brought to your true nature.*

TH: The saints speak about spiritual hedonism, where you want peace and joy, but you don't want reality. That's why Saint Paul says that you can give your body to be burned but if you have not love, you are nothing. Not only does it profit you nothing, you *are* nothing. Without God I am nothing. I'm brought out of nothing and without God can become nothing. And I can even become enamored of that nothingness.

P: *What of those who feel they love God and yet hate life?*

TH: They may love religion, they may love the Jesus Prayer, they may spend their whole life searching for pure prayer and miss the mark. I once met someone who had gone to Mount Athos and met a monk there who was in a very bad state, very dark, very bitter, very angry. When asked what was the matter, he said, "Look at me; I've been here for thirty-eight years, and I have not yet attained pure prayer." And this fellow was saying how sad he thought this was. Another man present said, "It's a sad story all right, but the sadness consists in the fact that after thirty-eight years in a monastery he's still interested in pure prayer." You can make pure prayer an idol, too. Those are the worst forms of idolatry.

A person must be helped to want joy, to see that it is possible. And then what is difficult is that all of these other things have to be acknowledged for what they really are, together with all the pain that has to be experienced. The other day a woman said to me, "It's not enough for me to say I have to forgive my father. I can't do that until I experience the rage and the sadness and the anger over how my childhood was. And that's what I have been afraid to do." Just because you know with your head that someone has offended you, that you ought to forgive them— that's not forgiveness. But how do you achieve the actual reconciliation where you are really at peace with the other? One must experience in full the pain of the actual harm that was done. That's the hardest part of forgiveness. That's the block for most people. It has to be gone through again and again, and layer after layer has to come up.

Many times when forgiveness is needed, one of the hardest things is to face the fact that the way I handled being harmed wasn't always the best, that I have a certain responsibility for allowing myself to have been harmed. One does have to admit, very often, that there were choices for one as well. There's always some form of symbiosis at work. That's why Chrysostom could write that the world is filled with evil but no one can harm him who does not harm himself.

The great example for Christians would be their martyrs, and Christ himself, who, although they are the greatest victims, have not allowed themselves to be touched by that evil, what Evagrios calls "allowing the devil to rejoice two times." You are sinned against; the devil rejoices. You react with vengeance or without forgiveness, and the devil rejoices two times. Never give the second joy.

So forgiveness is not just the healing of the other, it is the healing of yourself, too. If you don't forgive, you allow yourself to be poisoned. That's why Jesus says, "Do not resist the evildoer." The minute that you resist or react in kind, you become part of the evil yourself. That's the radical teaching of the cross.

P: *And you* can *be lost and destroyed. That's the other side. Forgiveness and communion are always offered, but "narrow is the way."*

TH: I think ultimately it comes to this. We are forgiven whether we like it or not. If we accept it, then we, too, become forgivers, and it's called

Paradise. But if we don't accept it, it is hell. In Tillich's language, being is gracious. When you reject the forgiveness, you destroy yourself. You refuse the communion.

P: *On my way here to see you I was thinking that forgiveness is not an act. As an "individual" I cannot forgive, but I can be acted upon, I can be forgiven, and I can participate in the current of communion.*

TH: Of course you can't grit your teeth and say, "I will forgive."

P: *It depends on grace?*

TH: Well, grace is given so that we would work. We co-work with God by grace. Grace comes not to do for us what we need to do, grace comes to enable us to do it. There isn't a God and a "me"—over and against each other. There is God who is God, and then there is "me" to the measure that I am full of grace. That's why whenever I do good, it is God in me, and really me. It is the Holy Spirit that allows me to be me. According to Saint Paul, when it is evil, it is not really me. It's *sin* in me. That's why devils are always spoken of as enslaving, captivating, whereas the Holy Spirit does not possess, it liberates. That's the great *kenōsis* of the Holy Spirit. To use the theology of our tradition, when it is really "me," it is the Holy Spirit and me in a union that is without separation or division, but without fusion either. This union is what gives us the freedom to act in a God-like manner.

Now it is true that there is nothing that we can do to make that happen. It's grace. What I have to do I is open myself to it. *Stop* doing things, if you like. As long as you keep thinking you can do it, you can't. The minute you say, "I am helpless but for this grace of God," then it happens. And it's really you. It is the real you. Not the false one that has been standing over and against God in some sort of mad independence.

According to the saints, every time you feel alone, dark, barren, it's always a sign that God is asking you to make another step. It's a spiral process.

P: *"Forgive us our trespasses as we forgive those who trespass against us." Is this simultaneous, or does one depend on the other?*

TH: Well, it's simultaneous, but because we are creatures, we always have to pray from our side. Any prayer that we make that we don't believe has already been granted from God's side is not a prayer. We say in the liturgy, "Lord have mercy," because we believe he *is* having mercy. In *Mark* 10, Jesus says that anything you ask in prayer, believing that you have already received it, it is yours. Everything that we need is already given from the side of God. Therefore, when it comes to forgiveness, we have to make an act of faith that the power to forgive has already been given to us. We just have to accept it. But it's there. It is there.

Our very nature includes the presence of God. As Saint Irenaeus said, we are body, soul, and Holy Spirit, or we are body, soul, and evil spirit, but we are never just body and soul. There is no autonomous humanity. There is either the law of the Holy Spirit and life working in our members, or the law of sin and death. There is always one or another law working within us—either the law of grace or the law of death, but we are not autonomous beings between the divine and the abyss who can pick and choose. That doesn't exist. It's either the real human state, which is full of the grace of God—that's what makes it human—or there is a state in which we reject our own being as rooted in grace and love.

Parabola
Volume: 19.1
The Call

THE CALL OF SERVICE

Robert Coles

In early December 1977, two years before she died, Dorothy Day agreed to speak with a group of nine Harvard freshmen at the Catholic Worker soup kitchen she had helped found at Saint Joseph's House on East First Street in Manhattan. The students in the freshman seminar I taught had been reading Agee's *Let Us Now Praise Famous Men* and Orwell's *Down and Out in Paris and London*, *The Road to Wigan Pier*, *Homage to Catalonia*, "How the Poor Die," and "Hop-Picking." We had also read Dorothy Day's autobiography, *The Long Loneliness*, and a collection of her nonfiction pieces, *From Union Square to Rome*. We piled into a van and drove to New York City to talk with her and with those who worked alongside her.

Before heading downtown, we stopped in Harlem to meet with Ned O'Gorman and the people who worked with him at the Storefront Learning Center, a college preparatory school located right in the middle of abandoned buildings and all too evident despair. O'Gorman, a poet and a marvelously vigorous and disciplined teacher, talked with us for three hours. We hoped to have time to come back and talk again, but we hastened on to see Dorothy, as all who knew her called her, in the early afternoon. At age eighty she suffered from coronary insufficiency and congestive disease, with occasional episodes of shortness of breath, tiredness, and "moodiness," as she told her friends. Still, there she was, standing up in the soup kitchen, cutting celery neatly and methodically with several bunches of carrots waiting their turn. I could see how pale, weak, and thin she was. She was quite chipper, though—more so than she had been for several weeks, according to Frank Donovan, an old, stalwart member of the Catholic Worker family. "She loves working, when she can. She especially loves sitting with the guests and just gabbing with them," he told us.

We had to wait until she finished the cooking tasks she'd assigned herself. Then we went to the dining room, where all those Bowery bums had eaten for so many years, found ourselves a long, long table, and sat down to the coffee and bread that had been set aside for us. The students were in awe of Dorothy at first, but it didn't take long for her to help us get through that mix of admiration and secular idolatry. On our drive down to the big city, the students had spoken of her "saintly" nature and her "awesome altruism." That phrase was turned into a playful chant as we plowed through an early winter snow on the interstate highway: "Three cheers for the awesome altruist!"

The "awesome altruist" told us that she was lucky to be alive although she had been looking forward with increasing eagerness to meeting her Maker. She also told us that until that day came, she hoped she would be able to "be of some use, still, to our guests." We all nodded as if to give her a vigorous show of support. We also were telling ourselves that it was good for this elderly and ailing lady to keep busy, to have something to do during this last, prolonged illness.

But Dorothy had a different notion of what she was about then and what she had been about all those decades since the early 1930s, when the Catholic Worker was founded. "I pray that God will give me a chance to pray to Him the way I like to pray to Him," she told us at one point. As we tried to figure out what she meant and what strategies for prayer had worked for her, she elucidated: "If I pray by making soup and serving soup, I feel I'm praying by doing. If I pray by saying words, I can sometimes feel frustrated. Where's the action that follows the words or precedes them? I may be old and near the end, but in my mind, I'm the same old Dorothy, trying to show the good Lord that I'm working for Him to the best of my ability. The spirit wishes, even if the feet fail some days! When I'm in bed, and the doctor has told me firmly to stay there for a few days, I don't feel I've earned my right to pray for myself and others, to pray for these folks who come here for a square meal."

She stopped, and the students tried to understand her line of reasoning. One young man said, "You've done so much already for these people!" She smiled and slowly answered, "The Lord has done it all; we try to be adequate instruments of His." The young man was not at all pleased; he tried to be respectful, but he answered back, "Well, it's been *you folks* who have done all this."

She was quiet for a moment, then said, "Yes, at someone's behest." A strange way of putting it, I thought—and a clever way, too. She did not mention God this time around, in seeming deference to the sensibility of a Harvard science major, but she insisted upon making the point that the labor of all those who lived in that Lower East Side tenement building, which housed a soup kitchen, the offices of the *Catholic Worker*, and some dormitory rooms, was all being done in response to a larger will.

The student wouldn't retreat, either. Politely, he asked, "How do you know?" Not in the least offended, she replied, "He has told us—in His way." The young man persisted. "How?" She patiently answered, "Oh, when we pray, we are told—we are given answers to our questions. They [the answers] come to us, and then we know He has sent us the thoughts, the ideas. They all don't just belong to us. He lives in our thoughts, the Lord does."

The student was silent for a few seconds. Several of us were made nervous by their exchange and wanted to steer the conversation in a less provocative direction. But the student resumed, "How do you know whether it's the Lord who's in you or just you talking to yourself? And how do you avoid becoming pleased with yourselves—too pleased?" She wasn't set back by his outburst of analytic and phenomenological psychology. She smiled and told him, "I don't think it has to be either/or. I think that the Lord can speak to us through ourselves. He can inspire us to follow Him! He can persuade us to show our faith in Him by offering to Him what we can. As for smugness and the sin of pride—thank God you mention it, because we *do* fall victim often, a great danger, and one we need to be reminded of all the time. By the way, have you ever read *The Imitation of Christ*? It's a fairly popular book."

A strong and confessional reply. She went on to explain her affection for the book, which recounts the author's struggle for an honorable but not saccharine piety. When she fell quiet, the student told her, "No, I haven't—I haven't really heard of that book. Who wrote it?"

"Thomas à Kempis; he was an obscure priest who wrote of his struggle to be a good person, a good Christian, centuries ago." The youth was ready to let the matter drop in a manner befitting an incipient intellectual: "I'll try to find the book in Cambridge and read it." In a playfully sardonic mood, she said, "I hope you can find it there."

We laughed, she along with us. Then she turned to the young man, and much to his surprise, to the surprise of all of us, she apologized to him. "I'm sorry if I didn't make myself clear. I'm sorry if I'm getting sharp with you. I think you've put your finger on some of our weaknesses. I can see that you find it confusing—how we think about things here in this community. We're not all that sure ourselves of what we are doing! I don't want you to feel we're afraid to discuss our beliefs with you as fully as you wish. I was trying to tell you that for me, for us here—I think I can speak for many of us who live here—the work we do is not a sacrifice or something done because we are interested in doing good, or in finding an answer to the demands of our conscience. All that, yes—all that, true. But I think we are quite happy here a lot of the time, doing what we do, because we believe we feel the spirit of Christ at work—*in the work*. We are not so high on ourselves that we feel Christ is *in* us; no, we hope we are moving a bit closer to Him, to His spirit, through the work we do, and that gives us the strength, the desire, to keep working at it here. But, of course, we are human beings, and we can be hypocrites and phonies, no question about that!

"I know this—what I'm saying—is hard for some of you to understand. I wish I could be clearer. You know, we are groping in the dark here; it may be different for you people. When people ask me why I'm doing what I'm doing, in this last time left of my life, I try to tell them that I'm doing what I was put here to do by the Lord. But they think, so many I've talked with, that I'm an old lady who needs to keep active, and feels better when she's busy, and who would go into a state of senility or depression if she didn't have something to do. It's very hard to tell people who think of you that way—it's hard to say, For the Lord, time isn't what it is for us. When I was twenty, or now [when I'm] over seventy-five, it's all the same *in this one respect*: I'm a person who's trying to find out how to live. At twenty, I didn't know; now I *think* I do—so I *do*, I work. But the worst thing would be to try to tell others to do what I'm doing, and if they don't, to condemn them!"

The student who had engaged with her had no more to say. He had begun exploring with his eyes the dining area, noting the posters on the walls, the kitchen where people were both cleaning up and preparing for the next day's meal. In a sense, I began to realize, he was following her lead—paying attention not to what she was saying about her psychological and intellectual life, but to the world she inhabited, where she felt the daily desire to do the work we had glimpsed before she set it aside for this conversation.

•

CHAPTER SIX

"Worldly and Divine Work"

The time of action does not differ at all from the time of prayer;
I possess God as tranquilly in the bustle of my kitchen—where sometimes
several people are asking me different things at one time—as if I were on my
knees before the blessed Sacrament. ... It is not necessary to have great things
to do. I turn my little omelet in the pan for the love of God;
when it is finished, if I have nothing to do, I prostrate myself on the ground
and adore my God, who gave me the grace to make it, after which I rise,
more content than a king. When I cannot do anything else, it is enough for
me to have lifted a straw from the earth for the love of God.[1]

—Brother Lawrence

Parabola
Volume: 21.4
Play and Work

First Things

Eric Gill

It is no use, and no good, complaining about the world we live in and vaguely wanting something better, unless we are prepared to review the grounds of our life and its real meaning.

It is absolutely necessary to have principles, that is things that come first, the foundations of the house.

What we want to know is: what principles of common sense are relevant to the matter of human work.

What principles are in harmony with divine revelation and in harmony with the conscience of man and the light of human reason?

Some philosophy, some religion, is behind all human works and is their primary instigation. Without some philosophy, some religion, nothing is done, nothing made, because nobody knows what to do or what to make, nobody knows what is good or what is bad. It has been said that the Church exists in order that words may have a meaning; it is also true that without philosophy and religion there is no meaning in human action.

To the workman, the artist, the subject has always been all in all. Unless he knows what he is making he cannot make anything. Whether it be a church or only a toothpick he must know what it is; he must have it in his mind before he can begin, before he can even choose his material or lay his hand on a tool. And what a thing is, what things are, and, inevitably, whether they are good or bad, worth making or not, these questions bring him without fail to the necessity of making philosophical and religious decisions. We may accept the conclusions of others, it may, indeed, be better that we should do so—provided "we know in whom we believe"—but conclusions must be accepted or the workman can make no beginning. So far from it being true that religion and philosophy have no concern for the artist or he for them, it is only when a religion and philosophy have become the unifying principle of a nation that any great works, whether steel bridges or stone shrines, are possible, and the decay of human art follows immediately upon the weakening of men's grasp upon the motives of action.

It has been said, and it is Catholic doctrine, that man is a bridge connecting the material and the spiritual. Both are real, both are good. God is spirit; man is matter and spirit. Man is therefore able to see, to present in material terms things spiritual and, conversely, though he cannot represent it, he is able to comprehend, though not fully, the spiritual significance of the material. He can show the spiritual in terms of matter, but he cannot show the material in terms of spirit.

The art of man, though ultimately unimportant, for, like all material things, works of art will return to dust, has therefore two claims to attention. In the first place, it is the only activity of which man is capable which is in itself worth pursuing and, in the second, it is man's sole abiding solace in this vale of tears.

Action is for the sake of contemplation, the active for the sake of the contemplative. To labour is to pray.

Work is the discipline (the yoga) by means of which "body holds its noise and leaves Soul free a little."

Recreation is for the sake of work. Leisure time is for the sake of recreation—in order that the labourer may the better return to work. Games are like sleep—necessary for the health of body and mind—a means to health, the health of the workman, the labourer, the man who prays, the contemplative. Leisure is secular, work is sacred. Holidays are the active life, the working life is the contemplative life.

The object of leisure is work. The object of work is holiness. Holiness means wholeness—it does not mean emaciate or emasculate. The holy man is the complete man—merry because "he nothing lacks"—sad because of the sufferings, failures and penury of others. The holy man is the poor man; having nothing he possesses all things; the Kingdom of Heaven is within him.

Reprinted from Eric Gill, *A Holy Tradition of Working* (Hudson, N.Y.: Lindisfarne, 1983), pp. 39–45. Reprinted by permission of Lindisfarne Books.

Parabola
Volume: 17.1
Solitude and
Community

BETWEEN WORK AND PRAYER, PRAYER AND WORK

Thomas Merton

The monastery conformed to a well-established type and was always a simple, four-sided group of buildings around a cloister garth, dominated by the monastic church with its belfry generally perched on top of the transept crossing. There was usually a rose window in the façade of the church, another at the end of each transept, and a fourth at the end of the apse if, as was so often the case, it happened to be rectangular. But on the whole, one was struck by the lack of large windows in the rough stone walls of the exterior. All around the outside of the buildings you met a sober, austere bareness, broken up by small windows arching to rounded tops, as if questioning the traveler with the simplicity of peasant children. The sun poured down on the mellow brown tiles of the roofs. The place was so quiet you wondered at first if it were inhabited, until you heard the sound of hammering or sawing or some other work.

Not till you got inside did you realize, suddenly, that the whole monastery was lighted from within. That is to say, it was centered upon a quiet pool of pure sunlight and warmth, the cloister garth. All around this central court, invisible to anyone outside, the wide bays and handsome open arches of the cloister allowed the light to pour in upon the broad flagstones of the floor, where monks walked quietly in their hours of meditation or sat in corners with vellum manuscripts of St. Augustine or the Old Testament prophets.

For the rest of the buildings, light was no particular problem. In church the monks chanted the offices mostly from memory, and in any case, the most important of the canonical hours were sung in the middle of the night. Often the windows did not open into the nave itself but into the side aisles. The sanctuary, however, was lighted by a big, simple rose window or by three or more small arched windows, through which the morning light poured in upon the altar as the ministers ascended for the conventual Mass. Since the church was always orientated, the rays of the rising sun shone into the apse and shot long spears of light at the monks gathered under the bare stones to sing the hymn of Prime, *Jam lucis orto sidere.* In most Cistercian churches all the side altars were so arranged that the priest saying Mass faced the rising sun.

The chapter room opened into the cloister and had some fair-sized windows of its own. The refectory was sufficiently lighted by a few high windows. The only person who really needed a good light in the refectory was the monk appointed to read aloud to his brothers. He usually sat in a lectern built into the wall and reached by a flight of steps let into the wall itself, and lighted by its own little window. Light was not important in the warming room. This was where the monks were allowed to gather around the only fire accessible to them in cold weather, although they could not stay there for any length of time or read books there. Still less were large windows needed in the dormitory; here, the high stone ceiling gave the monks a cool and pleasant gloom for the midday siesta so necessary in summer, when they had longer hours of work and less nighttime sleep.

Everything in the monastery was centered on the cloister and dominated by the church. It was in the church that the monks prayed, in the cloister that they lived. The cloister was, in a certain sense, the most important of all. It was the meeting place of all the different elements of the monk's life, the clearing-house where he passed from material to spiritual things and settled down for the moments of transition between work and prayer, prayer and work.

He came in from the fields, took off his wooden *sabots,* and sat under the sunny arches to read and meditate while the tension induced by activity seeped out of his muscles and while his mind retired from exterior things into the peaceful realms of thought and prayer. Then, with this preparation, he passed into the dark church, and his mind and will sank below the level of thoughts and concepts and sought God in the deepest center of the monk's own being as the choir began to chant, with closed eyes, the solemn, eternal measures of the liturgy.

When the monk returned from the inscrutable abyss of a contemplation which he himself could scarcely fathom, he emerged once more to the cloister, to sit or walk silently under those sunny arches or in the open garth itself, while the fruit of his prayer expanded in him and worked through his whole being like oil in a woolen fabric, steeping everything with its richness and life.

Yet, we must not think of the cloister as something altogether esoteric, a place filled with the same kind of sacrosanct hush you expect in a museum. It was a place where men *lived*. And the monks were a family. The cloister was not exempt from the noises of a society that was at the same time monastic and rustic. The young monks might practice difficult passages of chant that they had not yet mastered by heart. Others might be engaged in their laundry (for each monk washed his own clothes) or in repairing their shoes. Others might take it into their heads to bring their blankets down from the dormitory and beat the dust out of them. So, although they did not speak, the monks had to know how to be contemplative in a busy and not altogether noiseless milieu.

The monk's life was lived on three different levels. On each, there was the common element of constant prayer, constant union with God by the simple intention of love and faith that sought Him in all things: but apart from that, the three levels were characterized, respectively, by the predominance of *bodily* activity out at work; of *mental* activity in the readings and meditations of the cloister, and *spiritual* and *affective* activity in the church. If the monk happened, also, to have the grace of infused contemplation, he would be able at times to rise above all these levels and all these activities to a pure contact with God above all activity. But ordinarily speaking, even the contemplative monk lives and loves and therefore *acts* on these three levels.

Now, the cloister was the scene of the monk's most characteristically human mode of being. It was there that he met God and his brothers as a social and thinking and affective and perhaps affectionate creature: St. Ailred testified that the bond between brothers might be expected to be warmed by a glow of genuine and holy fondness. But in any case, all these elements made the cloister the place where the monk was most truly on his own level as a human being. That was why it was the solvent, the common denominator, of everything else in his monastic life.

Parabola
Volume: 24.2
Prayer and
Meditation

THE LIFE OF SPIRITUAL COMBAT

Interview with Abbot Hugh Gilbert, O.S.B.

The Right Reverend Hugh Gilbert, O.S.B., is abbot of Pluscarden Abbey, an ancient, cloistered Roman Catholic monastery in the remote reaches of northern Scotland. Pluscarden's stone walls enclose a community of some thirty Benedictine monks, bound together by Christian faith, sacred vows, and an ardent desire to pray. Following the Rule of St. Benedict, the fifth-century founder of the order, the monks gather in the church seven times a day to chant the Divine Office (also known as the opus Dei*), a medley of psalms, canticles, scriptural passages, and hymns. In addition, the monks spend part of every day in sacred reading (known as* lectio divina*), manual labor, meditation, and contemplation. They can be defined simply as men who pray. With this in mind, I visited Pluscarden Abbey recently to taste something of the life of the community and to talk to Abbot Gilbert about the nature of prayer.*

—Philip Zaleski

Philip Zaleski: *Perhaps we could begin with St. Benedict's observation that the monastery is a school of prayer. How do you understand this?*

Hugh Gilbert: Yes, the monastery is a school of prayer. The exact phrase that St. Benedict uses is "a school of the Lord's service." He thinks of the monk as a servant, a soldier, and a workman, all in the Lord's service. First and foremost, St. Benedict is concerned with Christian life as a whole, and the whole takes precedence over any of the parts, even the holiest part, which is prayer. He sees the monk as on a journey toward perfection in this life and, ultimately, toward the perfection of heaven. This end takes precedence over the means. But we should remember, as St. Thomas says, that prayer is a means that partakes of the nature of the end. So the Benedictine monastery is certainly a school of prayer, because prayer is the principal service, combat, and work that the monk offers as servant, soldier, and workman.

PZ: *To say that prayer is combat—that's certainly a provocative phrase.*

HG: Prayer is a combat with one's own reluctance to pray, with one's own fallen nature, if you like; with one's own sloth, negligence, and so on. And then also, of course, it's a combat with the powers of evil, the vices of thought and of the flesh. So there are two dimensions to this combat.

PZ: *Are monks meant to be aware at all times of this combat? Would you call the monastic life a constant struggle?*

HG: Yes, I would. One finds the smooth with the rough, of course. It would be pretty grim otherwise. But yes, it's a spiritual combat, and one is more or less always aware of that. I think St. Benedict intends one to be so. Military imagery is quite important in the Rule and in the monastic tradition generally. It's interesting that in *Vita Consecreta*, the Pope's recent apostolic exhortation to those leading a consecrated life, he speaks about the importance of spiritual combat and how it is an element of the tradition that has been somewhat neglected recently.

PZ: *St. Benedict counsels a life of prayer, lectio divina [sacred reading] and manual labor. It seems to me that in the Benedictine context, reading and labor can be understood as modes of prayer.*

HG: Certainly lectio divina and manual labor both connect with prayer in the narrower sense of the term. Reading is the food of prayer. Or perhaps one can say that reading is fuel for the fire. Prayer is the flame, but you won't have a fire if you don't have fuel. If the monk is not feeding himself with the word of God, if he is not putting the logs of the word of God into the hearth of his heart, there won't be prayer. The fire will just die out in one way or another. And manual work seems necessary as a balance here. Perhaps you remember a story about Antony the Great: He was trying to pray all the time, but he was afflicted by acedia and felt unsettled and depressed. Then an angel appeared to him and showed him how to weave a basket. The angel said, "Weave a basket for a bit and then go back to your prayer for a bit, and then weave a basket again and then pray again." And this proved to be the answer. St. Benedict is heir to this tradition that says that work is indispensable for the spiritual life of the monk. We have to use our hands and our body because we are body, soul, and spirit. You could say that in work we are using our body, in reading we are using our soul and our mind, and in prayer we are using our spirit. But what matters, as St. Benedict makes clear, is the whole person. It is the *via media*; St. Benedict's idea is always to find a balance.

PZ: *Jean LeClercq, writing about lectio divina as it was practiced during the Middle Ages, said that it was considered to be an athletic activity. This certainly suggests that it, and the other forms of prayer that you've mentioned, involve the whole person.*

HG: Lectio divina involves the idea of *meditatio*, which is not quite the same thing as meditation in the modern sense. In meditatio, one takes a psalm verse, or perhaps something that one has heard during the Office, and one keeps returning to it throughout the day. I don't know if you have in the States what we used to call gobstoppers. They were large sweets that would change color as you sucked on them. They started out as red, but if you took them out after five minutes they would be purple. And later on they might be green. In the same way, if you have a phrase from the Psalms or the Mass or from scripture, and you turn it over in the heart and mind while you are working, you've got something to come back to, and you can discover new things each time. St. Benedict often talks about this, saying that the good monk will be constantly repeating something or other in his heart. John Cassian [fourth-century Christian monk] talked about the phrase, "Oh God, come to my aid; Lord, make haste to help me." He thought that the monk should be saying that all day long. The classic example of this is, I suppose, the Jesus Prayer.

PZ: *It seems that the Eastern Orthodox tradition has focused on the Jesus Prayer, while the West has maintained a wider repertoire.*

HG: I do know some monks who repeat the Jesus Prayer and are very happy with it. But other monks—and this requires a considerable degree of self-organization—will pick up each morning a phrase that has struck them from Vigils, and they will keep that phrase with them throughout the day. And that is what is known as meditatio. It has been compared to a cow chewing the cud.

PZ: *Perhaps you could break down the average day of a monk at Pluscarden and indicate how much time is spent on each of the types of prayer that you've mentioned.*

HG: The day is quite long, a sixteen-hour day, from 4:30 in the morning until 8:30 in the evening. We spend about four hours a day for liturgy in the church and about five hours a day for work, half in the morning and half in the afternoon. As for reading, it's always been the element that's most easily sacrificed, but I'd estimate that we read for two or three hours a day. You have to fight for it a bit; it requires more self-discipline. If you don't come to choir, someone will come and fetch you or the abbot will ask where you were. If you don't work, that will be noticed and won't go down very well. But you can be in your cell, staring at the wall or doing whatever you like, and ignoring your reading. By the way, you know that lectio divina was only rediscovered in the 1920s, after centuries of neglect. Yet by the 1950s, Louis Bouyer was saying that lectio divina was the chief activity of the monk, which is overstating things a bit.

PZ: *Would you say instead that the Divine Office is the monk's chief activity, the core of the monastic vocation, or do you insist upon a balance between all these different works?*

HG: It's better to look upon the monastic life as a whole before one looks at any of the parts. But I think that one should accord a special place to prayer. Prayer is what the monk is about. It is his first work, his chief work, and his specific work. And there is no doubt that the opus Dei—the Divine Office—is the principal support and expression of the life of prayer. One of St. Benedict's great suppositions is that if you want to pray, you pray as simply and directly as possible, by saying prayers out loud. He believes in vocal prayer very much. St. Benedict is always concerned with what we need as beginners, and when we are beginning the life of prayer, we need things to pray, as it were. We need words. Just as we need good works to do, we need prayers to say. He's very realistic about that. So he has us pray at various times of the day and night. No matter what we are feeling at the time, no matter what our state, we come to pray, to discover the mystery of prayer.

PZ: *Well, let's consider the opus Dei, which can be translated as "the work of God." How do you understand this phrase?*

HG: One can understand it as the work that God is doing, or the work that we are doing for God. I think it's both. I prefer to go behind both of these understandings and say that God is at work in the world and the opus Dei—the liturgy in the narrow sense—is a privileged participation in this work of God. We are working with God as He works to bring the created world and the human race to the end to which He has destined us.

PZ: *In what way is the Divine Office a participation in this work?*

HG: Through praise, it is an acknowledgment of what God has done and is doing, and through intercession, it is striving to complete that work in historical circumstances and in the here and now.

PZ: *This leads directly to the mystery of intercessory prayer [prayer on behalf of others], which has befuddled human beings since we first began to pray. Why does God seem to answer some prayers and not others? Admittedly, this is a human perspective on a divine mystery. But so it seems. How odd to petition God for something, when He already knows what we want and need. There are difficult issues here.*

HG: Yes, it's a great mystery. I love the passage from John 15, when Christ says "No longer do I call you servants, for the servant does not know what his master is doing; but I have called you friends, for all that I have heard from my Father I have made known to you." God wants us to work with Him; He wants us to know His work and participate willingly in it. That is what is going on in intercessory prayer. It's not that we tell God what He already knows; rather, He tells us what He knows and enables us, through intercession, to say "Yes, this is what I want too." Intercession is the first work of the Christian, the first work of the Church. The fallen man prays for himself, the redeemed man prays for others, as Newman points out. The exemplar is Christ himself. Early Christian writers, in the second and third centuries, said that God keeps the world in being because of the prayers of all people. Later on in the tradition, this got narrowed down to monks. Monks pray that the world goes on; it's an old idea—if you give me ten pure hearts that pray, that will save the world. Intercessory prayer grows upon one. When you begin the monastic life, you live it for yourself. You've got an idea of holiness, and you feel that God wants you to be holy so you must go about it. But as time goes on, you live as a monk more and more for other people. And intercessory prayer is an expression of that.

PZ: *Could you tell us a bit about the practical arrangement for the Divine Office here at Pluscarden?*

HG: We celebrate the Divine Office as St. Benedict lays it down in his Rule, the full quotient of hours that he recommends—seven daily hours and one night hour—and we use the psalms that he prescribed. It is a demanding schedule, especially if you sing most of it, as we do. It adds up to about 220 psalms per week.

PZ: *What, ideally, would be the state of being of the monk when he chants?*

HG: St. Benedict says that the monk's mind should be in harmony with his voice. So there's an ideal of unity there. One should be at one with the psalms, with their meaning and action. Of course one rarely is, but that's the ideal.

Each psalm is different. I sometimes think that each is like a person who is talking to you. You have to enter sympathetically into this person, to identify with this person and come with him or her before God. So one enters into a psalm in that way—or the psalm enters into one. There's a beautiful passage in John Cassian where he says that over the years the monk will identify with the Psalms from within his own experience. Sometimes when I pray the Psalms that is what it's like. I feel that this is what I want to say to God. Other times the psalm is the voice of someone I know, a voice of joy or trouble. Other times it is the voice of Christ. And at other times it's general—I know that somebody, somewhere, in China or Paraguay perhaps, needs to be praying the psalm at this moment, and that the psalm is his voice.

In the Divine Office, the whole world is present. The whole of mankind is there, as well as the angels and the saints. The whole world is there, and each of us is a microcosm who contains the whole. At the end of Lauds every day, we sing Psalms 148–150, which include everything on heaven and earth—the birds, the fish, everything. It is very beautiful and it has a transfiguring effect, so that when you go out and see the hills after the Office, you think "Ah, yes." And you take the Office out to the hills. It couldn't be otherwise. If the liturgy weren't cosmic, it wouldn't be worth doing.

PZ: *It seems to me that one of the marks of the Divine Office is that it's done throughout the day and night, so that it gathers up all of time, and then the psalms within the Office speak of every possible shading of experience and emotion, so the Office gathers up all of space as well, it embraces all of creation and brings it to God.*

HG: Yes, absolutely. In the Psalms one hears the voice of humanity. All of human experience is echoed in the Psalms in some mysterious way. The Psalms are to the Office what bread and wine are to the Mass. And both of these are more than they appear to be.

PZ: *Perhaps that's another expression of the unity that St. Benedict talks about, the unity of all beings gathered into the Psalms. And this unity seems to be connected to the balance that St. Benedict is looking for also, because in order to have balance, you need to have every component in relationship with every other component. So unification and balance go together, and this seems to be a hallmark of the Benedictine life.*

HG: Yes, I would say so.

PZ: *What about silent prayer?*

HG: St. Benedict had this lovely picture—it's almost like a little cartoon—of the monk who may wish to remain behind in the church after the Divine Office is over. He says that the other monks must be silent when they depart out of reverence for God, and so as not to disturb a monk who may wish to remain to pray in silence. Columba Marmion, the famous Benedictine abbot from the beginning of this century, was well known for this. He would often stay behind in choir to continue his meditation. St. Benedict's idea seems to be that the Office will extend in the heart of the monk, that what the monk is doing with his fellow monks during the Office he will continue to do privately in his heart afterwards.

PZ: *Would you say, then, that silent prayer is the same as verbal prayer but in a different mode, or is it a different species of prayer altogether? Being by oneself and turning inwards, and standing with others to sing the Office, seem to be dramatically different actions.*

HG: I wonder if, among people who have been singing the Office for thirty, forty, or fifty years, there isn't more similarity than difference. An experienced monk will have silence within him even when he is in choir. The psalmody will induce silence, and in the silence the psalmody will carry on. One of the Syriac Fathers has a beautiful passage about the three liturgies. He says that there is the liturgy that goes on in church, and then there's the liturgy of the heart, and then there's the liturgy of heaven. There are three levels of liturgy. And you can't enter into the second without passing through the first, or the third without passing through the second.

The Divine Office is sometimes seen as the source of silent or contemplative prayer. It's said that the real activity of the monk is the prayer of the heart, and that the Office supports that. It can be likened to the pillars of a bridge. The pillars are the different times of day when we return to the Office; the bridge is prayer, which leads us to God. Others, however, say that this doesn't do justice to the Office. In any case, it comes back to the question of balance, or what we call the "threefold cord." The threefold cord is lectio divina, the opus Dei, and quiet private prayer. This threefold cord is not easily broken.

PZ: *Does a monk receive training in each of these three kinds of prayer, or does he simply sink or swim?*

HG: Well, the monastic way of training is rather to throw you in. The approach is "This is what we do, so start doing it." Practice comes first. And after you have been doing it for twenty-five, thirty, or forty years it might start to make sense to you. You begin to see, and you begin to see why. But of course one is given books to read, and talks or conferences, about the Divine Office and particularly about lectio divina, because often people do need help on that when they first come in.

PZ: *What kind of help?*

HG: If people have come from an academic background, they've got to learn to read in a less acquisitive way. Not read just to make notes and gain information and write an essay about it in the end. But to read for reading's sake, as it were; to read with an eye to meeting God. And often, of course, scripture is new to people, and therefore some kind of introduction is necessary. A novice nun said to me recently that she was having terrible trouble because the library in the novitiate had very few books. So I said, "What a wonderful opportunity for you to get to know that library well!" I don't think she liked that, but that's the idea—to withdraw from other books to discover scripture, and, ultimately, to discover how to pray.

Parabola
Volume: 4.1
The Trickster

Our Lady's Tumbler

D. M. Dooling

Retold from the twelfth-century French legend

Once long ago in France, the legend tells us, there was a minstrel who wandered from here to there throughout the land, earning his living by dancing and tumbling to entertain whoever would gather to watch him on the village greens and in the country fairs. So much he wandered and so much of life he saw that at last in his later years he tired of the world and entered the holy order of the monks of Clairvaux.

At first he was happy in the peace of the monastery, but soon he became aware that among all the monks he was the only one who had no skill of any kind to contribute to their common life. He knew no trade except that of tumbling, and he had no learning at all nor training in the service of the church. All the others had their work in the garden or the kitchen or the forge, or among the ancient manuscripts in the library of the monastery; but he could not even join with the others in their chants and prayers, for he could not read and had never learned the words or music of the holy offices. He became very ill at ease and felt he had no place there and no right to the bread he was given to eat, yet he longed to be a part of that life and could not bear the thought that he might be reproached for his idleness and cast out again into the world.

One day at the hour of compline, having fled the company of his brothers, he found himself in the crypt before the altar beside a statue of the holy Virgin, and sad at heart he knelt down to pray for help. "O sweet Lady Mary," he cried, "tell me how I can serve you and not remain idle and useless. I am good for nothing but my foolish trade. The skill to leap and tumble and dance is all I have; will you allow me to offer it to you?" Then he rose with determination and stripped himself down to his shift, and began to vault and tumble with all his might before the altar of the Virgin. "I will give you all I have," he cried, "do not despise it!" And he strove to perform feats he never tried before. Often he fell on the hard stones of the floor but he picked himself up again without rest and tried again his leaps and somersaults, praying all the while and adoring the Queen of Heaven. At last he fell exhausted with sweat pouring from him, unable to do more. But daily then at each of the monastic hours while the other monks were engaged in the holy offices, he went down to the crypt and performed his leaps and dances before the Virgin until he fell half fainting, bathed in sweat, and could not move again.

With this life he would have been happy had he not dreaded that he would be seen and scorned and sent away. So he went to the crypt with the greatest secrecy. Nevertheless it was noticed that he disappeared and never performed the offices with the others, and one of the monks spied him out and followed him secretly to the crypt, where, hiding behind a pillar, he saw all that the man did. Then this monk went laughing to the Abbot and told him what went on.

"Hold your peace," said the Abbot, "and we will go together and see." So they came together to the crypt and waited in concealment, and presently came the man and began his dancing, his leaping and his praying until he fell at last in a faint. Then the Abbot and his companion saw a marvelous thing: the image of the Virgin stirred and came to life, and Our Lady herself, surrounded by her angels, stepped down beside the unconscious man, and wiped his face tenderly with a linen napkin, and ministered to him until he came to himself and rose to put on his clothes and went his way without seeing her or knowing that he had had visitors from Heaven.

Then the Abbot stood struck dumb, and the monk who led him there fell weeping at his feet, saying, "God have mercy upon me, for this is indeed a holy man."

"I charge you to tell no one of this," said the Abbot, and they went away amazed at what they had seen.

After a few days the Abbot sent for the man who came weeping and trembling, for he was sure he had been found out and would be sent away. The Abbot made him confess what he had been doing as his service in the monastery, and when he had done he raised him up and kissed him and bade him to continue, for it was good and pleasing to God. Then the man was so overcome with joy that his heart leaped up with such a bound that it began to break. Nevertheless he continued night and day joyfully to do his service before the Virgin until he became so ill that he could not leave his bed. The Abbot came at each of the monastic hours to chant the office beside his pallet, and great was his joy in this also until he came to the hour of his death. And at that moment the Abbot and all his monks beheld a glorious sight, for the Holy Virgin and her angels came, visible to them all, to receive the soul of her minstrel as it departed from his body, and to bear it with her to Heaven.

Parabola
Volume: 14.4
Triad

Singer, Text, and Song

Rembert Herbert

Gregorian chant is the traditional music of Western Christianity. For several hundred years, until the later Middle Ages, it was the *only* music allowed in Christian services. It is sung in unison, without accompaniment, to Latin texts, most of them from the Bible. It is ancient, and its history abounds in fascinating puzzles and enigmas. The music notation we use today was invented (probably in the Frankish Empire, during or just after the reign of Charlemagne, in the ninth century) in order to write it down and preserve it. But no one knows when the music itself was composed. Current scholarship is humming with speculation as to the places, times, and manner of its origin, but little can be said with certainty.

St. Gregory the Great, whose name became associated with the chant at least as early as the eighth century, died in 604, about two hundred years before music notation was invented. We have no way of knowing what music was used in the liturgy in Gregory's day, though we do know that the services were sung. Could the chant, which consists of hundreds of melodies, have been transmitted orally for centuries? Could it be even older than Gregory? Scholars aren't sure.

Intriguing as the historical questions are which surround the early history of Gregorian chant, its important mystery has more to do with what it is than with where it came from, as is audible to any sensible listener today. That essential mystery lies in the unmistakable sacred quality of the chant, a quality which can touch anyone with a reminder of something beyond the ordinary.

If we are to understand the chant, it is this sacred quality we must approach more closely, and here we encounter a problem. There is little in modern aesthetic theory that can help us understand what we feel in this ancient music. More surprisingly, we find little help in medieval treatises on music either. But if we turn to medieval writings on scripture and immerse ourselves in these works, especially those of St. Gregory the Great himself, we begin to realize that we are in the presence of "sacred qualities" reminiscent of the chant. Even though St. Gregory seldom mentions music, we soon realize that his commentaries are sister works to the chant. The chant is a "musical commentary" on its scriptural text as Gregory's is a verbal one, and the style of the commentaries is somehow the same. Both arts, commentary and music, are concerned with bringing about a certain kind of meeting between text and person, a meeting based on prayer. When we recall that the commentaries and related monastic writings on prayer are products of exactly the same setting as the chant—the early medieval monastery—we find this common concern less surprising. The study of scripture was the foundation of monastic life, and "to study" meant to grow into a living relation to the text.

If we approach the monastic writers cold, however, we may find them as alien and impenetrable to our modern minds as the chant is mysterious. Fortunately, the authors themselves, called monastic "Fathers of the Church," have pointed out the way of entrance into their ancient grounds. As St. Bernard put it, "In matters of this kind, understanding can follow only where experience leads."[1] Today, *our* source for that essential experience, that living link with these early writers, can be the singing of the chant. Drawing on the experience of singing, we gradually find ourselves able to recognize in the Fathers' writings a wide-ranging and systematic understanding of the inner life of a human being in search of the Divine. In this search, we find that we are the same as our Fathers were, if we "walk in their way" and accept a similar discipline. It is to this way that the chant can be a guide and within the context of this way that its special qualities are entirely at home.

To take a simple example, John Cassian (d. 435) describes how monks "while singing psalms and kneeling in prayer ... have their thoughts filled with human figures, or conversations, or business, or unnecessary actions."[2] Anyone who has recited psalms in the lengthy liturgy of the Matins using Gregorian tones has some idea of what he means. The quiet, repetitious character of the music allows the instability of the mind to become clearly visible. The moment we believe we're attending to the chant we find, like Cassian, that our mind is in fact off wandering among "figures and conversations." By seeing in ourselves, through the stillness of the music, something of what Cassian saw, we are able to follow his descriptions with better understanding and considerably more interest.

As we become more attentive to the experience of singing, our under-standing of the Fathers' description of our own inner life deepens. We see, for example, that the instability of mind which Cassian described is due to the fact that we have taken the outer world into ourselves. We have become attached to opinions, ideas, emotions, and images of ourselves and the world which have very little substance. In fact, if we have glimpsed the image of God, which we are seeking in ourselves, we may suspect that by comparison with that image even our deepest feelings, our best ideas, our most religious emotions, have very little sub-stance. And we find, once again, that the monastic Fathers have been here before us and have both described this experience and explained its consequences. St. Gregory calls these images "fantasies of the worldly imagination" and writes: "While the delighted mind wholly precipitates itself into these [images of visible things], it waxes gross [and] loses the fineness of the inward sense."[3]

Much to our disadvantage, we take this lightweight inner mate-rial as the truth, as a reflection of our real selves. The psalms call this unhappy attachment "idolatry." St. Gregory in another passage calls this lightweight material the "water of the world" which must be resisted by an "ardent striving" within. Ecclesiastes calls it "vanity," meaning "emp-tiness," suggesting this paradox: we are full of this material, in fact so crammed with it there's room for little else, and therefore we are empty. St. Gregory explains that for this reason, according to scripture, only the empty or "hungry" can be filled with the Holy Spirit.

To be filled with the Spirit of the sacred text, then, we must prepare ourselves by resisting our attachments to external images, thoughts, and feelings. We must somehow restrain the aimless mental wandering which these attachments cause in us. The chant, whose stillness began to show us our inner condition in the first place, now supports our need for preparation by offering more extreme demands for our attention. To maintain the still, unison character of the music, we must listen, and focus our listening without interruption on the sound of the music. But the more we try, the more we discover again, as Cassian did, that the mind "insensibly returns to its previous wandering thoughts" or "slips from the inmost recesses of the heart swifter than a snake." Our recourse, according to tradition, is simple but demanding: to restore that lost attention.

As this exercise of constantly calling the mind back to listening is continued, gradually something in us begins to ease and change. Even the physical body begins to open, slowly, slightly, to the sound, so that the sound penetrates more fully; one draws closer to it. One finds also that as the attention is called back to the sound, an additional quiet watchfulness appears inside, so that one can actually see one's listening disappear and return. St. John Climacus (seventh century) writes: "Sit in a high place and keep watch if you can, and you will see the thieves come, and you will discover how they come, when and from where, how many and what kind they are as they steal your clusters of grapes"[4]—that is, steal your listening attention.

As this individual discipline becomes more serious with each singer, one finds that a transparency appears in the sound of the group, so that impulses or inflections of meaning can move through the choir almost instantaneously. In this way it becomes possible for the choir, through its singing, to touch the text with a new intimacy and immediacy. While singing in this way the choir begins to discover what St. Gregory called "the voice of psalmody directed by the intention of the heart" which becomes a means by which "a way to the heart is prepared for almighty God, so that he may pour into the attentive mind the mystery of prophecy or the grace of compunction."[5] In this condition of receptive quiet, the Spirit of the sacred text may begin to stir toward the singer's awakening intelligence, not as an idea or interpretation but as an action. Origen compares its movement to the divine Lover in the Song of Songs, "leaping upon the mountains, skipping over the hills."[6] Other writers speak of a "sudden brightness" or an "aroma" or "taste." In this condition, according to Cassian, "The eyes of the heart, as if the veil of the passions were removed, will begin as it were naturally to gaze on the mysteries of scripture." By sensing the mystery, the heart intuits the divine source and nature of the text and is able, for a short time, to rest in that nourishing presence, to "gaze on the mysteries."

In a real way, the purpose of Gregorian chant is to teach us to speak the sacred text in such a way that we perceive its divine source and nature. The "schola cantorum" or "singing school," which is the traditional name for a chant choir, teaches not so much "singing" as "sacred speaking." By means of music, the inner ear of the person is brought very close to the divine word, in order to hear it directly. The sacred character of the chant, then, is based on a threefold relationship—not just words and music, but words, music, and the inner condition of the singer. When we include all three elements, we see clearly that we are dealing not with an aesthetic phenomenon, but a spiritual one. The discipline of the chant allows this "triad" in a way to close, so that the three elements become one—text, singer, and song. As St. Gregory wrote: "Let us rejoice that what was written by Isaiah has now been fulfilled in us: 'And the bit of error which was in the jaws of the people [shall be destroyed], and you shall have a song like the voice of a sanctified solemnity.'"[7]

Considering the chant in context, then, we see that its purpose is to allow a special interaction to take place, by means of music, between the divine text and a deeper intelligence within a person. The chant begins to live when this triad begins to live, when its parts become absorbed in a larger unity. To learn to sing the chant is to learn to allow that process to take place. And in the course of this learning, one encounters other, related triads, one of which is of special importance. It lies at the heart of the chant and many other aspects of traditional monastic life as well.

According to the Fathers, the life of anyone who takes up the "way of perfection," as monastic life was called, is double—active and contemplative. At its simplest, this duality corresponds to a practical division of activity into work and prayer. But the same duality is also understood in more subtle ways. Prayer itself, for example, has its active and contemplative aspects, its giving and receiving, doing and waiting. But at all levels, the contemplative aspect is the more valuable. St. Gregory writes: "The active labors in the manner of our ordinary efforts, but the contemplative indeed savors now, by means of a deep inner taste, the rest to come."[8]

Among traditional writers the most common symbol for these two lives is the story of Mary and Martha in the Gospel of Luke (10:39–42, Douay-Rheims translation). When Jesus comes as a guest into the house, one sister, Martha, keeps busy in the kitchen serving the guests, while the second sister, Mary, "sitting also at the Lord's feet, heard his word." Martha, of course, is irritated because she's been left to do all the work, and she complains to Jesus. He answers: "Martha, Martha, thou art careful, and art troubled about many things. But one thing is necessary. Mary has chosen the best part, which shall not be taken away from her." Of this incident, St. Gregory writes:

> So one was attentive to work, the other to contemplation. One was serving the active by a more external ministry, the other the contemplative by suspension of the heart into the Word. And however good the active work might be, the contemplative nonetheless is better, because the first dies with this mortal life, but the second truly grows more complete in the life of immortality. Hence is it said, "Mary has chosen the best part, which shall not be taken from her. …" For even though by action we accomplish something good, nevertheless by contemplation we awake to the desire for heaven. Hence also with Moses the active life is called service, but the contemplative is called freedom.[9]

The Fathers believed that contemplative prayer was essential in the life of a monk. Perfection in the contemplative life, however, did not lie in leaving the active behind. Pure contemplation was not considered possible in this world. Perfection lay in finding the proper relationship or balance between the two, and from that balance arose a third condition which St. Gregory describes as "blessed." This balance can never be permanent, and so one must continually search for and rediscover it. When the balance is disturbed, it disappears. So this triad is always in a sense in motion, dynamic.

One could describe the chant as an exercise in the search for this balance. Without going into technical detail, one could say that the musical material of the chant contains both elements of speech (activity) and elements of quiet (contemplation). The elements of quiet are found both within the music itself and in the pauses which the music requires regularly, especially in the recitation of psalms.

If we understand the articulation of the text as the "active" life of the singer in this situation, careful listening and watchfulness during the elements of quiet become the "contemplative." For singers who have been trained to be sensitive to this process, there is no mistaking these two different directions. The contemplative direction is clearly one of gathering in toward oneself, what the monastics call "recollection." (St. Teresa of Avila described it as a turtle pulling into its shell!) The active direction, the recitation of the text with enough lightness and freedom to be responsive to its meaning, is clearly outward. It demands energy. A tired singer must work to find that energy.

Singers discover further that each of these directions depends on the other. The feeling of recollection—a sense of life in the silence—doesn't appear until a certain freedom of recitation is sustained, and vice versa. And singers discover that here, too, the contemplative element is the more precious: attention to silence is the life of the chant, without question. As St. Gregory wrote: "the censure of silence is a kind of nourishment of the word ... we ought not to learn silence by speaking, but rather by keeping silence we must learn to speak."[10]

The third element of the triad, which St. Gregory called "blessed," is also unmistakable when it is present in the choir, when the perfect balance is found between silence and speech, action and contemplation, giving and receiving. This third element, however, cannot be controlled. Its appearance is a gift, but a gift for which we must prepare. It is, the Fathers would say, a movement of the Holy Spirit.

It is by this movement that the larger intelligence of the singer can open and the text speak with its active, symbolic voice. It is then that the "bit" is, perhaps briefly, removed from the singer's mouth and the singer is shown, at least for an instant, how to speak the sacred text with the "eyes of the heart" open, like "the voice of a sanctified solemnity." It is the sound of this speaking, I believe, that we instinctively recognize in the chant as "sacred."

Notes:

1 Bernard of Clairvaux, *On the Song of Songs II*, tr. Kilian Walsh (Kalamazoo, Michigan: Cistercian Publications, 1983; Cistercian Fathers Series: Number Seven), p. 15.

2 John Cassian, The *Conferences*, tr. Edgar C. S. Gibson (Grand Rapids, Michigan: William B. Eerdmans, reprint 1982; The Nicene and Post-Nicene Fathers of the Christian Church, Second Series, Volume XI), p. 528.

3 Gregory the Great, *Morals on the Book of Job*, Volume I, tr. Anon. (Oxford: John Henry Parker, 1844; A Library of Fathers of the Holy Catholic Church), p. 288.

4 John Climacus, *The Ladder of Divine Ascent*, tr. Colm Luibheid and Norman Russell (New York: Paulist Press, 1982; The Classics of Western Spirituality), p. 263.

5 Gregory the Great, *Homiliae in Hiezechihelem Prophetam*, ed. Marcus Adriaen (Turnholti: Brepols, 1971; Corpus Christianorum, Series Latina, Volume 142), p. 12.

6 Origen, *The Song of Songs: Commentary and Homilies*, tr. R. P. Lawson (New York: Newman Press, 1956; Ancient Christian Writers, Volume 26), p. 79.

7 Gregory the Great, *HHP*, p. 310.

8 *Ibid.*, p. 37.

9 *Ibid.*, pp. 37–38.

10 *Ibid.*, p. 170.

Parabola
Volume: 21.3
Peace

Zeal in Detachment
The Paradox of Peace in Christianity

Stratford Caldecott

> *Peace I bequeath to you,*
> *my own peace I give you*
> *a peace which the world*
>   *cannot give*
> *this is my gift to you.*
> *Do not let your hearts be*
> *troubled or afraid.*
>   *—John 14:27*

Blessed are the peacemakers, for they shall be called sons of God (Matthew 5:9). The peacemaker is one in whom the peace of Christ, the gift of the Holy Spirit, is actively present. To become a peacemaker is to have peace within, to be a source of peace. Restoring unity to our fragmented souls, the Spirit centers us on Christ. Peace in the world can certainly come from no other source, for a person centered on himself cannot do the will of God nor live at one with others.

Yet do we truly understand the peace to which we are called by this passage? Compare the quotation from John's Gospel to the one that follows, from Matthew.

> *Do not think that I have come to bring peace on earth; I have not come to bring peace, but a sword. For I have come to set a man against his father, and a daughter against her mother, and a daughter-in-law against her mother-in-law; and a man's foes will be those of his own household. He who loves father or mother more than me is not worthy of me; and he who loves son or daughter more than me is not worthy of me; and he who does not take his own cross and follow me is not worthy of me.*
> —*Matthew 10:34–38*

In Luke's Gospel, Jesus puts it even more strongly: "If anyone comes to me and does not *hate* his own father and mother and wife and children and brothers and sisters, yes, and even his own life, he cannot be my disciple" (Luke 14:26).

The Gospels are full of paradoxes. Words shift their meanings: indeed often *new meanings* for words are forged in the heat of the Gospel paradox itself, and the very light that shines from this "furnace of meaning" reveals a deeper level of reality. Such is the case with Christ himself. To believe that he is both God and man is to give a radically new meaning to human life, and to understand God as a Trinity. But it is true also of Christ's teaching on peace. Such words as we have quoted are meant to shock, and they do. We may soften the impact by glossing the text. For example, we might say that all Jesus *really* means is that God comes first, and that if a choice *has* to made between following him and following the way of the world, we must choose Jesus, even at the cost of our most intimate and comfortable relationships. But in such pious explanations, however helpful they may be in one way, something important has been lost. The purpose of using the violent language of paradox is partly to reorient the hearer, to stop him in his tracks and turn him around. The purpose of the Gospel is to change lives, and that cannot be done by theology alone. There is something in the way the Gospels are written that is reminiscent of the Zen *koan*. To understand them, you have to enter imaginatively into the position of the one to whom the words are addressed—not hide behind a commentary.

In the book which closes the New Testament canon we read:

And now I saw heaven opened, and behold, a white horse! He who sat upon it is called Faithful and True, and in righteousness he judges and makes war. His eyes are like a flame of fire, and on his head are many diadems; and he has a name inscribed which no one knows but himself. He is clad in a robe dipped in blood, and the name by which he is called is The Word of God. And the armies of heaven, arrayed in fine linen, white and pure, followed him on white horses. From his mouth issues a sharp sword with which to smite the nations, and he will rule them with a rod of iron; he will tread the winepress of the fury of the wrath of God the Almighty. On his robe and on his thigh he has a name inscribed, King of kings and Lord of lords.
—Rev. 19:11–16

For John, who is said to have written this text as an old man on Patmos, the terrifying Rider on the white horse is the self-same Jesus who had walked and talked with him in Galilee, who had called him from his trade as a fisherman, at whose side he had reclined at the Last Supper in Jerusalem. John sees him now with the inner eye of prophecy—an eye akin to the same "eyes of fire" with which the Rider himself will one day see and judge, setting the world ablaze with the justice of God.

Peace which the world cannot give. … The peace of Christ may give us peace in this world, and it may even contribute to peace between men, but it is not what the "world" means by peace. The peace of Christ cannot be shaken by misfortune; it is not a mood or emotional state, nor a state of physical security. In fact it could be described as the very opposite of worldly peace: it is a state of *danger*. As Adrienne von Speyr writes, "No one knows into what adventure the Lord's peace may lead him. We seek peace out of fear of war. But nothing is fundamentally more insecure than a worldly peace treaty. For it gives the enemy time to make his preparations in secret. One never has to be more alert and suspicious than during the world's peace. But the Lord has no fear, nor has he any fear of fear."[1]

We have to put aside, then, our normal associations with the word "peace" if we are to understand the gift of peace that Jesus offers his disciples. The peace of Christ, like Christ himself, is paradoxical. It is described by two seemingly incompatible metaphors: the metaphor of *human breath* and the metaphor of the *sword*. They are combined in this image from the Book of Revelation: the breath of the Rider is a sword that issues from his mouth—the "sword of the Spirit," Paul calls it (Ephesians 6:17). We remember the "flaming sword" that God placed on the eastern borders of Eden to mark the boundary of our exile from Paradise, and to prevent us from reaching the Tree of Life (Genesis 3:24). At some level, these swords are the same. Our only way back to Paradise, to the peace of God's kingdom, is through the death to self that the sword represents.

After Christ's Ascension to heaven, Mary his mother and the disciples are gathered together in prayer—no longer afraid, but simply in a new state of attention and expectation. Suddenly "a sound came from heaven like the rush of a mighty wind, and it filled all the house where they were sitting. And there appeared to them tongues as of fire, distributed and resting on each one of them. And they were all filled with the Holy Spirit and began to speak in other tongues, as the Spirit gave them utterance" (Acts 2:2–4). Here the image of human breath and the contrasting image of the "flaming sword which turned every way" are combined in an image of "tongues as of fire" given to each of the disciples at the birth of the Church.

Although Jesus has breathed the Spirit upon them many times before, and given them the greeting of peace on several occasions since his Resurrection (e.g., John 20:22), the disciples have until this first Pentecost been incapable of *receiving* the tongues of fire. An inner process was necessary first. They needed to witness not only his Resurrection but also his Ascension—to see with their own eyes both the reality of his presence and the reality of his absence, to feel his closeness and his distance from them—before they could become receptive to the "baptism from heaven" that they had been promised.

The inner process is described by Maximus the Confessor. The true disciple, he writes, must attain a type of dispassion that excludes from the mind all "sensible images" in order to make room for God (the inner equivalent of the Ascension). "When the contemplative intellect enters this state, it gives the incensive power and desire their freedom, transmuting desire into the unsullied pleasure and pure enravishment of an intense love for God, and the incensive power into spiritual fervor, an ever-active fiery *élan*, a self-possessed frenzy."[2] It was in this inspired yet controlled frenzy that the apostles led by Peter ran out into the street and spoke in many languages, so powerfully that "about three thousand souls" were added to their number (Acts 2:41).

The peace of Christ, then, has an inner and an outer manifestation. Exteriorly it manifests as fire, as zeal, as transformation, as death and rebirth. Interiorly it manifests as silence, as knowledge, as joy, as union with the Beloved: a joy of union that is capable of communicating itself to others. This is the real key to the early spread of the Christian faith. Here is the secret of the paradoxical peace of the true Disciple: "not an amalgam or a compromise, but both things at the top of their energy; love and wrath both burning."[3] We see it at work in Jesus himself when he drives the moneychangers, the traders, and their cattle out of the Temple (e.g., John 2:13–17). This is passion, the passion of a lover who is jealous for the honor of his beloved. "You shall worship the Lord your God and him only shall you serve" (Matthew 4:10). With these words, and with all the energy of transformed Eros, we too may expel the traders and beasts from the Temple of the heart.

Notes:

1   Adrienne von Speyr, *The Farewell Discourses: Meditations on John 13–17* (San Francisco: Ignatius Press, 1987), pp. 149–50.

2   Cited in *The Philokalia: The Complete Text*, Vol. II (London: Faber & Faber, 1981), p. 223.

3   G. K. Chesterton, *Orthodoxy* (Wheaton, Ill.:Harold Shaw Publishers, 1994), p. 97.

Parabola
Volume: 3.2
Sacrifice and
Transformation

Transformative Suffering
Sacrifice and Will

Christopher Fremantle

The idea of sacrifice as a *making sacred* has always been very much a part of Western thought. Today the word remains, but it is more often used in the political and economic sense of belt-tightening or of accepting inconveniences necessary for the common welfare; or even as a sort of trade-off or exchange. There is no other word to carry its primal meaning so it is necessary to restore the word to its original significance and bring it back into currency; for it is not only a word but a dynamic idea, as alive now as ever, although seemingly out-of-date. And it is also a paradox.

If, as tradition says, the universe is created, then everything must be sacred, because this quality derives from the Creator; so the idea of "making sacred" is redundant. But if in accord with some present-day thought, our universe is accidental, arising from an unknown beginning, then nothing in it is or will become sacred. And our understanding of this contradiction is not helped by the traditional Christian outlook which, leaning on the words, "Greater love hath no man than this, that a man lay down his life for his friends," speaks of death as "the supreme sacrifice"; nor is it helped by traditional sacrificial rites in which the blood of victims is offered. How can the destruction of life—whether on the altar or the battlefield—render life itself sacred?

I think the reconciling elements between these conflicting aspects of meaning must be looked for in the view of sacrifice as an essential part of the life process, rather than as an isolated act of expiation. There is a striking, though very brief, passage in the Gospel of St. John in which Christ says (apparently referring to the Eleusinian mysteries, since Philip had just announced that two Greeks wished to speak with him): "Except a corn of wheat fall into the ground and die, it abideth alone, but if it die it bringeth forth much fruit." In this statement, and in the context of the Greek mysteries, the idea of sacrifice and death is linked together with that of rebirth and fulfillment. That is, the idea of sacrifice and that of immortality, life beyond time; "before Abraham was, I am." In joining sacrifice, suffering and death with the concept of transformation and of the continuity of life as a total process, all the apparent contradictions are resolved. The perspective that life itself does not die, but is expressed in constant transformation and movement, lies at the root of major religious traditions in both East and West.

Here in the light of modern investigative thought, the question arises: what actually is the transforming action of sacrifice and suffering upon the person who offers it? The first contemporary teaching to have posed this question seems to have been that of Gurdjieff, with his emphasis on "conscious labors and intentional suffering." Every sacrifice involves suffering, sometimes beneficial and sometimes not; what seems to distinguish "useful," strengthening and transformative suffering from that which is useless and distorting is precisely its intentional quality. If the suffering is not voluntarily accepted, it turns into bitterness, as Lot's wife turned into salt.

But with the idea of voluntary sacrifice other questions arise. Today, the medieval Christian asceticism that expressed itself in self-torture seems remote; any such tendency is suspect, as masochism or at best just another ego-trip. So the question becomes important: what is the nature of, and whose is the *will* behind this voluntary action? What is the transforming role of personal will in sacrifice? What, indeed, is it that we call "will"? We know so much more about "self-will," with its ego-motivations, than about human will itself; and how are we to separate real will from the conditioned responses and defenses formed around a person from birth?

Ramana Maharshi, who died in 1952, once commented that to gain control of the attention is the sole aim of all spiritual exercises and disciplines—thus aligning himself with Ramakrishna who, a century earlier, had followed for twelve years different disciplines of great traditional religions and concluded that they did not differ in essence. Gurdjieff, too, pointed to attention as the unique tool for acquiring objective, non-egoistic will. The attention to which they refer is certainly not that which is continually darting from one thing to the next, distracted by every happening and every association; nor that which is helplessly absorbed in some problem. Neither kind has the activity and stability capable of resisting the automatic, conditioned responses which rule our behavior. When suffering appears, these automatic impulses push us towards escape; where sacrifice is involved, towards compromise or complacency. Only an independent and stable attention can be aware of the moment of decision and choice, and detect a deviation from the decision before it gathers momentum.

Perhaps it can be said that real will is the product of intention and of the strong forces released in us by suffering. Suffering and danger free vast amounts of fine energy which have observable physical manifestations: under threat from a charging bull a man leaps obstacles he could never clear in cold blood; when a child is in danger a mother can forego sleep for days and nights because an extraordinary energy is present. But except at such moments we are not in control of these capacities and not even aware of them, so they are not available to us.

All teachings regarding conscious transformation seek ways of coming into relationship with these inner powers. Traditional counsels of "action without attachment," ascetic practices of various kinds, deep meditation and contemplation, are means proposed for reaching and studying an attention which can transform: that is, an attention which can link a man with his deepest aspiration and the power to resist the automatism of flight in the face of suffering.

Modern scientific psychology has begun to study those areas crucial to development in man's psyche, and to acquire some information about them. This direction interested the late Abraham Maslow and other researchers who have pursued it through psychological studies or through laboratory measurement of the physiological effects of meditation; but not nearly enough is yet known. In medicine, current research is reported to be revealing the part played by fine energies—subatomic particles—in the processes of physiological and neurological response. Looking further ahead, particle physics will surely throw new light on the action on man's psyche of fine energies entering our world from the cosmos. When these aspects of the natural sciences reach their flowering, it may well be found that they restate, more lucidly and in contemporary terms, ancient traditional teachings concerning the true role of sacrifice. The last thirty years have brought about a rapprochement between metaphysical and scientific thought, and it seems quite possible that a new understanding, confirmed by research, will show the role of sacrifice and suffering as vital forces in the chain of life's evolution and transformation.

Parabola
Volume: 2.1
Death

LEARNING TO DIE

Brother David Steindl-Rast

Brother David told us that he did indeed have something that he would like to say about death, but that he would prefer to tell it rather than write it. The following is an edited version of what he had to say, and it retains an oral quality. It thus should be read as much with the ears as with the eye.

The only point where one can start to talk about anything, including death, is where one finds oneself. And for me this is as a Benedictine monk. In the rule of St. Benedict, the *momento mori* has always been important, because one of what St. Benedict calls "the tools of good works"—meaning the basic approaches to the daily life of the monastery—is to have death at all times before one's eyes. When I first came across the Benedictine Rule and tradition, that was one of the key sentences which impressed and attracted me very much. It challenged me to incorporate the awareness of death into my daily living, for that is what it really amounts to. It isn't primarily a practice of thinking of one's last hour, or of death as a physical phenomenon; it is a seeing of every moment of life against the horizon of death, and a challenge to incorporate that awareness of dying into every moment so as to become more fully alive.

I have found that this approach is present—sometimes more explicitly, sometimes more implicitly—in all the different spiritual traditions that I have come into contact with. It is certainly very strong in Zen Buddhism; it is present in Hinduism and Sufism. It is one of those basic human gestures by which one confronts meaning in order to live religiously. As I use the term "religious," it refers to the quest for *ultimate meaning*. Death has evidently to be one of the important elements in that, for it is an event that puts the whole meaning of life into question. We may be occupied with purposeful activities, with getting tasks accomplished, works completed, and then along comes the phenomenon of death—whether it is our final death or one of those many deaths through which we go day by day. And death confronts us with the fact that purpose is not enough. We live by meaning. When we come close to death and all purpose slips out of our hands, when we can no longer manipulate and control things to achieve specific goals, can our life still be meaningful? We tend to equate purpose with meaning, and when purpose is taken away, we stand there without meaning. So there is the challenge: how, when all purpose comes to an end, can there still be meaning?

This question suggests why in the monastery we are counseled (or challenged) to have death at all times before our eyes. For the monastic life is one way of radically confronting the question of life's meaning. In it you cannot get stuck in purpose: there are many purposes connected with it, but they are all secondary. As a monk you are totally superfluous, and so you cannot evade the question of meaning.

This distinction that I am making between purpose and meaning isn't always carefully maintained in our everyday language and thought. In fact, we could avoid a good deal of confusion in our lives if we did pay attention to the distinction. It takes only a minimum of awareness to realize that our inner attitude when striving to achieve a purpose, a concrete task, is clearly different from the attitude we assume when something strikes us as specially meaningful. With purposes, we must be active and in control. We must, as we say, "take the reins," "take things in hand," "keep matters under control," and utilize circumstances like tools that serve our aims. The idiomatic expressions we use are symptomatic of goal-oriented, useful activity, and the whole of modern life tends to be thus purpose-oriented. But matters are different when we deal with meaning. Here it is not a matter of using, but of savoring the world around us. In the idioms we use that relate to meaning, we depict ourselves as more passive than active: "It did something to me"; "it touched me deeply"; "it moved me." Of course, I do not want to play off purpose against meaning, or activity against passivity. It is merely a matter of trying to adjust the balance in our hyperactive, purpose-ridden society. We distinguish between purpose and meaning not in order to separate the two, but in order to unite them. Our goal is to let meaning flow into our purposeful activities by fusing activity and passivity into genuine responsiveness.

Death puts our responsiveness to the ultimate test. Unless our dying becomes our full and final response to life, activity and passivity must ultimately clash in death. Because we are so one-sidedly active in life, we think of death one-sidedly as passive. In death we are indeed passive: obviously, dying is the most passive thing that can happen to us. It is the ultimate passivity—something that will happen to us inevitably. We will all be killed in one way or another, whether it be by disease or by old age or by an accident or in some other way. We are well aware of this aspect but not too many people realize that death is also ultimate activity. Again, some "symptomatic idioms" can help make this clear. It is, for example, very significant that the one act that is the most passive in our experience, namely dying, cannot be expressed in English by a passive form. There is no passive voice to the verb *to die*. We can *be killed*, but we have *to die*. There is imbedded into our very language the realization that dying is not only passive, maybe not even primarily passive, but also the ultimate activity. Dying is something we have to *do*. Perhaps we can be killed without dying, which would explain those ghost stories in which a house or a room is haunted by the continuing presence of a person who has been killed but hasn't really died. These two things have to come together in death: we *do* something and we suffer something. More than that: we must suffer what we do and do what we suffer. This doing and suffering, this give and take, which constitutes responsiveness, is brought into focus by our confrontation with death, but it has a far wider range. It characterizes life in all its aspects. Life, if it isn't a give and take, is not life at all. The taking corresponds to the active phase, to our "purpose" when we do something; while the giving of ourselves to whatever it is that we experience is the gesture by which meaning flows into our lives. It must be stressed that this is not an either/or; life is not a give *or* take, but a give *and* take; if we only take or only give, we are not alive. If we only take breath in we suffocate, and if we only breathe out we also suffocate. The heart pumps the blood in and pumps it out; and it is in the rhythm of give and take that we live. In practice, however, the balance is often upset in our lives. Our emphasis falls far too heavily on the taking, on the doing, on the purpose. We belong to an "underdeveloped nation" with regard to meaningful living. Because we keep cultivating only one-half of the give and take of life, we are only half alive.

Here again the idioms we use are symptomatic of our preoccupation with *taking* and with purpose. We have scores of idioms that speak of taking but few that speak of giving yourself; we take a walk, take an exam, take a trip, take a course, take a bath, take a rest, take a meal. We take practically everything, including many things that nobody can truly take, such as time. We say we take time; but we really live only if we *give* time to what *takes* time. If you take a seat, it is not a very comfortable way of sitting down but if you let the seat take you that's more like it. Taking a nap is the surest way to insomnia, for as long as you insist on taking it you will never get it; but the moment you give yourself to it you will fall asleep.

We might begin to suspect that our one-sided insistence on taking not only prevents us from living balanced lives and living peacefully, but also from dying a balanced death and dying peacefully. Faced with the prospect of death, we must say "I can't take it." After a life in which we take and take, we eventually come up against something which we can't take; death takes us. This is serious. One can go through life taking, and in the end all this will add up to having taken one's life, which is in a real sense suicide. But we can learn to give ourselves. It doesn't come easy, conditioned as we are to be fearful of giving ourselves, but it can be learned. In learning to give ourselves we learn both to live and to die—to die not only our final death, but those many deaths of daily living by which we become more alive.

This is precisely the point: whenever we give ourselves to whatever presents itself instead of grasping and holding it, we flow with it. We do not arrest the flow of reality, we do not try to possess, we do not try to hold back, but we let go, and everything is alive as long as we let it go. When we cut the flower it is no longer alive; when we take water out of the river it is just a bucketful of water, not the flowing river; when we take air and put it in a balloon it is no longer the wind. Everything that flows and is alive has to be taken and given at the same time—taken with a very, very light touch. Here again we are not playing off give against take, but learning to balance the two in a genuine response to living as well as to dying. I remember a story told me by a young woman whose mother was close to death. She once asked her: "Mother, are you afraid of dying?" and her mother answered, "I am not afraid, but I don't know how to do it." The daughter, startled by that reply, lay down on the couch and wondered how she herself would do it if she had to; and she came back with the answer: "Mother, I think you have to give yourself to it." Her mother didn't say anything then but later she said, "Fix me a cup of tea and make it just the way I like it, with lots of cream and sugar, because it will be my last cup of tea. I know now how to die."

This inner gesture of giving yourself to it, of letting go from moment to moment, is what is so terribly difficult for us; but it can be applied to almost any area of experience. We mentioned time, for instance: there is the whole problem of "free time," as we call it, of leisure. We think of leisure as the privilege of those who can afford to take time (this endless taking!)—when in reality it isn't a privilege at all. Leisure is a virtue, and one that anyone can acquire. It is not a matter of taking but of giving time. Leisure is the virtue of those who give time to whatever it is that takes time—give as much time to it as it takes. That is the reason why leisure is almost inaccessible to us. We are so preoccupied with taking, with appropriating. Hence, there is more and more free time, and less and less leisure. In former centuries when there was much less free time for anybody, and vacations, for instance, were unheard of, people were leisurely while working; now they work hard at being leisurely. You find people who work from nine to five with this attitude of "Let's get it done, let's take things in hand," totally purpose-oriented, and when five o'clock comes they are exhausted and have no time for real leisure either. If you don't work leisurely, you won't be able to play leisurely. So they collapse, or else they pick up their tennis racket or their golf clubs and continue working, giving themselves a workout as they say.

We can laugh about it, but it goes deep. The letting go is a real death, a real dying; it costs us an enormous amount of energy, the price, as it were, which life exacts from us over and over again for being truly alive. For this seems to be one of the basic laws of life; we have only what we give up. We all have had the experience of a friend admiring something we owned, when for a moment we had an impulse to give that thing away. If we follow this impulse—and something may be at stake that we really like, and it pains for a moment—then for ever and ever we will have this thing; it is really ours; in our memory it is something we have and can never lose.

It is all the more so with personal relationships. If we are truly friends with someone, we have to give up that friend all the time, we have to give freedom to that friend—like a mother who gives up her child continually. If the mother hangs on to the child, first of all it will never be born; it will die in the womb. But even after it is born physically it has to be set free and let go over and over again. So many difficulties that we have with our mothers, and that mothers have with their children, spring exactly from this, that they can't let go; and apparently it is much more difficult for a mother to give birth to a teenager than to a baby. But this giving up is not restricted to mothers; we must all mother each other, whether we are men or women. I think mothering is just like dying, in this respect; it is something that we must do all through life. And whenever we do give up a person or a thing or a position, when we truly give it up, we die—yes, but we die into greater aliveness. We die into a real oneness with life. Not to die, not to give up, means to exclude ourselves from that free flow of life.

But giving up is very different from letting someone down; in fact, the two are exact opposites. It is an upward gesture, not a downward one. Giving up the child, the mother upholds and supports him, as friends must support one another. We cannot let down responsibilities that are given to us, but we must be ready to give them up, and this is the risk of living, the risk of the give and take. There is a tremendous risk involved, because when you really give up, you don't know what is going to happen to the thing or to the child. If you knew, the sting would be taken out of it, but it wouldn't be a real giving up. When you hand over responsibility, you have to trust. That trust in life is central to all the religious traditions. It is called by different names; Christians know it as faith, and in Zen Buddhism, to my surprise, it is also called faith, though with a connotation different from the one it has in the Biblical tradition. It isn't faith in anything or anyone, but there is a lot of emphasis in Buddhist monasteries on the tension between faith and doubt, faith always being a nose's length ahead of doubt. The greater your doubt, the greater your faith will be—faith in ultimate reality, faith in yourself, if you wish, your true Self. But in the Buddhist as well as in the Christian tradition faith is courage—the courage to take upon yourself the risk of living, and dying, because the two are inseparable.

Thus, one could distinguish between two ways of dying: a mere giving in, which means you are being killed without really dying; and a vital way of dying, a giving up, which is this giving of yourself and so dying into deeper life. But that takes a great deal of courage, because it is always a risk, a step into something unknown. It also takes a great deal of vitality, and that is why I am a little reluctant to accept what Karl Rahner and Ladislas Boros have to say about death. They are two German Catholic theologians who have written with a great deal of insight on death, but both put much weight on their ideas of what happens in a person's last moments. I would much rather say: Die when you are alive, because you don't know how well you will be able to do something that takes all your energy when you are senile, weak, or very sick.

Here again is one of the points where I think birth and death come very close to one another: neither of the two events can be precisely pinned down to a moment in time. We don't really know when a person is born. We can point to the physical fact of the umbilical cord being cut, but some people come to life maybe after forty years, or even later. When does a person come to life? I can imagine that the very moment in which someone comes to life is also the moment in which he really dies. And everything that led up to that, for forty-five years perhaps, is time spent in practicing for the important moment; and everything that follows is time spent letting nature run its course. Maybe in some people's lives this happens all of a sudden, at one moment, while with others it is a gradual thing that goes laboriously through many stages.

Most of what I have said simply means: let's learn to die so that, when our last hour comes and if we are still alert to it, we will be able to die well. But at any rate let's learn it, and that means let's learn to give ourselves over and over again to that which takes us; let go of things, or rather give up as a mother gives up. Let go is a little too passive, it comes too close to *letting down; giving up* is the truly sacrificial gesture. So in many traditions you have this notion that throughout our lives we train for a right dying; and that means to train for flowing with life, for giving ourselves. And this suggests some more symptomatic idioms of taking and giving that show ways we can make the inner gesture of dying: *giving thanks* instead of *taking for granted; giving up* rather than *taking possession; for-giving* as opposed to *taking offense.* What we take for granted does not make us happy; what we hold on to deteriorates in our grasp; what we take offense at we make into a hurdle we can't get past. But in giving thanks, giving up, forgiving, we die here and now and become more fully alive.

We speak, for instance, of a good death versus a bad death: I suppose the death we call bad is the one in which we struggle and cannot die peacefully. There are many cases when the doctor says: "I don't know how this patient keeps on living," but perhaps he never learned to let go, so he hangs on for *dear life*, as we say. He will eventually be killed, but he has not learned to give himself freely. After all, it is not a dogma or a theory but something that anyone can check out and experience in his own life, that when we really give up and actively die, we die not into death but into a richer life; and when we drag on and hang on to something that we should have already let go of, we are dead and decaying. Thus we know—not from any revelation but from our own personal daily experience—that the fruit of a good death, a death to which we give ourselves, is greater fullness of life, and the fruit of a death against the grain, in which we are just killed and do not give ourselves, is destruction, or what the Bible calls the second death.

Now the difficulty that comes in here is that when it is a matter of our final physical death, what is given up by us is all of life. I feel rather strongly that we sometimes fail—especially, I think, people who speak from a religious perspective—to stress the seriousness of dying. It may be a beautiful image, but it just won't do to say that "we fall asleep." Death is no falling asleep; there is a rather drastic difference. Nor is it the same as going into a tunnel and coming out on the other side. I do not like to speak of "afterlife." I have seen this book, *Life After Life*; it is interesting, and I think that there may be whole dimensions, a whole world of things going on after what we observe as dying; but I am not concerned with all that. As I have said, I am convinced that we cannot pinpoint our real death. It is that real death, however, which concerns us here: the event through which all we know of life comes to an end, in every respect. To speak of life after death makes no sense if death is the end of time for the one who dies. And that is just what I mean. Death is the event which has no *after*. To blur this fact means losing sight of the seriousness of dying.

It is an all too harmless picture of death if we think that the body dies but the soul lives. Is there really an independent soul over against a body with its own independent existence? Concretely we experience ourselves as body-soul beings. The total person, experienced from the outside, is body. Experienced from the inside, that same total person is soul. In that event we call death, the total person comes to an end. But the total person that sits here now and talks, knows that whenever in his life anything truly died, it did not mean destruction, but always a step into greater life; and therefore, that total person can take the leap of faith and can say yes, I believe that in this ultimate death also, what I am going toward is ultimate life. And that is faith in the resurrection, in the Christian context, because resurrection is not survival; it is not revivification, or coming back to life, or any sort of reversal at all. The flow of life cannot ever be reversed. By faith we die *forward* into fullness of life.

This is why eminent Christian theologians today can dispense with the notion of an immortal soul without jeopardizing the Good News of resurrection and eternal life. In fact, as soon as we no longer feel obligated to hold on to such intellectual abstractions as the notion of an immortal soul, we are able to enter more freely and more fully into the existential approach on which Biblical statements about the resurrection are based. We might be surprised to discover that even the Christian belief in the resurrection of the body is simply based on the experience that the soul and body are existentially one in the human person. It is not possible to speak of a disembodied human being, because that is no longer a human being. The body absolutely belongs to it. Therefore, when St. Paul speaks of resurrection life—life *beyond* death as I would call it, rather than *after* death (if death is the end of time, then what's after it?)—he speaks about life that must be embodied. What happens in the course of our lives is that we become somebody. Who we become will depend on the decisions we make and somehow bodily enact. It will depend on the responses we give to God's calling which reaches us in many different forms, and these responses, too, will be bodily enacted. That in this way we become somebody is obviously as much a statement about our bodies as it is a statement about our souls. But the body we call our own in this sense is not limited by our skins. It comprises all those elements of the cosmos by which we have expressed our own personal uniqueness; it is the total person, seen from the outside. But if the total person has died, resurrection of life, as St. Paul sees it, must be a new creation of the total person—soul and body—by God who alone provides the continuity between the old and the new life. All St. Paul can say about our immortal life, the Christ-life within us, is that it is "hidden with Christ in God" (Cor. 3:3). This holds true whether we have died or not. In either case, "your real life is Christ," as St. Paul puts it in the same passage.

Passages like these make it clear that the Christian vision of immortal life is far closer to what has been branded as "Eastern" notions than it is to those popular Western beliefs tied to an immortality of the soul. When Christians practicing under some guru from the East learn to realize "I am not my body, I am not my mind," they are making room for an understanding of St. Paul's words: "Your real life is Christ." All too often this understanding is blocked by the misconception "I am not my body, but I am my mind," a misconception perpetuated by the doctrine of the immortal soul.

This is closely connected with another area in which current Eastern influences tend to help Christians recover their own authentic tradition regarding life beyond life. It sometimes appears as a threat to Christians that Oriental thought seems to challenge the Western emphasis on individual survival. But is that popular emphasis really in tune with the Christian message? The one thing that is certainly true about it is that *personhood*, what we have made of ourselves in becoming somebody, is something that will never be lost; but that is a different thing from individuality. We are born as individuals and we become persons, laboriously so. We become persons through relationships with others—interrelationship is what defines you as a person. What separates us defines us as individuals, but what relates us to others makes us persons. It is in the relationship of a deep love that we become most truly persons. When we give and lose ourselves, we paradoxically find our true self. What St. Paul calls our real life, the Christ-self within us, is universal interrelatedness in love; and it is not difficult to see that this is more readily compatible with "Buddha nature" or "Atman" than with insistence on perpetuating individual separateness.

But now St. Paul says of that Christ-self, which is our real immortal life, not only that it is hidden with Christ in God, but that "when Christ appears, then you too will appear with Him and share His glory." This seems so central to the Christian message that I for one feel that I cannot be agnostic about it. I cannot say: "Well, just give me the rest of Christian life and teaching and forget about eschatology." To do something right we must start out with the end clearly in mind. If not even a meal will turn out right if we start with the ingredients instead of a clearly planned menu, we had better keep our eyes on the end of our spiritual life also, which means we ought to clarify our eschatology. Our problem at the moment seems to be that we have outgrown our child-like integrity in dealing with eschatological myths, but have not yet achieved the integrity of mature minds capable of accepting these myths more fully than the child could. We are like awkward adolescents who laugh at fairy tales that were deeply meaningful to them not long ago and will be more meaningful still a short time hence.

We might do well to take a fresh look at what we might call the Christian mythology of heaven, hell, purgatory, judgment, and so on. It is more important than we might guess. We cannot assume that it is just something we have outgrown; we have only seen that certain images must not and cannot be taken literally any longer. On the other hand, a Christian can still fully believe in the reality these images try to depict. I can say that I believe in the resurrection of the body and in the last judgment; I do believe in these truths, but I wouldn't press the imagery. I believe in the reality that stands behind it and I take the expression very lightly. It is meant to be an image, a beautiful poetic image, but no more. Actually the myth of purgatory comes very close to the myth of reincarnation; it tries in general to answer the same questions and it comes up with largely the same answers—that there is justice and that you have to work out your karma. But just as I would not press the image of purgatory as if there were actually a fire burning somewhere with so many degrees of heat, so I personally would not press the imagery of reincarnation. But I can say that I do believe in both.

One reason why Christian tradition has always steered me away from preoccupation with reincarnation has not so much to do with doctrine as with spiritual practice. The finality of death is meant to challenge us to decision, the decision to be fully present here now, and so begin eternal life. For eternity rightly understood is not the perpetuation of time, on and on, but rather the overcoming of time by the *now* that does not pass away. But we are always looking for opportunities to postpone the decision. So if you say: "Oh, after this I will have another life and another life," you might never *live*, but keep dragging along half dead because you never face death. Don Juan says to Carlos Castaneda, "That is why you are so moody and not fully alive, because you forget you are to die; you live as if you were going to live forever." What remembrance of death is meant to do, as I understand it, is to help us make the decision. Don Juan stresses death as the adviser. Death makes us warriors. If you become aware that death is right over your left shoulder and if you turn quickly enough you can see him there, that makes you alive and alert to decisions.

As human beings, here and now, not as believers of this or that doctrine, we all know what life beyond time means. If we can say *now*, and know what we mean when we say *now*, we are speaking about a reality that is not in time. The *now* is; time is only possibility for becoming. Dying in all its forms and stages is our opportunity to pass from time into the *now* that does not pass away, from the mere possibility of becoming to being real.

In our human experience time is, to use a fine expression I heard somewhere, a measure for the energy it takes to grow. In that sense it has nothing to do with minutes and hours, years and eons, with clock time. And growing means to die to what we are in order to become what we are not yet. The seed has to die to become a plant, and we have to die to being children in order to become adolescents, and so on. But our most important death has to do with dying to our independence, as individuals, and so coming to life as persons in our interdependence. We find this terribly difficult because we always want to retain our independence, the feeling that "I don't owe anybody anything." Then comes the moment of death, whether it is the ultimate death or a moment in the middle of life, and we give up our independence and come to life in interdependence, which is the joy of belonging and of being together. This is what we really most want, but except for such moments we hang on to something which we don't really want and yet are afraid to let go of—our independence and the isolation which necessarily goes with it. The moment we let it go, we die into the joy of interdependence. The importance of our physical death fades away in comparison with this dying into what St. Paul calls the real life, Christ in us. He says in another passage: "I live, yet not I: Christ lives in me." This is not a private statement about himself; he means that each one of us ought to be able to say that. As believers, you and I can say that as well as St. Paul; and that means that it is the true Self that lives in all of us; I—"yet not I; Christ lives in me." The face we had before we were born, as the Buddhists put it, is the Christ-reality. That doesn't mean, narrowly, Jesus Christ, Jesus of Nazareth; it means *the Christ*. It is not separated from Jesus of Nazareth but is not limited to him. It comes very close to what Buddhists call Buddha nature, and Hindus call Atman, the lasting reality. But we are still afraid of losing our individuality in this all-embracing unity. I think we could overcome this fear by seeing that Divine Oneness is not achieved by the imposition of uniformity, but by the embracing of limitless variety; there is room for all our personal differences within it.

One time I talked with Eido Roshi about the question of the personality or impersonality of this ultimate reality, for here there seems to be what is generally thought of as an important difference of concepts between East and West, or between the Buddhists and the Christians. The Buddhists use the image of waves on the sea; each of us is just one wave that comes out and goes back into the sea. I told him that a Westerner does not readily accept this; he says, "I am somebody with self-consciousness, awareness, and self-possession. Am I just going back into some cosmic custard? If that sea out of which I came is impersonal and I am personal, then I would be more than the sea." The answer Eido Roshi gave me was simple enough: "If the sea did not have all the perfection of personhood, from where would the waves have gotten it?" That is a beautiful Buddhist answer, and it does full justice to the Christian concern. But we could also say: All right, the wave goes back into the ocean, and that is a beautiful picture; but that high point, when the wave was cresting, the moment when it was most alive, that, as T. S. Eliot said, is a moment that was not only in time but "in and out of time." It was one of those *now* moments that does not pass away, that is eternity. And therefore anything that happens, at that moment of the fullest personhood, simply is; it does not belong to *was* or *will be* but to that which can never again be lost; maybe because it never was unrealized, maybe because it is a bursting forth of the eternal *now* into time. I experience it as being realized, but perhaps it is my homecoming.

I like the suggestion too that the virgin energy of a life in which personhood was never developed simply returns to the source, a wave that never crested. This image somehow connects with the idea of time running out. But the turning point of the spiritual life is the moment when time running out is turned into time being fulfilled. It rests with us whether death will be a fizzling out when our time runs out or an explosion of the fullness of time into the *now* of eternity. In the book of *Deuteronomy* God says: "I place before you today life and death; choose life." Choose life! Life is something we have to choose. One isn't alive simply vegetating; it is by choosing, making a decision, that you become alive. In every spiritual tradition life is not something that you automatically have, it is something that you must choose, and what makes you choose life is the challenge of death—learning to die, not eventually, but here and now.

•

CHAPTER SEVEN

TRANSFORMATIONAL KNOWLEDGE

When you make the two one, and
when you make the inner as the outer
and the outer as the inner, and the above
as the below, and when
you make the male and the female into a single one,
so that the male will not be male and
the female not be female; when you make
eyes in the place of an eye, and a hand
in the place of a hand, and a foot in the place
of a foot, and an image in the place of an image,
then shall you enter the Kingdom.[1]

—The Gospel According to Thomas

Jesus said:
If they ask you
"What is the sign of the Father in you?"
Say to them:
"It is a movement and a rest."[2]

—The Gospel According to Thomas

Parabola
Volume: 3.4
Androgyny

THE GNOSTIC VISION

Elaine H. Pagels

From the nine Muses one separated away. She came to a high mountain, and spent some time there, so that she desired herself alone, in order to become androgynous. She fulfilled her desire, and became pregnant from her desire. He was born. The angels who were over the desire nourished him. And he received power and glory there.[1]

This myth, included in the *Apocalypse of Adam*, an ancient text recently discovered in Upper Egypt, claims to tell the birth of the savior. Yet the image of androgyny contained in this ancient source bears a meaning that recurs often in contemporary works—the autonomy of the female. Desiring "herself alone," she becomes self-sufficient and productive. Perhaps the myth also intends to suggest that she brings forth the male that is within her.

Other sources from the same discovery tell a similar myth—that Wisdom, severing her relationship with her male companion, became pregnant by herself. Yet the poet who tells this story, Valentinus, takes this as evidence of a fundamental disharmony in the universe, which, in his view, properly consists of masculine and feminine energies in harmony with one another.[2]

If the *Apocalypse of Adam* describes androgyny as an achievement to be attained, another text, the *Interpretation of the Soul*, describes it as the original condition of the soul:

> *The wise, of old, gave the soul a feminine name. Indeed, she is female in her nature as well. She even has her womb. As long as she was alone with the Father, she was a virgin, and, in form, androgynous. But when she fell down into a body and came into this life, then … she prostituted herself … As long as the soul keeps running around everywhere copulating with whomever she meets, … she exists in suffering. But when she weeps and repents, then the Father will have mercy on her and will make her womb turn from outside and will turn it again inward, and the soul will receive her individuality … then the soul becomes again what she was before.*[3]

This has a different message about human autonomy. It suggests that the soul in everyone, men and women alike, recovers its original androgyny—its "individuality"—by withdrawing from mere sensation, and turning inward.

Discovered by accident in 1947, these texts—and about fifty others—disclose astonishing new evidence of the early Christian movement. These texts claim to reveal secret traditions about Jesus, including sayings, myths, poems, dialogues, philosophical and mystical treatises—all of which were banned, burned, and destroyed as "heresy" as early as 80–140 A.D. For the first time, this discovery offers evidence of forms of Christian teaching that the orthodox church attacked and suppressed.

Yet the people who wrote and revered these texts did not consider themselves to be heretics; they insisted that they, not the orthodox, understood the true meaning of Christ and his teaching. The movement they represent is called gnosticism, from the Greek word *gnosis*, translated as *knowledge*, or *insight*, since these Christians claimed to "know" secret traditions that were kept hidden from "the masses." The discovery includes the secret *Gospel of Thomas*, the *Gospel of Philip*, the *Gospel to the Egyptians*, and the *Secret Book of John*, to name only a few. Written originally in Greek in the late first or early second century, some may have been contemporaneous with the gospels of the New Testament;

Professor H. Koester, of Harvard University, suggests that some of these texts may be even earlier.

Many striking differences separate these sources from what we know as orthodox Christian tradition. Here we can consider only one of these differences: these texts, which abound in sexual symbolism, frequently use the image of the androgyne. But when we begin to investigate this image in gnostic texts, we discover that it occurs in a variety of different ways that suggest different meanings.

Besides connoting the person who has achieved autonomy, as in the examples above, we find that often the image is used in a second way: to express a new vision of humanity. According to the gnostic teacher Simon, since the divine source of all things consists of a "bisexual power,"

> *What came into being from that Power, that is, humanity, being one, is discovered to be two: a male-female being that bears the female within it.* [4]

This refers to the story in Genesis 2, which relates Eve's "birth" out of Adam's side; thus Adam, being one, is "discovered to be two," an androgyne who "bears the female within him." Rabbis in Talmudic times had made a similar inference from the Creation account in Genesis 1:27: "So God created humanity (*Adam*) in his own image, in the image of God He created him, male and female he created them." Rabbi Samuel bar Nachman, perhaps influenced by Plato's myth in the *Symposium*, speculated that:

> *When the Holy One, Blessed be He, first created humankind, he created him with two faces, two sets of genitals, four arms and legs, back to back: then He split Adam in two, made two backs, one on each side.* [5]

The gnostic author of the *Gospel of Philip* agreed with Nachman that originally humanity lived in harmony as an androgynous being. But when the two elements, male and female, became separated from one another, this, he explains, was the "fall" that brought death into being. To overcome death, humanity must recover that original androgyny:

When Eve was still in Adam, death did not exist. When she was separated from him, death came into being. If he again becomes complete and attains his former self, death will be no more.[6]

According to the *Gospel of Thomas*, Jesus teaches that whoever achieves the state of perfect consciousness perceives the male and female as "one and the same":

Jesus saw infants being suckled. He said to his disciples, "These infants being suckled are like those who enter the Kingdom." They said to him, "Shall we, then, as children, enter the Kingdom?" Jesus said, "When you make the two one, and when you make the inside like the outside, and the outside like the inside, and the above like the below, and when you make the male and the female one and the same, so that the male will not be male and the female not be female ... then you will enter the Kingdom."[7]

Later, Salome asks Jesus, "Who are you, man ... that you have come up on my bed, and eaten from my table?" Jesus replies to Salome that whoever sees differences between male and female has not achieved enlightenment. But whoever recognizes them as the same is "filled with light."[8]

Some gnostic teachers, agreeing that Adam, existing in original perfection, was an androgyne, drew from this a more radical inference. They pondered the verse that precedes the account of creation, Genesis 1:26: "And God said, Let Us make humanity in Our image, after Our likeness." How, they asked, could a masculine, single God say this—and to whom? Since the account goes on to say that humanity was created "male and female," they conclude that the God in whose image we are made must likewise be both masculine and feminine—both Father and Mother!

Besides expressing an image of autonomy, or of the unity of humanity, then, androgyny often bears a third meaning in these ancient sources: it expresses the true nature of the divine being. The teacher Valentinus begins with the premise that God is essentially indescribable. Yet, he suggests, the divine can be imagined as a Dyad consisting of two elements: one he calls the Ineffable, the Source, the Primal Father; the other, the

Silence, Grace, the Mother of all things.[9] The gnostic Simon celebrates the divine Source as the

> ... one Power that is above and below, self-generating, self-dis-covering; its own mother; its own father; its own sister; its own son: Father, Mother, Root of all things.[10]

What do gnostic teachers mean when they describe God in this way? Different teachers offer different interpretations. Some maintain that the divine image is to be considered masculo-feminine—"the great male-female power." Others insist that the terms serve only as metaphors, for, in reality, the divine is *neither* masculine nor feminine. A third group suggests that one can describe the Source of all things in *either* masculine or feminine terms, depending upon which aspect one intends to stress.[11] Proponents of these diverse views agree, however, that the divine is to be understood as consisting of a harmonious, dynamic relationship of opposites—a concept that may be akin to the Eastern view of *yin* and *yang*, but remains antithetical to orthodox Judaism and Christianity.

The third context for the image of the androgyne, then, intends to describe the "fullness of being," of which we, in our limited sexual self-definition, usually experience only a part. Sometimes the image of androgyny is implicit, as in the account in the *Secret Book of John* that tells how John, the brother of James, went out after the crucifixion with "great grief," and had a mystical vision of the Trinity:

> As I was grieving ... the heavens were opened, and the whole creation shone with an unearthly light, and the universe was shaken. I was afraid ... and behold ... behold a unity in three forms appeared to me, and I marveled: how can a unity have three forms?

To John's question, the vision replies:

> It said to me, "John, John, why do you doubt, and why do you fear? ... I am the One who is with you always: I am the Father; I am the Mother; I am the Son."[12]

John's interpretation of the Trinity—as Father, Mother, and Son—may startle us at first, but, upon reflection, we can recognize it as a natural and spontaneous interpretation. Where the Greek term for the spirit, *pneuma*, being neuter, virtually requires that the third "Person" of the Trinity be asexual, the author of the *Secret Book* has in mind the Hebrew term for spirit, *ruah*—a feminine term. He thus concludes, logically enough, that the feminine "Person" conjoined with the Father and Son must be the Mother! The same text goes on to describe the spirit as an androgyne, the Father-Mother:

She is … the image of the invisible, virginal, perfect spirit. … She became the Mother of the all, for she existed before them all, the Mother-Father (matropater), the first Humanity, the holy Spirit, the thrice-male, the thrice powerful, the thrice-named androgynous one.[13]

According to another of the secret texts discovered at Nag Hammadi, *Trimorphic Protennoia* (literally, the "Triple-formed Primal Thought"), when one discovers the presence of the divine within, one experiences its presence as androgynous. The text opens as a divine figure speaks:

I am Protennoia, the Thought that exists in the Light. … She who exists before the All. … I move in every creature. … I am the Invisible One within the All. … I am perception and knowledge, uttering a voice by means of Thought. I cry out in everyone, and they know that a seed dwells within.[14]

The second section, spoken by a second divine figure, opens with the words:

I am the Voice … it is I who speak within every creature. … Now I have come a second time in the likeness of a female, and have spoken with them. … I revealed myself in the Thought of the likeness of my masculinity.[15]

258 THE GNOSTIC VISION

Later the Voice explains that:

> *I am androgynous. … I am both Father and Mother, since I copulate with myself … and with those who love me.*[16]

We have noted, then, three different ways in which the image of the androgyne occurs in gnostic sources: first, to indicate a state of human autonomy; second, to describe the original unity of humankind, or its state of ultimate perfection; third, to represent the "fullness" of the divine. Yet we have sketched here only a few examples of the extraordinary range of images that these newly discovered texts offer. Published in English for the first time in 1978, as *The Nag Hammadi Library* (Harper & Row), they are currently attracting great attention: the discoveries they will make possible, perhaps especially in the study of literary imagery and in the history of religion and culture, are only beginning.

Notes:

1 *The Apocalypse of Adam*, in *The Nag Hammadi Library* (hereafter cited as NHL), ed. James M. Robinson (San Francisco: Harper & Row, 1977), p. 262.

2 For discussion and references, see E. H. Pagels, "What Became of God the Mother? Conflicting Images of God in Early Christianity," in *Signs*, 2.2 (1976), pp. 293-303. For a fuller and more technical discussion of androgyny, see W. Meeks, "The Image of the Androgyne: Some Uses of a Symbol in Earliest Christianity," in *History of Religions* 13 (1974), pp. 165–208.

3 *The Exegesis of the Soul*, NHL, pp. 180–185.

4 Hippolytus, *Refutationis Omnium Haeresium* (hereafter cited as *Ref.*), ed. L. Dunker and F. Schneidewin (Gottingen, 1859), 6.18.

5 *Genesis Rabba* 8.1, also 17.6; cf. *Leviticus Rabba* 14.

6 *Gospel of Philip*, NHL, p. 141.

7 *Gospel of Thomas*, NHL, p. 121.

8 *Ibid.*, pp. 124–125.

9 Irenaeus, *Adversus Haersus* (hereafter cited as AH), ed. W. W. Harvey (Cambridge, 1857), 1.11.1.

10 *Ref.*, 6.17.

11 AH 1.11.5–21.1.3; *Ref.*, 6.29.

12 *Apocryphon of John*, NHL, p. 99.

13 *Ibid.*, p. 101.

14 *Trimorphic Protennoia*, NHL, p. 462.

15 *Ibid.*, pp. 465–466.

16 *Ibid.*, p. 467.

Parabola
Volume: 30.1
Awakening

THE HIDDEN UNION

Jacob Needleman

One of the most momentous archaeological finds of our time was the discovery in 1945 of manuscripts that have come to be known as the Gnostic gospels. Accidentally unearthed by an Egyptian peasant near the desert village of Nag Hammadi and dating from the very beginnings of the Christian era, these texts have exerted a profound influence on our thinking about the origins and nature of Christianity, an influence that continues to grow with every passing year.

One of these documents is the Gospel of Philip. Like many of the Gnostic documents, it consists mainly of sayings and doctrines attributed to Jesus, which point to an astonishing body of knowledge about man and the cosmic world and about the practices leading to inner freedom and the power to love. As is common in all the great spiritual traditions of the world, this knowledge is expressed mainly in allegory, myth, and symbol, rather than in the intellectual language we have become accustomed to in science and philosophy.

How are we modern men and women to understand these ancient sayings and symbols? What are they telling us about the illusions that suffocate our minds and freeze our hearts—and about the way of life that can actually awaken us to what we are meant to be?

Perhaps such texts as the Gospel of Philip contain, necessarily in the form of symbolic language, a treasury of *answers* that we as individuals might have all but given up hope of finding. In a time when the role of religion in human life has become one of our world's most agonizing concerns, texts such as the Gnostic gospels invite us to risk stepping back in a new way from many of our most cherished opinions not only about the teaching and acts of Jesus, but about who and what we are as human beings. It is in this specific new effort of separating from our own thoughts and feelings that an entirely unexpected source of hope may be glimpsed, both for ourselves and for our world.

To begin to understand this text, we need to have a question, and to question ourselves. That said, the issue then becomes not only what are our questions, but *how* do we ask them? What does it really mean to have a serious question of the heart and to ask it from the whole of ourselves, or at least from the part of ourselves that is able to hear an answer? For one of the most remarkable aspects of spiritual knowledge (in the ancient meaning of the term *gnosis*) is that its answers can be fully received only in response to a real question, a real need. And it is no doubt true—and also often forgotten—that the inner meaning of all scripture, whether canonical or not, can be received only in the state of spiritual need. If approached without this need or genuine state of questioning, texts such as the Gospel of Philip are likely to be either regarded at arm's length as mere scholarly and archaeological riddles or curiosities, or greedily appropriated as fuel for fantasy.

The first step then toward a new kind of questioning, a new kind of knowing, is a step back into ourselves, apart from all that we think we know about ourselves. If there is such a thing as transformational knowing (and this is the true meaning of the term *gnosis*), its first stage is the inner act of *not knowing*.

This hitherto "hidden" and "secret" text may be regarded as pointing to the hidden or *subconscious* teachings of Christianity; in the sense that what is ontologically subconscious in human life is what secretly influences and directs that which we call our consciousness. This is to be contrasted with the well-known or, in this limited sense of the word, conscious canonical Gospels. We might also think of the subconscious and the conscious as *essence* and *manifestation*—what we are in the depths of our hidden being and how we act and manifest in the conditioned and relative realm of time and the world we live in. It might also be suggested that in our own individual lives, as well as in the life of a great tradition that compassionately struggles to penetrate the worldly life of humankind, essence and manifestation often drift apart from each other, to the point that outer expression or manifestation loses or "forgets" its source and essence—and thereby, knowingly or unknowingly, even contradicts or denies the authority of its source. In that case, to confront essence and manifestation together, especially in their accrued mutual contradiction, is nothing less than a great shock of awakening—and it is there where we may experience the state of self-questioning that is both joyous and bittersweet.

In this sense, speaking in terms of *gnosis* or sacred knowing, a genuine question that corresponds to a state of spiritual need involves the experience in ourselves of our own essential being together with our actual manifestation. It means being present to both the divine essence within and how we manifest or act in ways that generally serve only the illusions and attachments of the ego. There can be great suffering in this awareness of how we forget or betray the truth of what we are. But this awareness itself, when it is deep enough, opens the way to a reconciliation of these two opposing currents in ourselves, and this awareness can lead us toward "the peace that passes understanding." Here knowledge and love fuse.

Jean-Yves Leloup, the translator of the text excerpted below, has written that, "It is not my intention to set the canonical and the apocryphal gospels against each other. ... My aim is to read them together: to hold the manifest together with the hidden, the allowed with the forbidden, the conscious with the unconscious." Such an honest approach to this text, which open-heartedly examines subversive ideas with patience, humility, and respect, allows us to *hear* the way Yeshua speaks of the meaning of sacramental bread and wine; of the *true* and "*illusory*" human body; of the meaning of death and resurrection as stages on the path of inner work; of the purity of the Virgin as the immaculate and fertile silence (*parthenos*) or void within the human soul; or—in what is bound to attract much attention—in the way Jesus is allowed to speak about marriage and sexuality. There is a teaching here that is very deep and very high, and woe to us if we too hastily attach ourselves to one or another surface meaning of what is expressed in these pages. The text speaks of the sexual act in marriage as "the holy of holies," and at the same time we find such passages as the following:

Even the worldly embrace is a mystery;
Far more so, the embrace that incarnates
the hidden union.
It is not only a reality of the flesh,
For there is silence in this embrace.
It does not arise from impulse or desire
[epithumia];
It is an act of will.
It is not of darkness, it is of light.

At this point we may recall the oft-repeated warning of Jesus in both the canonical and apocryphal gospels: "Let those who have ears to hear, hear." For at the very least, what seems to be spoken of here is the meaning of sexuality in its highly evolved, fully human form. Who among us is yet able to claim enduring access to such a quality of the fully human?

Christian or not, we are all children of our era and we have heard that Truth is for all who seek it—whether in Christian terms, in the language of any of the other great spiritual traditions, or in the language of a new, authentic revelation of spiritual knowledge; whether through the sacredness of nature as science reveals it to us, or simply through people, individual men and women whose presence radiates the light of hope in the darkening night of our world.

Nearly every page of the Gospel of Philip can evoke intense self-questioning, offering directions of personal search for Truth that are as profound as they are startlingly new and challenging. The words of Jesus stand to meet us there: "Seek and ye shall find." Perhaps, then, the one real question we all can share and ponder is not *whether* to seek, but *how* to seek, how to discover and accept our own real need. I can think of no better platform from which to approach this powerful text.

Excerpts from The Gospel of Philip

What you say, you say in a body;
you can say nothing outside this body.
You must awaken while in this body, for everything
exists in it:
Resurrect in this life.

It is impossible for anyone to see the everlasting reality
and not become like it.
The Truth is not realized like truth in the world:
Those who see the sun do not become the sun;
those who see the sky, the earth, or anything that exists,
do not become what they see.
But when you see something in this other space,
you become it.
If you know the Breath, you are the Breath.
If you know the Christ, you become the Christ.
If you see the Father, you are the Father.

The bridal chamber
is not for animals, nor for slaves,
nor for the impure;
it is for beings who are free, simple, and silent.
It is through the Breath that we come into being, but we are
reborn by the Christ two by two. In his Breath,
we experience a new embrace; we are no longer in duality
but in unity.

What is the bridal chamber,
if not the place of trust and consciousness in the embrace?
It is an icon of Union,
beyond all forms of possession;
here is where the veil is torn from top to bottom;
here is where some arise and awaken.

Those who have become free through knowledge

become loving servants of those who do not yet have
this knowledge and freedom.
Knowledge [gnosis] makes them capable of this
because they are free, even of their freedom.
Love refuses nothing, and takes nothing;
it is the highest and vastest freedom.
All exists though love.
It does not say "this is mine," but "this is yours."
Spiritual Love [agape pneumatikos] is a drunkenness
and a balm;
those who are anointed by it rejoice.

You who are with the Son of God do not love worldly
things; love the Teacher, so that what you engender
will resemble the Teacher, and not some other thing.
Humans mate with humans,
horses with horses, donkeys with donkeys,
each species with its own.
Likewise, our breath seeks another breath,
our intelligence seeks intelligence,
and every clarity seeks its light.
Become more human, and humans will love you;
become more spiritual, and the Spirit will unite with you.
Become more intelligent, and the Logos will unite with you.

Grace is transmitted to us in four ways:
the work of the earth, the taste of the heavens,
and love and truth, which are beyond the heavens.
Blessed is the one who makes no sadness in the soul.
That one is Jesus Christ.

Those who were separated will reunite and become fertilized.
All those who practice the sacred embrace [koiton]
will kindle the light;
They will not beget as people do
In ordinary marriages, which take place in darkness.
The fire that burns by night flares up, and then is gone;

but the mystery of that embrace is never extinguished;
it happens in that light of day which knows no sunset.
If someone experiences Trust and Consciousness in the
heart of the embrace,
they become a child of light.
If someone does not receive these,
it is because they remain attached to what they know;
when they cease to be attached, they will be able
to receive them.
Whoever receives this light in nakedness will no longer
be recognizable;
none will be able to grasp them, none will be able to make
them sad or miserable,
whether they are in this world, or have left it.
They already know the truth in images.
For them, this world has become another world,
and this Temple Space [Aeon] is fullness [pleroma].
They are who they are. They are one.
Neither shadow nor night can hide them.

Parabola
Volume: 4.2
Sacred Dance

To the Universe Belongs the Dancer

Elaine H. Pagels

> *To the universe*
> *belongs the dancer.*
> *Whoever does not dance*
> *does not know what happens.[1]*

These lines, attributed to Jesus, occur in the "Round Dance of the Cross," the ritual for a sacred dance included in the *Acts of John*, one of the most remarkable texts that survived from the early Christian movement. The *Acts* tells how Jesus, anticipating arrest, gathered his followers into a circle, holding hands, to dance, while he himself stood in the center, intoning a mystical chant:

> *Before he was arrested ... he assembled us all, and said, "Before I am delivered to them, let us sing a hymn to the Father, and so go to meet what lies before us." So he told us to form a circle, holding one another's hands, and he himself stood in the middle and said, "Answer Amen to me." So he began to sing the hymn and say,*
>
> > *Glory be to thee, Father.*
> > *And we circled around him,*
> > > *and answered him,* Amen.

Glory be to thee, Logos:
Glory be to thee, Grace. Amen.

Glory be to thee, Spirit:
Glory be to thee, Holy One:
Glory be to thy Glory. Amen.

We praise thee, Father:
We thank thee, Light:
In whom darkness dwelleth not. Amen.

And why we give thanks, I will tell you.
I will be saved,
And I will save. Amen.
I will be released,
And I will release. Amen.
I will be wounded,
And I will wound. Amen.
I will be born,
And I will bear. Amen.
I will eat,
And I will be eaten. Amen ...[2]

Although they claim to be based on early traditions (c. 100–300 A.D.) concerning John, the disciple of Jesus, the *Acts of John* were condemned as heresy. Pope Leo the Great, in the fifth century, decreed that such writings, which "contain a hotbed of manifold perversity, should not only be forbidden, but altogether removed and burnt with fire."[3] But the *Acts* survived, copied and shared secretly among Christians who dared to risk heresy.

But those who revered the *Acts of John* did not actually consider themselves heretics. They insisted that they, not the orthodox, understood the true meaning of Christ and his teaching. The movement they represent is called *gnosticism*, from the Greek word *gnosis*, translated as *knowledge*, or *insight*, since these Christians claimed to "know" secret mysteries kept hidden from "the masses." So the *Acts of John* takes up a saying of Jesus from the New Testament ("... this generation ... is like children sitting in the market places and calling to their playmates, 'We piped to you, and you did not dance; we wailed, and you did not mourn,'" Matthew 11.16–17) and places it in a new context:

I will pipe,
Dance, all of you. Amen.

I will mourn,
Beat you all your breasts. Amen.

The twelfth number
dances on high. Amen.

To the universe
belongs the dancer. Amen.

Whoever does not dance
does not know what happens. Amen. ...[4]

Was the "Round Dance of the Cross" actually danced? Whether Jesus himself danced with his disciples we do not know; so far as I know there is no other testimony that claims he did. But early Gnostic Christians used the "Round Dance" to enact a sacred ritual dance. The leader of the group, representing Christ, stood in the center, speaking Jesus' lines; the others circled around, chanting "Amen" in response to his singing. When the text directs that Christ himself joins in the dance, the leader danced before them. By identifying himself as Christ, he demonstrated the "mystery" that, Jesus says, "I showed to you and to the rest in my dance." What is that mystery? According to the *Acts of John*, Jesus explains that everyone who dances—not just the leader—is to "see yourself in Me who am speaking," and to recognize that Christ's suffering is actually the suffering of all humanity:

I am a mirror to you
who know me. Amen.
I am a door to you
who knock on me. Amen.

I am a way to you,
the traveler. Amen.

Now if you follow
my dance,
see yourself
in Me who am speaking,
and when you have seen what I do,
keep silence about my mysteries. ...

You who dance, consider
what I do, for yours is
the passion of humanity
which I am to suffer.

For you could by no means
have understood what you suffer
unless to you, as the Word,
I was sent by the Father ...
What I am you shall see
when you come yourself.[5]

As each participant comes to recognize his own mystical identification with Christ, he learns to transcend human suffering. The dance closes as Christ declares:

As for me,
if you would understand what I was,
by the word I mocked at all things,
and I was not mocked at all,
I exulted;
but understand the whole,
and when you have understood it, say,
Glory be to thee, Father.

Say again with me,
Glory be to thee, Father.

Glory be to thee, Word.
Glory be to thee, Spirit. Amen.[6]

John explains that:

> *After the Lord had danced with us, my beloved, he went out. And*
> *we were like people amazed or fast asleep, and we fled this way and*
> *that way. And so I saw him suffer, and did not wait by his suffering,*
> *but fled to the Mount of Olives and wept at what had come to pass.*
> *And when he was hung (upon the cross) on Friday, at the sixth hour*
> *of the day there came a darkness over the whole earth.*[7]

John relates that as he sat in a cave grieving during the crucifixion,
Christ suddenly appeared to him in a vision:

> *And my Lord stood in the middle of the cave and gave light to it*
> *and said, "John, for the people below in Jerusalem I am being given*
> *gall and vinegar to drink. But to you I am speaking, and listen to*
> *what I speak."*

In this vision, Christ explains to John the paradox of human experience—that while the mortal being suffers, the divine being within
simultaneously transcends suffering:

> *So then I have suffered none of those things which they will say*
> *of me; even that suffering which I showed to you and to the rest in*
> *my dance, I will that it be called a mystery. For what you are, I have*
> *shown you. … You hear that I suffered, yet I suffered not; and that*
> *I suffered not, yet I did suffer; and that I was pierced, yet I was not*
> *wounded; that I was hanged, yet I was not hanged; that blood flowed*
> *from me, yet it did not flow …*[8]

Having received this vision, John relates that he went out, and laughed
at the crowds who saw only the physical events of Christ's torture and
execution, failing to perceive his spiritual triumph over suffering:

I laughed at them all, since he had told me what they said about him, and I held this one thing fast in my mind, that the Lord had enacted everything as a symbol.[9]

What did this ritual dance mean to those who performed it? First, they came to recognize their own identification with Christ; second, they learned the paradox of human suffering, and so claimed to transcend it. But orthodox Christians condemned this mystical writing, convinced that such teaching would rob Christ of his uniqueness, and deprive Christian traditions of its reverence for his human vulnerability—and our own.

Notes:

1 *Acts of John* 95.16–17, in Hennecke-Schneemelcher, *New Testament Apocrypha* (hereafter cited as *NT Apocrypha*), volume 2.229 (Philadelphia: 1964). Translated from the German *Neutestamentliche Apocryphen.*

2 *Acts of John* 94–95.8, in *NT Apocrypha* 2.227–228.

3 Leo the Great, *Letters*, 15.15.

4 *Acts of John* 95.12–17, in *NT Apocrypha* 2.229.

5 *Acts of John* 95.25–96.40 in *NT Apocrypha* 2.230–231.

6 *Acts of John* 96.47–51, in *NT Apocrypha* 2.231–232.

7 *Acts of John* 97, in *NT Apocrypha* 2.232.

8 *Acts of John* 101, in *NT Apocrypha* 2.234.

9 *Acts of John* 102, in *NT Apocrypha* 2.234–235.

CHAPTER EIGHT

•

Fullness of Being

Gather up the fragments that remain, that nothing be lost.[1]

—John 6:12

The primary mystery is the birth of God in man (who includes the world in himself) and the birth of man in god. In our imperfect language this means that there is in God a need for a responsive creative act on the part of man. Man is not merely a sinner; the consciousness of sin is but an experience which moves him as he treads his path; man is also a creator. The human tragedy from which there is no escape, the dialectic of freedom, necessity, and grace, finds its solution within the orbit of the divine Mystery, within the Deity, which lies deeper than the drama between Creator and creature, deeper than representations of heaven and hell.

*Here the human tongue keeps silence. The eschatological outlook is not limited to the prospect of an indefinable end of the world;
it embraces in its view every moment of life.
At each moment of one's living, what is needed is to put an end to the old world and to begin the new. In that is the breath of the Spirit.*[2]

—Nicholas Berdyaev

Parabola
Volume: 17.4
Power and Energy

DIVINE ENERGY

Father Symeon Burholt

Energy is fullness of being. By my energy I go beyond mere existence and come to life. I surpass the limits of my self and affect the world around me. In doing this I truly become myself, doing and suffering, making my unique contribution, meeting the challenges each day brings, giving myself to others and receiving others into myself.

But how can one speak of divine energy? To attribute energy to God seems to be nothing but a projection, a fashioning of God after our own image and likeness. Yet in the Christian tradition the belief that God has overflowing life and energy is vital not only for a right understanding of God but also for knowing what it means to be a human being, since the human person is seen as made for participation in the divine energy. This dimension of Christianity is unknown to many people.

Existence on its own, devoid of energy, is hard to envisage. Even apart from the insights of modern physics we see that everything has a characteristic mode of being and behaving, which we may call its energy. This is especially true of people, whom we come to know from what they do, not by some intuition of their essence. We experience the way they act. We are affected by their distinctive properties, their size, weight, or color. If I am told that someone or something exists without these, I am forced to hypothesize a substance which is inert and lifeless, which in fact cannot be known, any more than could the *pura materia* about which the medievals speculated and which is not found in the real world. And when in common parlance we say that someone is merely existing we mean that he is in a sorry state: he carries on, but not much more. His existence is hardly a life. A person is fully living, on the other hand, insofar as his or her energies are heightened. We become and manifest who we really are to the extent that we realize our potentialities. A tree is known by its fruits.

But if by "God" we mean a reality far surpassing our own fullness of being we must envisage the divine as total realization, abundance of life and actuality, energy unfailing, of which our mode of being is a pale reflection, and at best a symbol. Yet people persist in asking whether or not God *exists*. As Dostoyevsky pointed out, their question never finds an answer, because it is wrongly put. Its proper context is the experience of active loving, but it is confined within the narrow limits of a notion of existence which is as irrelevant to life as it is unreal and reductionist. The concept of God as a remote entity which does nothing served as a postulate for some philosophers of the eighteenth century, but it is foreign to all the great religious traditions of humankind. For these the question—and it is a burning question—is not of God's existence but of his presence, and this implies his power or energy. Yet even today deism is not dead. The reductionist notion of God, which was formerly the preserve of academics, is uncritically accepted by ordinary people in our society, who on the whole do not reject belief that God exists but have little sense of the divine presence and of communion with him. This reductionist point of view is in direct opposition to the religious instinct and mystical impulse, which suffers widespread atrophy in our times.

In spite of all this, the human heart senses that "God" is not a mono-syllabic blob but the Ever-present One. How are we to understand, and live, this sense? Christianity is sometimes seen as nothing but a collec-tion of moral duties and soothing reassurances about salvation, rather than as a summons to the deification of the human person.

St. Athanasius of Alexandria, a pillar of orthodoxy during the fourth century, insisted upon the divine being's exuberance. The divine being, ineffably more alive that we are, cannot be self-contained and barren but has to be *Father*, forever bringing forth his son from the womb of his own substance. This continual begetting is a movement of being which is essentially fruitful. Our human experience of parenting is only an analogy for the perfect generation in the divine being, where there is no before and after, no differentiation into male and female, and where the one brought forth is not inferior to the parent. This vision of God continually pouring forth his very being would inspire Meister Eckhart a millennium later to speak of God in terms of molten metal which is always boiling over. The son's coming forth from the Father is a non-stop act of both begetting and giving birth.

Thus for the Christian tradition the divine reality is essentially personal. The three are not merely aspects of some impersonal substrate, nor are they separate individuals. The doctrine of the Trinity states that ultimate reality is a *communion of persons*, each dwelling in the others. Here relationship is of the essence. And this communion of persons is the truth and exemplar of all being. In particular it is the hope to which we human beings aspire. We come alive when our eyes meet those of the one who loves us, for we then find our center outside ourselves in the other, and in so doing we touch the mystery of transcendence. By falling in love we leave behind our own isolation and break away from our old, limited way of life, which is now revealed as loneliness and incompletion. And, even more, in the unromantic daily struggle of active loving, in relationship, we find out who we really are. That is the context in which we can ask about God for it is then that we most resemble God. The Trinity goes beyond both solitude and the mutual opposition of Dualism, for God, as St. John says, is love.

Strictly speaking, the divine energy is something more than God's life. It is the natural expression, or abundance, of the divine being, which is common to the three and overflowing with power, goodness, love, life, and innumerable other attributes. All of these are dynamic energies. We could sum them up by the statement that God is almighty. But all too often this smacks of our own notions of power and of the arbitrary right of might which we project, making God out to be basically angry, if not plain bad-tempered. The more authentic Christian understanding is that God's energies are modes of the divine presence. The three make their home in each other; but they also overflow, so to speak, beyond themselves, and this means the possibility of our participation in God. St. Athanasius wrote of this two-fold presence when he said of the son:

> *In His Substance He is indeed outside the Universe, but by His Powers He is in all things, ordering everything … containing all things without Himself being contained: only in His Father is He totally present in every respect* (De Incarnatione *17*).

And again, in a very different context:

> *He is in all things with respect to His goodness and power, but according to His Nature He is outside all things* (De Decretis *11*).

To express this vision St. Athanasius uses Plato's image of the sun, but with an important difference. Whereas Plato emphasizes the human struggle to emerge from the cave and finally attain the dazzling vision of the sun, St. Athanasius stresses the descent of the sun's rays to the earth where they permeate and nourish all things. Just as the sun's rays reach down to us without being separated from the sun, so the son of God remains one in being with his father yet is really present in the world by means of his "condescension," *sygkatabasis*, which one could well translate as "loving descent."

This understanding of the act of creation as a continual descent and presence of the creator by his power, or energies, is a far cry from the common idea that God works by some kind of remote control or that he merely started things off in the beginning, as a man may wind up a watch and then leave it to tick away. When we make something, we simply act upon what already exists, giving it a new form, and then we go on our way. The Christian doctrine of creation out of nothing, however, means that the very being of things is imparted by God, who is ever actively present, sustaining them in being. It involves a relationship which is ineffably more intimate that that of a craftsman with his artifact. God is not pantheistically equated with the world, but neither is he separated from it in dualistic fashion.

God by his nature overflows with abundant life in his energies, like the sun, which cannot but pour forth its light and heat: he is not an inert essence, an impotent object, but exists in three subjects who continually shine forth in the divine energy. Hence all God's dealings with the world are radically forms of divine self-communication. Thus we read in Psalm 19:

> *The heavens declare the glory of God: and the firmament sheweth*
> *his handywork.*

The world is radiant with God's presence, with divine energy. He is dynamically present in all things as their creator and all things participate in the divine energy to the extent that he acts upon them and they are patient to his touch.

In the Christian tradition it is the human person who is most capable of this participation. We are believed to be made in the image and likeness of God and, on the basis of the ancient axiom that knowledge and vision occur with likeness, the Church has affirmed that man can behold God with the eye of his soul, or heart. So our heart's gaze can be fixed upon God. To sin is, literally, to "fall short" of this vision of God and to deal with things merely as objects of our own gratification and convenience.

Exactly what human life would be like if we partook fully of the divine energy by being open to the vision of God in things is difficult to imagine, for we experience human nature only in its more or less fallen-short condition. Our guesses about ourselves easily become clichés and idealizations. For the Christian the paradigm is not an ideal but the person of Christ. The son of God is believed to have taken up our human nature to himself, making it his very own. This is the supreme act of his loving descent. It is not a mere appearance in our form but a real union of the divine and the human in himself. Like the union of marriage, there is a complete sharing. This means that he could experience and undergo all that human life brings, including death; and also that our flesh is united to him and becomes the vehicle of the divine energy, experiencing and undergoing the works of God.

The right understanding of this mystery was proclaimed at the Third Council of Constantinople in 680. The union of the human and the divine in Christ does not mean our nature is swallowed up or in any way diminished. Rather in Christ our human energy is united with the divine energy so that God can suffer in our flesh and our flesh can be deified by participation in God's energy. Christ could be weary and distressed as we often are, yet he could also heal the sick and raise the dead by his word or touch. On one occasion he allowed his disciples to behold this deification when, on a high mountain he was transfigured in their presence, his flesh and even his garments becoming radiant like lightning.

Thus the body of Christ becomes the source for our own transfiguration. The saints are those who allow the divine energy to become their own through renunciation of their "own" will, in the sense of inordinate fears and cravings, and through the practice of prayer and active love of their enemies. But their food for this divine life is the body of Christ. Believers partake of this deified body in the mysteries of the Christian religion; and by assimilation, their own humanity can become deified by divine energy. Whether this process has its full effect depends upon the individual's openness to the growth of the divine begun in him or her.

Speaking in the person of the flesh, St. Athanasius replied to an imaginary objector:

> By nature I am indeed mortal and of the earth, but then I became the flesh of the Logos, who Himself bore my passions, although He was not liable to passion. I have become free from them and not left as their slave because of the Lord Who set me free from them. If you accuse me of laying aside my natural corruption, see that you do not accuse the fact that the Logos of God took my form of slavery. For as the Lord put on a body and became man, so we humans are being deified by the Logos and taken up through his flesh. And in the future we shall inherit eternal life (Contra Arianos, 3, 34).

The word "spirituality" is a recent addition to the Christian vocabulary. In fact the centrality of the body and physical objects and the community of persons in the Church constitutes a kind of sacred materialism which has always offended those who look for a more ethereal and other-worldly path, and such trends have sometimes found their way into Christian thinking. But the mainstream of the tradition, shown in the lives of the saints, is a summons not to leave the world and the body but to transfiguration, to more abundant life and energy.

Parabola
Volume: 13.4
The Mountain

THE THRESHOLD OF THE MOUNTAIN IN DANTE'S *DIVINE COMEDY*

Helen Luke

There are three images in Dante's *Divina Commedia* which unforgettably symbolize the three stages of the inner journey of every human soul. In the *Inferno* is the dark wood of the lost and unconscious state in which some may choose to stay; in the *Paradiso* is the white rose, the mandala of the final vision of unity, of the totality, of eternity; and rising between them in the central *cantica* is the mountain of the *Purgatorio*.

Marie Louise von Franz, in one of her lectures on fairy tales, said, "Often the mountain is the goal of a long quest or the site of transition into eternity. The mountain also marks the place—the point in life—where the hero, after arduous effort (climbing) becomes oriented and gains steadfastness and self-knowledge, values that develop through the effort to become conscious in the process of individuation."[1] The mountain of the *Purgatorio* is precisely such a place. We may realize how vital a symbol it is in Dante's imagination when we remember that it first appears for a moment at the very beginning of the poem, on the threshold of the entire journey. Before the poet has made any movement at all to emerge from the dark wood of his fear and despair, he awakens to the acknowledgment of his powerlessness, his loneliness, his self-pity, and dares to *look up* and out of this absorption in the ego; immediately there comes to him a glimpse of a great mountain rising into the heavens, and the sun of consciousness is shining upon it.

At this point of sudden vision, Dante did three things. He forced himself to look back with eyes wide open at his fear; he rested awhile, then he tried his best to climb the mountain. He wanted, as we all want, to go the shortest and the quickest way to his goal; but "*la diritta via*" of the utterly childlike and innocent is for few in any age, for the very few in ours. That it was the wrong way for him Dante very speedily found out; but if he had not made that courageous effort to scale the mountain, simply putting one foot in front of the other in the direction which seemed to him the right one, he would never have learned his true path. He was hindered and finally turned back by three beasts—the leopard, the lion, and the wolf—by his love of pleasure, by his fierce pride, and by the terrifying latent greed and avarice of the ego. So indeed do we learn, struggling out of the dark wood, that we cannot hope to find wholeness by repressing the shadow sides of ourselves, or by the most heroic efforts of the ego to climb up, to achieve goodness. The leopard, the lion, and the wolf will not allow it, we may thank God. It is when we admit our powerlessness that the guide appears. For Dante it was Virgil, sent by Beatrice to his help—Beatrice, through whom he had as a very young man briefly but deeply experienced the meaning of both mountain and rose, and the darkness of loss without which they can never be incarnate in human life.

We do not see the mountain again until, having passed through the fog and murk of the darkness of Hell, Dante, climbing on the body of Satan himself, emerges with Virgil into another kind of darkness and approaches the threshold of the great mountain under the stars.

It is near dawn as the poets climb out of the narrow opening and look upon the stars. Behind them is the darkness of the pit, monotonous, dirty, a blackness of meaningless confusion and clamor; before them is the clean, sapphire-blue darkness out of which the great stars shine—Venus, the planet of love, and the four brilliant stars of the southern pole to which fallen man is blind. It is thought possible that Dante had heard of the Southern Cross: but, whether he had or not, the symbol of the fourfold nature of reality springs from his unconscious, shining upon the threshold of the great climb to the Earthly Paradise where man regains his innocence.

The effect upon us of this image is far more powerful than if the poets emerged from the dark pit into clear sunlight, for implicit in it is the whole meaning of this crucial transition-point in the life of a man or woman. We do not suddenly exchange our thralldom to the unconscious fogs and suffering of neurosis for a wholly conscious and sunlit climb to the heights. What we do experience at this moment is a total transformation of the nature of darkness itself—or rather of our attitude towards it. As long as we seek to escape from our various "hells" into freedom from pain, we remain irremediably bound; we can emerge from the pains of Hell in one way only—by accepting another kind of suffering, the suffering which is purging, instead of meaningless damnation. The souls in the *Purgatorio* suffer the same kinds of torments as those in the *Inferno*; but they suffer with willing acceptance instead of with bitter resentment, because they have dared to recognize meaning and to accept responsibility. They have glimpsed from afar the planet Venus, the true nature of love, and deep in their hearts is born the vision of the four stars of the pole, the pattern of wholeness. Thus the moment when a man or woman steps over the threshold onto the shore of Purgatory is the moment in which he or she is ready in the core of his or her being to follow *at any cost* the way to the realization of this vision in his own individual life. It is a way which will inevitably lead him through the agony whereby the "I want, I must have" of the ego is transmuted into the love whose "center is everywhere."

In the lifetime of every man or woman there surely comes, at the deepest level, such a moment of choice, whether fully recognized or not. Sometimes it comes very early, sometimes not until the moment of physical death. Yet, as T. S. Eliot says, "the time of death is every moment," and so therefore is the time of choice. However, even when the basic choice of direction has been truly made, nevertheless in our weakness we are continually falling back into the neurotic, ego-centered torments of Hell, and so the new attitude must be constantly reaffirmed. Almost daily this great image of Dante's passage from the blind murk to the shining dark may come to our aid. We have but to turn ourselves upside down, reverse our attitude, for Satan's legs, the evil itself, to become the ladder to the narrow opening, for the misery and shame that engulf us to become the very way to the vision of the stars. We fail, however, and lose heart, because we so quickly forget that this change is impossible without a total willingness to "pay the uttermost farthing"—if necessary over a long period of time. Instead we expect to be transported immediately into an infantile paradise as Dante did in Canto I of the *Inferno*. Purgatory is not an outmoded doctrine invented by the Roman Catholic Church; it is an immediate reality in the life of everyone who chooses the way to consciousness.

Anyone who has experienced this emergence from an attitude of remorse and resentment to an attitude of repentance and acceptance knows the extraordinary sense of a total change of atmosphere that goes with it. In place of a grey monotony and heaviness, everything and everyone around us is bathed in freshness and filled with meaning. From the first words of the *Purgatorio*, through all the descriptions of suffering, until we reach the forest at the summit, Dante evokes with extraordinary vividness the clean and sparkling *delight* of the atmosphere. We are pierced through and through with wonder at this sense of clarity; and, by the mere reading of such "angelic verse," feel cleansed and purged ourselves. "Within the all-pervading atmosphere of 'delight renewed' the change of outlook defines itself with endless subtlety. Courtesy is everywhere the key-note."[2]

There is a clear distinction between this atmosphere of delight in the midst of pain and the unclouded joy of the blessed in the *Paradiso*, for which the mountain is the training ground. As far as words can define the difference, "delight" and "joy" must serve. On the first page of the *Purgatorio*, Dante writes:

> *For to the second realm I tune my tale,*
> *Where human spirits purge themselves, and train*
> *To leap up into joy celestial.*
> *(I, 4-6)*

He continues, though the sun has not yet risen:

> *Colour unclouded …*

Brought to mine eyes renewal of delight,
So soon as I came forth from that dead air
Which had oppressed my bosom and my sight.
(I, 13-18)

There are no dreams in Hell; there are no dreams in Heaven; for both realms are outside time. When we are possessed by the archetypes in the unconscious we cannot relate to them, and there is no process, no dialogue between dream and consciousness; the dream world has swallowed us up, and we are driven round and round forever at the mercy of instinctive drives and ego-desires. At the other end of the scale, when we shall have come to the state of bliss, these same archetypes will be known as the great angelic and human powers of the psyche, their ambivalence transcended as they revolve around the center. Again this state is beyond time and the opposites, and each individual will have found his place in the eternal dance.

Purgatory, however, is the way between these two states, and is symbolic of the work we do in the dimension of time—the day by day suffering of the tension between the opposites and the long battle for consciousness. On the mountain, therefore, there is the alternation of night and day and a very urgent sense of time.

The souls are unwilling to waste one moment of the daylight in spite of their great pleasure in talking to Dante. It is a point which awakens us to a truth so easily forgotten in this age—the truth that the way of individuation demands *attention*, not just for a few hours or weeks, or a few minutes a day, but, ultimately, during every moment of our lives. I am reminded of the Zen master who was so disconcerted when he realized he had put his umbrella down without noticing the exact place. How he would have approved of Dante's extreme precision in his descriptions of the images of bliss! The experience of immortality will spring ultimately from constant attention to the "minute particular," in Blake's phrase. The point lies not in *what* we do, as the Puritans mistakenly defined this truth, but in the degree of our conscious awareness of every act and every impulse in their contexts outer and inner. True spontaneity is born of this awareness alone.

In the daytime, then, in the *Purgatorio*, when the sun is shining, we feel the necessity of unremitting effort. But there is another law of the mountain: during the night it is impossible for anyone to take one step upward. The traveler must be still and wait, unless he or she chooses to walk down the mountain again. Theologically this is interpreted to mean that when the light of grace, the sun, is withdrawn, the pilgrim falls into a spiritual dryness and aridity during which time he must simply wait in faith for the sun to rise again and resist the temptation to fall back. True indeed; but there is another depth of meaning—particularly for us in this century, individually and collectively, caught as we are in the tremendous overemphasis placed by our society on activity, intellectual, physical, or emotional. In the few words which define this law of the mountain, it is made abundantly clear that if we do not spend the nights—that is, half of our time—being still, we shall effectually extinguish the possibility of growth and walk backwards. In other words, if we do not give validity to the dark, the yin, the feminine and the receptive; if we do not consent to do nothing, to allow time for dreaming, for listening to the voice of the unconscious, then we shall be in far worse case than if we waste time during the "day"; for our excessive activity will lead us backwards, and all will be to do again. On each of the three nights that Dante spent in Purgatory he dreamed. We cannot climb the mountain at all without the cooperation of the unconscious.

It seems that the symbol of divine grace, without which all our activity is of little avail, comes as powerfully to us nowadays through Dante's dreams as through the image of the daytime sun. Each dream represents a leap in Dante's individual awareness—wisdom from the unconscious given and heard in the passivity of the dark, nourishing the hard conscious work of the day and being nourished by it. Dreams, the images which spring out of the dark, are the free gift of grace, falling on us like dew from Heaven, bringing freshness and strength for our striving under the sun.

As Dante and Virgil stand on the shore of the mountain and look upon the stars, it is well to reflect upon the nature of the torments they have left behind in the pit and of those they are about to see as they climb.

There are no punishments in the *Inferno* or in the *Purgatorio*. Punishment is something imposed from without, and the popular idea of sinners punished by a condemning deity is totally alien to Dante's vision.

The word "penalty," however, means the payment of a debt; every act or attitude, insofar as it does not spring from the wholeness beyond the opposites, carries within itself its own penalty. This truth is defined by the East in the doctrine of karma and by Dante through the extraordinary fitness of his images of suffering. The souls, whether in Hell or Purgatory, are tormented either by the true nature of the sin itself or by its opposite, which is the same thing in reverse.

If we compare the condition of Paolo and Francesca in the second circle of Hell with the suffering of the lustful on the seventh cornice of the mountain, we see clearly how the torment in both states springs from the nature of lust itself. In Purgatory the redeemed souls walk in the fierce heat of the fire, whereas in the *Inferno*, the lovers were mercilessly blown by the cold wind. Desire is hot, but lust which remains unconscious is ultimately cold. The fire of Purgatory is not a condemnation of desire: Dante knows that there is no redemption through cold repression. On the contrary, it symbolizes the free acceptance of the terrible burning of the desire itself endured with the full realization of its redemptive meaning; so, passing through the fire, the soul finds love.

To take one more example: the wrathful in Hell lie choking and spluttering in sticky black mud; the wrathful in Purgatory are blinded by a thick and gritty smoke. We might expect punishment by fire for anger, but anger is never a bringer of light and warmth; on the contrary, it is essentially a cold and blinding thing, stifling all discrimination and warmth of heart, so that we cannot see things and people as they are, nor can we ourselves be seen. Dante says of the sullen wrathful in Hell that their "hearts smoldered with a sulky smoke." The difference between the sufferers in Hell and those in Purgatory is again only in their attitude. The angry shades in the mud of Styx shout curses. Marco Lombardo in the *Purgatorio* says, "… though the smoke has made us blind, hearing instead of sight shall neighbour us."

"Hearing instead of sight shall neighbour us." The literal translation is "Hearing shall keep us joined." These words, coming to us with such gracious courtesy out of the smoke, express a fundamental attitude of all the souls in the *Purgatorio*, an attitude of enormous importance to each one of us. Even after the consent to pay the price has been given, how easy it is to say, "I am in a fog—in the grip of my shadow side and I have to get rid of this or that weakness *before* I can be free enough to attend to other people or embark on some positive relationship; I am not yet ready." And so, forgetting that if we cannot see, we can hear, or if we cannot hear, we can perceive, we become obsessed with the smoke, or with whatever other form of tension and suffering the shadow creates for us; and soon we are back in the infernal dark. The souls on Dante's mountain, while they never allow themselves to be distracted from the pain and tension which awareness of the shadow brings, yet give to the travelers as they pass their full attention, with such of their faculties as *are* free to hear, to see, or to speak. There is no slightest hint of that deadly attitude, "I am no good because of this or that or the other weakness, and you can't possibly want to associate with me," nor of its opposite, "Stay with me, distract me, pull me out of this awful pain." The purging process is immediately halted when we lose that objective courtesy to others, to ourselves, to life in all its manifestations, which is conveyed in those words, "though the smoke has made us blind, hearing instead of sight shall neighbour us."

From the shore the poets have quite a long way to go before they pass the next gateway and enter Purgatory proper. "Peter's Gate" is not reached until they have climbed almost a third of the way up the mountain and have passed through the region which Dante calls Ante-Purgatory.

We left them standing beside the dark hole from which they have emerged; but before Dante can start at all on the new journey, he must pass a kind of entrance examination. He is confronted by Cato, the guardian of the threshold, who questions him somewhat roughly. Virgil answers and explains the situation with great respect, flattering Cato a little, for which the latter brusquely rebukes him.

Cato stands for the strict moral virtues of the Stoic. He is the only person on the mountain who speaks ungraciously, a hint that the Stoic virtues know nothing of grace, from which springs courtesy in action; and it is probable that Dante makes him the guardian of the approach to Purgatory in order to stress that in the ecstasy of that first vision of the stars lies a danger—the temptation to forget the necessity for discipline. The dour figure of Cato barring the way to the heights of being carries an apt warning for us nowadays, when such things as drug-induced visions lure men all too easily into the delusion that such ecstasies are ends in themselves, unrelated to life and behavior in this world. While ethical disciplines alone cannot ever rise beyond the shore of the mountain, as

Cato could not, nevertheless without them we cannot take one step on the way to individuation. Only after the long climb is an individual free from all law—free to love and do as he wills.

Two things, says Cato, must be done before the journey may be continued. Virgil must wash Dante's face and clean off the filth of Hell, and he must gird his pupil's waist with one of the reeds which grow in the water on the shore—reeds which can withstand wind and wave because they bend before the storm. The ego must be girdled with humility, without which all experience of the numinous must lead ultimately to the fate of Icarus. The rope girdle of "good resolutions," which Dante had to abandon in the pit, is now replaced by the girdle of the humble reed. Dante had to go down into the pit of fraud and look upon the ultimate darkness without any support from his hitherto noble intentions. Only when he has emerged from this black experience is he ready and able to know the humility without which all our visions of light lead only to an inflation of the ego. When we are girdled with the reed, we are safe, however high we mount, encircled by that which grows only from the waters in the low places of the earth.

Moreover, the sound of the reeds, the whisper of the wind blowing through them, often symbolizes in myth and fairy tale the voice of the inner wisdom. They whisper to the hero or heroine (as in the Eros and Psyche story) the solution to the impossible task, and no one can take a step up the mountain until he or she is quiet enough to hear and humble enough to listen to their message.

Since the Middle Ages we have climbed so high on the skyscrapers of the intellect that the image of climbing anything is apt to strike us as negative. We are desperately aware of our need to go down, to find the truth and wisdom which has sunk into the unconscious, having realized that our upward strivings lead only to false spirituality or empty theory. Nevertheless the climb is still an essential of the way; and the effort and hardship involved in mountain climbing speak as powerfully as ever to the imagination, especially when we think of this climb in contrast to the elevators which we construct to shoot us up to the top of the lofty buildings of our split thinking. In the *I Ching* there is a sign called Humility or Modesty; in our context we could call it the sign of the reed. The image for this sign is the Mountain *within* the Earth. This is surely the point of the reed girdle; we must stay, as it were, within the earth as we climb the mountain to reach "the site of the transition into eternity."

Notes:

1   Marie Louise von Franz, *Introduction to the Psychology of Fairy Tales* (New York: Spring Publications, 1970), chap. VII, p. 12.

2   Dorothy Sayers, *The Comedy of Dante Alighieri, Cantica I, Hell* (London/Baltimore: Penguin Books, 1955), p. 19.

Adapted by the author from Helen Luke, *Dark Wood to White Rose*, copyright Dove Publications, Pecos, New Mexico, 1975. Reprinted with permission.

Parabola
Volume: 10.4
The Seven
Deadly Sins

THE GARMENT

P. L. Travers

The bell rang in the outer court, a peremptory, musical summons. And with much jangling of keys, St. Peter unlocked the double doors, opened them a little way, and put out his head through the crack.

"Well?" he demanded. "What do *you* want?"

A man in a long white robe stepped forward.

"I want to come in," he said.

"What? Dressed up like an apprentice angel? Isn't that rather premature?"

"My garment represents myself," said the man. "You can read it as though it were a book. There is no stain on it anywhere."

"So I see. That makes the book difficult to read. Nothing to declare, as it were. I'm afraid you have come to the wrong place. We only cater for sinners."

"But surely I have a right to be here! I have led a blameless life."

"We do not deal in rights," said St. Peter. "Though there is grace abounding. Perhaps it would be more to the point if you told me about the wrongs."

"There are none. Guilt has passed me by. I have never practiced avarice, keeping only enough for my simple needs, giving alms to the beggar at the corner and tipping waiters generously. Moreover, I have envied no man nor been a source of envy. I eat sparsely, once a day only, a meager dinner of herbs. And as for lechery, I deplore it. When I see a woman, even the passing swing of a skirt, I quickly turn my back on the scene or look in the other direction. Pride, too, I likewise abhor, bowing both to king and peasant, not setting myself above another nor boasting of my possessions. And I fill my days profitably, never an idle moment. Compared with myself, the ant is a sluggard; sloth finds no place within me. Last of all, I have never lost my temper."

"Alas, poor ant!" St. Peter grinned. "I feel for you, my good sir. You have told me a tale that is all perfection. But perfection is a heavy burden. I have not known one who could carry it."

"But, surely," the man was clearly dismayed. "You must take account of virtue!"

"Ah, virtue. That is a different matter. Virtue is always equivocal, a field of opposing forces. It is not merely lack of shortcomings and certainly not an unstained garment. It belongs to a man's totality, the bad along with the good. Did you think to approach the courts of Heaven without passing through—yes, and reveling there—the hostelries of earth? If you take my advice, you'll ring the bell at the Other Place. They would certainly teach you a thing or two, not least the meaning of virtue." He pointed downwards with his thumb.

"Down there? Never!" the man shuddered. "There must be some alternative."

"There are always alternatives," said St. Peter. "For instance, you could return whence you came and begin again at the beginning. The garment which you call yourself might then have something to tell me."

The man drew his robe about him, with a fond possessive gesture.

"After all my self-denial!" he said, and sighed as he turned away. "I never thought it was possible that this could happen to me."

"You never thought—leave it at that."

St. Peter's face disappeared from the crack. The doors swung together again and a key turned in the lock.

And the sun rose and the sun set and the work of Heaven went steadily on, systole and diastole, the heartbeat of the universe.

And after a time, a lifetime, perhaps, the man who had gone dejected away came once more to the door.

"What—you again?" St. Peter exclaimed. "But what have you done with that vestal garment, yourself immaculate?"

For the man was clad in a threadbare robe, spattered with patches of brassy color all shades of the spectrum.

"I am wearing it," he replied, turning about like a spinning top in order to display himself.

"Are you, indeed?" St. Peter chuckled. "Well, this vestment has clearly done some living. Come closer so I can read it."

He pored over the splashes of insolent color as though they were a map. "Ha! Yellow—bright as a wasp's wing! This is avarice, if ever I saw it! I would guess that the beggar at the corner no longer gets his lucky penny, nor the waiter his generous tip. And this strip of green must surely be envy. Covetousness seems to have burned in you for the chattels and qualities other men have. Warp and woof almost worn away.

"Now, what have we here in this patch of blue—greed, would you say, yes greed indeed! No more dinners of herbs, eh, but gluttony at all levels, mind and stomach always a-clamor, calling, even when full, for more. And this—this broad explicit expanse of scarlet? Does the man who so deplored lechery still turn his back when he sees a woman, let alone the swing of a skirt? Who would have thought that virgin robe would have had such a tale to tell!

"And you are proud of its disclosures. See, the sin of pride declares itself here where the violet borders the red. Do you bow, now, both to king and peasant? I am inclined to doubt it. And what about the slug-gard ant that you so far outdistanced? This splash of black where the thread shows through assures me that he who was never idle has lain in the very lap of sloth. And this torn flap of brilliant orange—what could it be but the sin of wrath? What tempers! What tantrums! What fits of rage! Well, well! Now let me see. Is there not something else?"

"What could that be? You have seen the lot. The sins speak for themselves."

"I am looking," said St. Peter, gravely, "for some small unstained seg-ment—white, perhaps as the swan's wing—that would give them all their meaning."

"What could that be?" the man inquired. "I thought the list was complete."

"That which completes is repentance and I do not find it here."

"But these—?" The man gestured widely at the colors. "Aren't they enough? And what about *you*? Have you repented?"

St. Peter gave him a long deep look.

"I have wept," he replied, quietly. "At the crowing of the cock."

At that the man turned his head away and was silent for a moment.

"I thought to cast down a golden crown around the glassy sea. But that is not to be, it seems. I have never shed a single tear, nor learned aught of repentance."

"It cannot be taught," said St. Peter, gently. "It arises, of itself, in a man, when the time in him is ripe. Hitherto, as your robe tells me, you have let your life simply happen. You yourself have played no part in it. I have said there are always alternatives. Why not go and sit in the cave of your heart and confront whatever you find there—a caracole, maybe, of angels and devils. If so, you could join them in the dance, hand to one of them, hand to another, and so learn much that you now do not know. That garment will be your teacher."

The man drew his robe about him, and strode away shaking his head, clearly misliking the proposition.

And the sun rose and the sun set and the work of Heaven went steadily on, systole and diastole, the pulse of the Universe.

And after a time, a lifetime, perhaps, St. Peter, humming like a bee at his daily tasks—polishing the knobs of the doors, whitewashing the front step, shaking out the mat—looked up and saw a curious sight.

A man, naked but for some tatters of cloth, was sitting hunched up beside the entrance, head bowed, deep in thought.

St. Peter tapped him on the shoulder. "What's all this?" he demanded sternly. "Keep away from that fresh white step. I don't want footprints on it. Why, it's *you!*" he exclaimed, as the man turned, revealing a face that was now familiar.

The man assented wordlessly.

"But what are you doing sitting here with not a stitch of clothing on you but a handful of faded rags? What has happened to that famous garment?"

"It has gone," said the man, "except for these scraps. You told me to repair to the cave of my heart. This I did, but unwillingly. And as

I sat there pondering, telling over the beads of my life, seeing what I had dared not see and dancing with the opposites, my robe disappeared thread by thread, worn out by the strain of that confrontation and above all by the grieving: grieving for my sins, yes, in the measure that was needful—all men, in some degree, wear my many-colored gown—but mostly for that which had no color, the white and stainless garment I was pleased to call my virtue. I had fashioned it, I saw clearly, to hide myself, my pretentiousness, from my own eyes, let alone Another's. And I wept for shame who had never wept. That I could presume to come to this place, assuming the rights of one called and chosen. Alas, the pity of it!"

"The pity of it, indeed," said St. Peter.

"Yet, for all that, do not pity me. With my garment in shreds I am emptied out of all that I was, and am content to be so. Who am I? I ask myself and do not know the answer—no more than the worm on the leaf knows or bread cast upon the waters. And what, I also ask, is my purpose, without my protecting garment? That I do not know either but whatever it is I must try to serve it. If I have meaning it is there."

He hid his face in his hands again, lost in his own thoughts.

St. Peter regarded him silently for a long and brooding moment.

"Blessed are the poor in spirit. You must come in," he said.

The man raised his head, startled.

"But I am naked," he protested. "And of all men unworthy."

"Your nakedness shall be your passport. And none are worthy here."

St. Peter flung the doors wide.

"Step over the whitewash carefully and make your way to the inner court. They will give you a garment there."

Parabola
Volume: 30.2
Restraint

THE YOGA OF HESYCHASM

James S. Cutsinger

We know very little about Theophanis the Monk, not even when he lived. All we are sure of is that he was a monastic of the Christian East and the author of a short poem, "The Ladder of Divine Graces" (see page 303) into the seventy-one lines of which are distilled over a thousand years of spiritual teaching and ascetic discipline. There can be no question of providing an exhaustive interpretation of his insights, as concentrated and potent as an alchemical tincture. Our aim here is simply to hint at the vision he shared with his fellow monks of Mounts Athos and Sinai, whose quest toward *hesychia* or stillness has given rise to their designation as the Hesychast fathers.

In a sense, the title of the poem says it all: anyone who seeks union with God must understand before he even begins his search that a synergy or cooperation between Divine mercy and human effort is the key to his movement. If we would counter the gravitational forces of habit, we must like a climber commit ourselves to real struggle, real discipline, proceeding incrementally one step at a time. Whatever else, the poet means to prick the conscience of the man who assumes that doctrine can stand alone without method, theory without practice. On the other hand, we must not forget that our climbing is not only toward God; it is in and by God. Each of the rungs of the Ladder is a gift or a grace, a real and efficacious presence of the

Goal in the very midst of the way. "Work out your salvation with fear and trembling, for God is at work within you" (Phil. 2:12–13).

The subtitle confirms this synergy. The authority of the poem's teaching is at once human and Divine. What we are offered is no rarified speculation, concocted by a spiritual dreamer whose claims are untestable. It comes instead rooted in the concrete, the practical, the immediate, and it leads beyond mere credulity or acceptance to certainty. Notice that *experience* has made the Ladder *known*. But at the same time the knowledge is thanks to God, who has mercifully condescended to *those inspired* by Him. Authentic wisdom is never man's alone, an accomplishment or achievement for which he can take credit. The *wisdom born of God* is to know that God knows Himself in us.

Each of the ten steps of the Ladder is described by a single noun, the journey passing through the several stages of *prayer, heart, energy, tears, peace, purging, vision, light, illumination,* and *perfection.* But the nouns in each case are distinguished by adjectives. It is not just any prayer, but *purest* prayer that counts; not just any heart, but a *warm* one. So also one notes that the energy is *holy*, the tears are *God-given*, the peace is mental, the purging is intellective, the vision is mystical, the light is ineffable, the illumination is cardiac, and the perfection is *endless*.

Theophanis is careful to stress that the prayer of step one is of a most particular kind. In its *purest* form it is an imageless attention to the Divine presence, ontologically rather than discursively linked to its object, and often supported in Hesychast practice by the repetition of a short invocatory formula like the Jesus Prayer. It is important to realize that this opening step is itself a highly advanced spiritual state, presupposing a background not even hinted at in the poem and beginning at a point far beyond what most of us are probably ready for. Quintessential prayer is the bottom rung of a Ladder that must first be set on a living sacramental foundation, and its scaling assumes a deliberate and extensive propaedeutic under the guidance of a spiritual father. The Christian mystical tradition knows very well that individual initiatives and exploits are always ruinous in the contemplative life. Hence the author's deference to his own elders and betters: to *a saint inspired by God* and to *one of God's elect*.

Were we granted the grace of this first step, it would soon be discovered that true prayer is a transformative power, which begins to work its magic within the very tissues of the human body. This is noticed initially, the Hesychasts teach, in that central part of the body, the *heart*, where pure consciousness dwells, and the most common signal of change is a sensation of *warmth*. Warmth, like heart, is no metaphor. Something really begins to take place in the breast. One could say that it happens in and to the four-chambered beating muscle, but at the same time the sensation comes as proof that our true heart is always more than its concealment in matter, more than a physical pump. In either case the Ladder brings the whole man into play. The body is not left behind in our approach to full union, but is lifted up and drawn into its Divine prototype. Heaven is more, not less, solid than earth.

And then a strange, a holy energy. What was true at first for the central organ alone gradually makes itself felt throughout the entire human organism. A centrifugal radiation of power begins now to course outward through the various envelopes of the self. *Energy* is a technical term in this context. Western philosophy is accustomed to a distinction between form and matter; energy is the third that connects these two, the living and interior pulse through which essence communicates itself as substance. God has a pulse all His own, the effective and salvific presence of the Transcendent in the domain of the immanent, and we may participate fully in the Divine Substance and come to share in God's power through an assimilation of His *holy* energies. The nexus of this exchange is man's heart, an exchange that begins when our own center moves toward coincidence with the center of God.

Tears, the fourth step, are a mark of this concentrical shift. Not just any tears, however: only those that are *God-given*. Do not confuse the "gift of tears," as it is sometimes called, with ordinary grief or sorrow. Climbing the Ladder means mastering the passions, including the self-pity, resentment, and anger that often express themselves in weeping. We are to become objective toward our ego, no longer controlled by its sentimental involvement in the shifting play of the world. *Detach yourself from everything*, says Theophanis, *for without detachment nothing can be learnt*. The tears of the Ladder are not tears of selfish regret or refusal. On the contrary, they are the natural result of the ego's liquefaction. As the radiant energy of God carries the heart's warmth forward through the rest of our nature, the many layers of ice begin melting. We become the warm, soft water of our tears. The warmth is our fervor and longing for God; the softness is our yielding to the Divine influx; the water is the power of our newly found passivity.

The next pair of steps may be usefully treated as one, for they are two sides of a single coin: *peace from thoughts* and *purging of the intellect*. Note well that the peace is from thoughts of *every kind*. This is no power of positive thinking, which would simply replace bad or debilitating conceptions with good ones. Hesychasts follow a path leading beyond conception as such. By *thoughts* are meant the products of discursive mentation, that is, all the mental chatter which comes from the jostling and sorting of sensations, images, ideas, and feelings and which causes our waking life to be more truly a dream. Theophanis knows well that we are never simply now in the present, so fully occupied is our mind by the memory of what was and the *idle hopes* of what will be.

Against this must be placed an altogether different quality of attention, superintended by what the Christian East calls the *nous* or *intellect*. Unlike discursive thinking, which proceeds sequentially with the information it has gleaned from the surface of things, the intellective or noetic faculty goes straight to their core, contemplating the inner *logoi* or essences of creatures by direct apprehension. Present in all of us but dormant in most, the intellect is first awakened and set into motion by the efforts of prayer and ascetic discipline. Once purged of the encrusting dross that surrounds it, the noetic faculty becomes in turn a purging or purifying force of its own. Cutting through the veils of forgetfulness and piercing to the world's very marrow, it there discovers by recollection its own inward content. "For, behold, the kingdom of God is *within you*" (Luke 17:21).

The poet's aim thus far has been to describe the indispensable initial work of repentance, a negative movement away from illusion and death. Now we begin glimpsing the positive results of that work. There is a *vision of heavenly mysteries*, the perception of an *unheard-of light*, and an *illumination* of the heart itself.

We should stress that the *mysteries* Theophanis has in view are not secret facts or formulas, nor is the fruit of his path a knowledge of celestial statistics. He has counseled detachment not only from *what is senseless* but from *what seems intelligent*, and this latter category doubtless includes much of what passes for spirituality in this so-called new age. For the Hesychast tradition a true mystery exceeds the form of data, no matter how exotic or esoteric those data might be. The inner is always inner even in the midst of our seeing it, and therefore the *vision* of mysteries remains a vision of *mysteries*, of realities which necessarily elude the perception even of a mystic and which cannot be adequately conveyed by any language.

Whatever it is that one noetically sees, the poet and his fellow monks are unanimous about its being bathed in an extraordinary *light*. Once again we are using more than a metaphor, for the light in question is objectively real, its model being the light of Christ's transfiguration on Mount Tabor, when "his face *shone as the sun*, and his raiment was *white as the light*" (Matt. 17:2). Being born from one's vision *ineffably*, this dazzling darkness eclipses all description. And yet it is truly there, suffusing creation with the radiance of God, a sort of visible band in the spectrum of His *holy energy*.

Intimately tied to our transformed perception of this light all about us, there comes next a corresponding and complementary *illumination* within. *Beyond all telling*, the ninth step of the Ladder admits man to a degree of Divine participation where he himself begins to shine with Christ's glory. True to the maxim that like can be known only by like, the Hesychast strives by grace toward the moment when the body, now thoroughly steeped in God, bears witness in its own substance to the realities it has seen. The iconographical tradition of the halo or nimbus is no pious extravagance. Had we the eyes to see, we would realize that the true saint shines like the heaven he is.

And yet heaven is not enough. Heaven is a prison for the Sufi, say the mystics of Islam, for who wants the garden when there is also the Gardener? Theophanis agrees. There is more than illumination in the spiritual journey. We are not to rest satisfied with a contemplation of the splendor of God, nor with an appreciative spectator's place, however joyful and permanent, in the Divine proximity. A tenth step remains: coinherence in the Supreme Reality, deification. It is into the Infinite as such that human nature may eventually be drawn at the very top of the Ladder.

Like God Himself, this top rung has *no limit*, though its description may be *compassed in a single line*. For the end of the way is in fact the beginning of an immeasurable advance into the Love that loves Love and in Love all things. "God became man that man might become God": salvation is not just the restoration of an Edenic status quo. It is an unprecedented and *unheard-of life*, no longer constricted by the qualities and conditions of created existence in *this present world*. A reversion has taken place along the path of creation, a voluntary return of what we are into God. Two distinct circles remain, the human and the Divine, but their center is now the same.

Anticlimactic though they will seem, a few words must be added concerning the remaining lines of the poem. Why there is a remainder at all may be a puzzle, at least at first glance. Not content with his beautiful description of this wondrous Ladder, the poet turns his attention to what will be for many a surprising and somewhat tedious series of implorations, admonitions, and self-deprecations. Having been uplifted by so inspiring a guide, we are now dashed to earth. For Theophanis is now at pains to insist that he himself is the worst of hierophants: *indolent, hard of heart*, and *void of all these graces*, he is presumptuous in having *dared* to write on so sublime a subject and is therefore deserving of the fate of the Biblical *Uzzah*, who was killed for touching the *ark* of God (2 Sam. 6:6–7); indeed all he is worthy of are words that *condemn himself*, being an example of *utter fruitlessness*. Moreover a *note of terror* is sounded by his *fearful warnings*, which he deliberately intends to *strike* us *harshly* and *inspire* our *dread*. What is going on here? Why the vivid expressions of unworthiness and the fire and brimstone exhortations? Is this pious sentimentality? Is the author following some ancient stylistic precedent? Is he merely trying to frighten us?

Our answer in each case must be No. Admittedly the second half of "The Ladder" could be read in this way, as a network of platitudes, but such a reading would be quite mistaken. On the contrary, it should be obvious that anyone who understands the *purest* science of *prayer* as precisely as Theophanis, who is subtle enough to distinguish between *illumination* and *light*, and who from his own experience in wrestling with *thoughts* can speak so powerfully about the limits of language, is aware of what we ourselves have seen so clearly in our own not-so-subtle experience: that *terror* and *panic* are emotions belonging to the hardened, not the liquefied, *heart*, measures of the ego's continuing eccentricity in relation to God, and the result of our congenital complicity in a world that will inevitably disappoint every one of us. In Hesychast terms such passions are simply more *thoughts*, more psychic chatter, and our poet cannot possibly be construed as encouraging them. Nor can he be unaware of the fact that the ego has a way of feeding even on abjection and self-condemnation, of being proud of its sin. When he refers to himself as *the first* among those *who are hard of heart*, it would therefore be absurd to imagine that he expects us to think we are his rightful superiors. So what is the point?

Only the *via negativa*, so characteristic of Hesychasm and the Christian East as a whole, can make sense of these puzzling expressions. Both the self-reproaches and the warnings require transposing into the apophatic key of which we have already seen evidence in the first part of the poem: the vision was a vision of *mysteries*; the Divine light was *unheard-of*; the heart's illumination, *beyond all telling*. In short, *experience alone can teach these things, not talk*. All discourse is reduced to stammering and silence when confronted by God.

Therefore, having told us in positive terms what the Ladder consists of, Theophanis is now obliged to undercut the understanding we may have gained, extending the range of negation and deepening its intensity, lest we suppose ourselves wise. *Do not deceive yourselves*, he warns. The full force of the imperative will not be felt unless we first admit that our entire waking life is a web of delusion and vanity. Remember what was said on the subject of *thoughts*. The union we long for with the Absolute will come about only at the expense of all those *idle hopes* aroused by our present, passion-laden conceptions. This does not mean that a man should despair of making any progress toward God, believing himself condemned to a sort of total depravity. The apophatic path is still a path, and the poet is quick to insist that we make every effort in searching for the Truth right now *in this present world*. But what we shall find when we find it is *a wealth the world cannot contain*. The author means what he says: if you wish to enter God, you must *detach yourself from everything*, most especially that self.

It is helpful to recall the relative anonymity of the poet. We are not listening to the voice of someone whose biography might be used in checking the history of his opinions or the accuracy of his judgments. It is a voice that time has detached from all else and thus rendered impersonal, according perhaps to its own design. Theophanis the Monk is not such and such an ego. He is the ego as such, and with this in mind the assessment provided in the poem becomes perfectly intelligible. The ego is indeed *void of all graces*, not just in fact but in principle. Indeed, measured against the Supreme Reality at the top of the Ladder, it is much less than merely lacking in value: having but the pretence of being, it is a centrifugal tendency toward the "outer darkness" of destruction, the very root of blind and *fruitless* craving, and its mortification is essential to our realizing that God's is the only true center, competition with the Divine being no more than illusion.

The promises of *terror* and the *fearful warnings* may be interpreted along similar lines. Fear is often just a passion itself, of course, a feeling of malaise, consternation, or anxiety, and as such it too must be excluded from the soul of the man seeking *peace from thoughts*. But in an older and deeper sense, *fear* is awe. Rather than a subjective and blood-freezing fright, it points us toward an objective, liberating wonder. No mere reactive emotion, this kind of fear is a real organ for perception and participation in God.

Let us not expunge the common-sense meaning of the poet's words. Doubtless there will come a day of sheer emotional panic for those who in this life did *not ponder always on these things* and did not through serious spiritual struggle grow accustomed to the daily death of desire. But for those who did, the holy *fear* of awe, the exquisite joy of *dread*, will be itself among the *blessings promised*. Far from something they might wish to escape, it is among the many rewards of their journey, a delicious *fruit of all the books*. For these seekers know from repeated *experience* that negations of negations are something wondrously positive, gifts or *graces* to be enjoyed when the ego Theophanis has been stripped of its many layers of ambition and cowardice and resentment and greed and smugness and torpor, and our naked souls are ushered, beyond all possibility, into the *heart* of the living God.

The Ladder positioned at our very feet, the poet is showing us, with a precise and carefully selected apophatic language, what it means truly to climb. The denials—of himself and hence us—are but the spaces between the rungs.

THE LADDER OF DIVINE GRACES
Which Experience has Made Known to Those Inspired by God

Theophanis the Monk

The first step is that of purest prayer.
From this there comes a warmth of heart,
And then a strange, a holy energy,
Then tears wrung from the heart, God-given,
Then peace from thoughts of every kind.
From this arises purging of the intellect,
And next the vision of heavenly mysteries.
Unheard-of light is born from this ineffably,
And thence, beyond all telling, the heart's
    illumination.
Last comes—a step that has no limit
Though compassed in a single line—
Perfection that is endless.
The ladder's lowest step
Prescribes pure prayer alone.
But prayer has many forms:
My discourse would be long
Were I now to speak of them:
And, friend, know that always
Experience teaches one, not words.
A ladder rising wondrously to heaven's vault:
Ten steps that strangely vivify the soul.
Ten steps that herald the soul's life.
A saint inspired by God has said:
Do not deceive yourself with idle hopes
That in the world to come you will find life
If you have not tried to find it in this
    present world.
Ten steps: a wisdom born of God.
Ten steps: fruit of all the books.
Ten steps that point towards perfection.
Ten steps that lead one up to heaven.
Ten steps through which a man knows God.
The ladder may seem short indeed,
But if your heart can inwardly experience it
You will find a wealth the world cannot contain,
A god-like fountain flowing with
    unheard-of life.
This ten-graced ladder is the best of masters,
Clearly teaching each to know its stages.
If when you behold it
You think you stand securely on it,

Ask yourself on which step you stand,
So that we, the indolent, may also profit.
My friend, if you want to learn about all this,
Detach yourself from everything,
From what is senseless, from what seems
    intelligent.
Without detachment nothing can be learnt.
Experience alone can teach these things, not talk.
Even if these words once said
By one of God's elect strike harshly,
I repeat them to remind you:
He who has no foothold on this ladder,
Who does not ponder always on these things,
When he comes to die will know
Terrible fear, terrible dread,
Will be full of boundless panic.
My lines end on a note of terror.
Yet it is good that this is so:
Those who are hard of heart—myself the first—
Are led to repentance, led to a hold life,
Less by the lure of blessings promised
Than by fearful warnings that inspire dread.
'He who has ears to hear, let him hear.'
You who have written this, hear, then,
    and take note:
Void of all these graces,
How have you dared to write such things?
How do you not shudder to expound them?
Have you not heard what Uzzah suffered
When he tried to stop God's ark from falling?
Do not think that I speak as one who teaches:
I speak as one whose words condemn himself,
Knowing the rewards awaiting those who strive,
Knowing my utter fruitlessness.

From *The Philokalia: The Complete Text compiled by St. Nikodimos of the Hold Mountain and St. Makarios of Corinth*, translated by G. E. H. Palmer, Philip Sherrard, Kallistos Ware (London: Faber and Faber, 1984), Vol. III, pp. 67–69.

Parabola
Volume: 29.2
Web of Life

Epilogue

WITNESSING THE GREAT LIFE

Christopher Bamford

A few years ago, I was given the grace of accompanying my wife across the threshold. No matter how great the pain and the abyss of the loss endured, the gift that came with the physical loss—that of experiencing the abundance of life, the great life that includes and far surpasses birth and death—is something for which I shall always be grateful.

That great life was brought home to me one Sunday at church. I understood that in this one life that includes physical death, as it includes many little deaths and resurrections, all human beings, those in Heaven and those on Earth, are present at every moment with the great angelic hierarchy of beings. I understood that all of us are a single being, a single body, and are connected in such a way that each is responsible for all. That Sunday, celebrating the Eucharist, I recognized that just as all humanity (and also the Earth herself) was present in the sacrificial breaking of the bread, so too all the dead (and all the angels and spirits) were also present. I understood that humanity, embodied in Heaven or on Earth, was a single being, united with all beings. The sense of interconnection, kinship, and dynamic unity was overwhelming. I sensed what it meant to be members of one body, speakers in a single continuous conversation. In that instance, I knew that life was without end, our stories were endlessly interwoven, and every human was connected to, and in a sense part of and responsible for, every other. I realized that there was nothing to which I was not called to respond, for which I was not responsible. There was nothing of which I could say, "That's not my responsibility." I understood that we are all implicated in each other—and that only egoism cut us asunder. I understood that it was only a kind of egoism that allowed me to think of my feelings, thoughts, and actions as my own personal possessions—as existing for my sake. I knew that whenever I felt pain or joy—and did not hold onto and lay claim to my experience in a self-oriented way, but received it as a gift given for the sake of the world—then that pain or joy was the world's. I realized that whenever any one of us experiences pain or joy, that is an aspect of a larger and more important process than whatever it was I or another was going through—call it the pain or the joy or the learning of the world. Specifically, I recognized that another's suffering is all our suffering, as much mine as his or hers or yours, that I was somehow implicated in both its cause and its healing. I understood, too, that this one body that we are includes the whole world, the Earth itself and all its beings—mineral, vegetable, and animal—and that these are in conversation with Heaven and participate in the responsibility of each for all.

CONTRIBUTOR PROFILES

Christopher Bamford is editor-in-chief of Anthroposophic Press (Steiner Books) and Lindisfarne Books. His most recent book is *An Endless Trace: The Passionate Pursuit of Wisdom in the West.*

Cynthia Bourgeault is the principal teacher and advisor to the Contemplative Society. A retreat and conference leader, teacher of prayer, and Episcopal priest, she is the author of *The Wisdom Way of Knowing* (John Wiley & Sons, 2003), *Mystical Hope* (Cloister, 2001), and *Centering Prayer and Inner Awakening* (Cowley, 2004).

Father Symeon Burholt is engaged in psychiatric social work in Massachusetts. He has studied monasticism and Eastern Christian mysticism for many years.

Stratford Caldecott is a publisher, writer, and editor, and is the European Director of the Chesterton Institute for Faith & Culture and the editor of *Second Spring* (www.secondspring.co.uk).

Robert Coles is a child psychiatrist, and a professor at Harvard University. His books include the Pulitzer Prize-winning *Children in Crisis* series and *The Spiritual Life of Children.*

James S. Cutsinger is Professor of Theology and Religious Thought at the University of South Carolina. His books include *Paths to the Heart* and *Not of this World.*

D. M. Dooling (1910–1991) was the founder and editorial director of *Parabola: The Search for Meaning.* She edited a number of books; *The Spirit of Quest: Essays and Poems* is a collection of her own writings.

Christopher Fremantle (1906–1978) was a painter, editor, and translator. *On Attention* is a collection of his talks and essays.

Hugh Gilbert, O.S.B. is the abbot of Pluscarden Abbey, a Roman Catholic monastery in Scotland.

Eric Gill (1882–1940) was a British sculptor, engraver, typographic designer, and writer.

Bede Griffiths (1906–1993) is considered by many to be one of the greatest religious leaders of the 20th century. After becoming a Catholic and a Benedictine monk, Bede Griffiths went to India and established an ashram where he spent the remaining thirty-eight years of his life and where pilgrims from all continents came for enlightenment in prayer and meditation. He is the author of *The Golden String, River of Compassion*, and *Return to the Center*, among many others.

Kim Coleman Healy is a long-time reader of Thomas Merton and a contributor to *Parabola*.

Rembert Herbert is an authority on Gregorian chant. *Entrances: Gregorian Chant in Daily Life* is his latest book.

Thomas Hopko is Dean Emeritus of St. Vladimir's Seminary, Crestwood, N.Y., and author of the series *The Orthodox Faith, The Lenten Spring*, and *All the Fullness of God*.

Thomas Keating is an author, teacher, and monk. He directs retreats in the practice of Centering Prayer and is the author of many books, including *Open Mind, Open Heart; The Mystery of Christ; Invitation to Love;* and *Intimacy with God*.

Helen Luke (1904–1995) was a Jungian counselor and writer. *Old Age, Kalaidescope*, and *Dark Wood to White Rose* are among her books.

Thomas Merton (1915–1968), known in religion as Father Louis, was a Trappist monk of the Cistercian Abbey of Gethsemani near Bardstown, Kentucky. Merton's best-selling autobiography *The Seven Storey Mountain* has become a classic. His other works include *The Sign of Jonas, No Man Is an Island, New Seeds of Contemplation, Conjectures of a Guilty Bystander, The Way of Chuang Tzu*, and *Mystics and Zen Masters*. Since his death in Bangkok, Thailand, in December

1968, a number of his works have been published posthumously, including *The Asian Journal, The Collected Poems, The Literary Essays,* and five volumes selected from his letters.

James and Myfanwy Moran are Eastern Orthodox writers engaged in comparative religion studies.

Jacob Needleman is a professor of philosophy at San Francisco State University and the author of many books, including *The American Soul, The Wisdom of Love, Time and the Soul, The Heart of Philosophy, Lost Christianity,* and *Money and the Meaning of Life.* In addition to his teaching and writing, he serves as a consultant in the fields of psychology, education, medical ethics, philanthropy, and business.

Elaine H. Pagels is Professor of Religion at Princeton University. She is the author of *The Gnostic Gospels* and *Beyond Belief: The Secret Gospel of Thomas.*

Paul Quenon (1921–1963) has been a Trappist monk of the Abbey of Gethsemani since 1958. He is a poet and photographer, cantor and cook.

Alexander Schmemann was dean and professor of liturgical theology at St. Vladimir's Orthodox Theological Seminary. *The Eucharist: Sacrament of the Kingdom* and *For the Life of the World: Sacraments and Orthodoxy* are two of his books.

Brother David Steindl-Rast is a Benedictine monk who has written several books about the importance of gratitude, including *Gratefulness, the Heart of Prayer* and *A Listening Heart.* He is co-founder and adviser to A Network for Grateful Living (Gratefulness.org), based in Ithaca, N.Y.

Richard Temple is owner of The Temple Gallery in London and author of *Icons: A Search for Inner Meaning.*

Paul J. Tillich (1886–1965), one of the great theologians of the twentieth century, taught at Union Theological Seminary, New York, and then at the University of Chicago and Harvard University. His many works include *The Protestant Era*; *The Courage to Be*; *Love, Power, and Justice*; and *My Search for Absolutes*.

P. L. Travers (1899–1996), was an essayist, poet, and the author of *Friend Monkey* and the *Mary Poppins* books. She was one of the founding editors of *Parabola: The Search for Meaning*.

Norvene Vest is the author of *Preferring Christ, Bible Reading for Spiritual Growth*, and *No Moment Too Small: Rhythms of Silence, Prayer, and Holy Reading*. An oblate of a Benedictine abbey in Valyermo, California, she leads workshops and retreats on Benedictine spirituality in the United States and Britain.

Kallistos Ware is the Spalding Lecturer in Eastern Orthodox Studies at Oxford University. In 1982 he was consecrated titular Bishop of Diokleia and appointed assistant bishop in the Orthodox Archdiocese of Thyateira and Great Britain. *The Orthodox Way* is his best-known book.

Irma Zaleski is a Canadian translator, lecturer, and writer. *God Is Not Reasonable: And Other Tales of Mother Macrina* is her latest book.

Philip Zaleski is the author and editor of many books, including *The Recollected Heart* and *The Book of Heaven*, a senior editor at *Parabola*, and a research associate in the Department of Religion at Smith College. With his wife, Carol Zaleski, he wrote *Prayer*, a book about the nature, practice, and meaning of prayer across religious traditions and through the ages.

FOR FURTHER READING

General Accounts

Versions of the Bible and study guides are widely available on the Internet. An excellent entry into this vast literature is the *Christian Classics Ethereal Library's World Wide Study Bible* at http://www.ccel.org. The site also carries a enormous and growing collection of reference works and volumes in the public domain. An excellent place to begin exploring the ground.

The Classics of Western Spirituality series published by Paulist Press has year by year over the last several decades produced excellent versions of the original writings of the universally acknowledged teachers of the Western tradition. The volumes have been translated and introduced by prominent scholars and spiritual leaders, and each is recommended without reservation. The writings are selected and presented in accessible, contemporary language, and the reader is given access to teachings that might otherwise have remained obscure and difficult of access. A few essential titles from the series:

Augustine of Hippo: Selected Writings, translated and introduced by Mary T. Clark; preface by Goulven Madec.

Augustine of Hippo (354–430) was one of the most influential Christian writers and theologians.

Bernard of Clairvaux: Selected Works, translated and with a foreword by G. R. Evans; introduction by Jean LeClercq; preface by Ewert Cousins.

Writings of the great medieval spiritual teacher (1090–1153) who was the founder of the Cistercians. His power and spiritual attainments are tempered by an astute insight into human nature and sense of humor.

Jacob Boehme: The Way to Christ, edited by Peter Erb.

Jacob Boehme (1575–1624), a German Lutheran and one of the most original Christian mystics and visionaries. *The Way to Christ* is a collection of nine treatises intended to serve as a meditation guide.

Bonaventure: The Soul's Journey into God, The Tree of Life, The Life of St. Francis, translated and introduced by Ewert Cousins.

Bonaventure (1217–1274), friar and professor at the University of Paris, was considered a great spiritual master in his own lifetime. These works collected here demonstrate the poetry and passion of his mystical vision.

Meister Eckhart: Teacher and Preacher, edited by Bernard McGinn with the collaboration of Frank Tobin and Elvira Borgstadt; preface by Kenneth J. Northcott.

An enigmatic mystic whose influence has continued to inform the Western Christian tradition. Eckhart (c. 1260–1327) is represented here as teacher, with commentaries, and preacher, with sermons.

Hildegard of Bingen: Scivias, translated by Mother Columba Hart and Jane Bishop; introduction by Barbara Newman.

The 26 visions of Hildegard of Bingen (1098–1179). She was the first of the great German mystics, a healer, a poet, and a prophet.

John of the Cross: Selected Writings, edited with an introduction by Kieran Kavanaugh, O.C.D.

The "essential" St. John of the Cross (1542–1591), including selections from *The Ascent of Mount Carmel*, *The Dark Night*, and *Spiritual Canticle*.

Julian of Norwich: Showings, translated and introduced by Edmund Colledge, O.S.A., and James Walsh, S. J. Preface by Jean Leclercq, O.S.B.

One of the greatest of all English mystics, Julian (1342–c.1423) was an anchoress who lived in solitude in Norwich, England.

Mechthild of Magdeburg: The Flowing Light of the Godhead, translated and introduced by Frank Tobin.

Mechthild was a 13th-century (c. 1260–c. 1282/94) German Beguine of deep religious insight.

Pseudo Dionysius: The Complete Works, translated by Colm Luibheid; foreword, notes, and translation collaboration by Paul Rorem.

The complete works of the enigmatic 5th and 6th-century writer known as the Pseudo Dionysius, a primary teacher of the apophatic path.

Symeon the New Theologian: The Discourses, translated by C. J. DeCatanzaro.

Abbot, spiritual director, theologian and church reformer, St. Symeon (942–1022) was a great spiritual master of Eastern Christianity. His Discourses were preached to his monks.

Johannes Tauler: Sermons, translated by Maria Shrady, introduced by Josef Schmidt.

An influential German mystical writer of the 14th century, Johannes Tauler (c. 1300–1361) was an impassioned and inspired preacher.

Celtic Spirituality, translated and introduced by Oliver Davies, with the collaboration of Thomas O' Loughlin.

Saints' lives, monastic texts, poetry, devotional texts, liturgical texts, and theological treatises from the 6th through the 13th centuries.

Pursuit of Wisdom and Other Works by the Author of The Cloud of Unknowing, translated, edited, and annotated by James Walsh, S. J.

Modern English translations of essays by the unknown 14th-century mystic who wrote *The Cloud of Unknowing*, and of equal interest.

Quaker Spirituality: Selected Writings, edited and introduced by Douglas V. Steere; preface by Douglas V. Steere and Elizabeth Gray Vining.

The major voices of the Quaker movement from the 18th to the 20th centuries, including the *Journals of George Fox*, *The Journal of John Woolman*, *Thomas Kelly's Testament of Devotion* and selections from Caroline Stephens and Rufus Jones.

Additional works of the *Parabola* authors collected here can be found in the contributor profiles.

Eastern Orthodox Tradition

For further reading in the Eastern Orthodox tradition, the following books are helpful:

Anonymous, *The Way of a Pilgrim*, translated from the Russian by R. M. French (Milwaukee, Wisc.: Morehouse Publishing, 1931).

Ephrem the Syrian, *The Luminous Eye: The Spiritual World of Saint Ephrem*, translated by Stephen Brock (Kalamazoo, Mich: Cistercian Publications, 1992).

Vladimir Lossky, *The Mystical Theology of the Eastern Church* (Crestwood, N.Y.: St. Vladimir's Seminary Press, 1998).

Writings from the Philokalia on the Prayer of the Heart, translated by E. Kadloubovsky and G. E. H. Palmer (London: Faber & Faber, 1951).

The Syriac Fathers on Prayer and the Spiritual Life, translated by Stephen Brock (Kalamazoo, Mich: Cistercian Publications, 1987).

Christian Eschatology

The titles below explore Christian eschatology, the beginning and end; what Christians believe; and how they ought to love:

Anonymous, *Meditations on the Tarot: A Journey into Christian Hermeticism* (New York: Jeremy P. Tarcher, 2002).

Nicholas Berdyaev, *The Destiny of Man* (New York: Charles Scribner's Sons, 1937).

Dietrich Bonhoeffer, *Life Together* (New York: Harper & Row, 1954).

C. S. Lewis, *Mere Christianity* (San Francisco: HarperSanFrancisco, 2001).

Andre Louf, *Tuning into Grace: The Quest for God* (Kalamazoo, Mich: Cistercian Publications, 1992).

Karl Rahner, *Everyday Faith* (New York: Herder and Herder, 1968).

Pierre Teilhard de Chardin, *The Divine Milieu: An Essay on the Interior Life* (New York: HarperCollins, 1960).

Favorites

A few perennial favorites:

John Bunyan, *The Pilgrim's Progress from This World to That Which Is to Come; Delivered under the Similitude of a Dream.* Widely available in various editions.

Peter Kreeft and Blaise Pascal, *Christianity for Modern Pagans: Pascal's Pensées* (San Francisco: Ignatius Press, 1993).

William Law, *A Serious Call to a Devout & Holy Life* (Louisville, Kent.: Westminster John Knox Press, 1968).

Brother Lawrence, *The Practice of the Presence of God* (Boston: New Seeds, 2005).

Thomas à Kempis, *The Imitation of Christ* (N. Y.: Image, 1955).

Two fictional explorations of quite different character:

George Bernanos, *The Diary of a Country Priest* (New York: Carroll & Graf Publishers, 1984).

C. S. Lewis, *The Screwtape Letters* (New York: Simon & Schuster, 1996).

Modern works of devotion, guidance, and inspiration:

Anthony Bloom (Metropolitan Anthony of Sourozh), *Living Prayer* (Springfield, Ill.: Templegate Publishers, 1966).

Michael Casey, *The Undivided Heart: The Western Monastic Approach to Contemplation* (Petersham, Mass.: St. Bede's Publications, 1994).

Romano Guardini, *Prayer in Practice* (New York: Pantheon Books, 1957).

Søren Kierkegaard, *Purity of Heart Is to Will One Thing* (New York: HarperCollins, 1966).

Thomas Merton, *New Seeds of Contemplation* (London: Shambhala Publications, 2003).

Henri Nouwen, *Reaching Out* (New York: Doubleday, 1975).

Hans Urs von Balthasar, *Prayer* (London: G. Chapman, 1961).

Simone Weil, *Waiting for God* (New York: Harper Perennial Library, 1992).

Chapter Citations

Call of the Tradition
1 John 13:34 Revised Standard Version (hereafter cited as RSV).
2 Matt. 11:28–30 RSV.
3 Matt. 7:7 RSV.
4 Matt. 5:1–10 RSV.
5 Rev. 22:13 RSV.
6 From *The Marrow of the Gospel: A Study of the Rule of Saint Francis of Assisi* (Chicago: Franciscan Herald Press, 1958).
7 From *The Confessions of Jacob Boehme*, translated by Frederick D. Maurice (London: Methuen, 1920).
8 From *The Very Thought of Thee: From Three Great Mystics, Bernard of Clairvaux, Jeremy Taylor, Evelyn Underhill*, arranged and edited by Douglas V. Steere and J. Minton Batten (Nashville, Tenn.: The Upper Room, 1953).
9 From *Bonaventure*, translated and introduced by Ewert Cousins; preface by Ignatius Brady (New York: Paulist Press, 1978).

Christian Imagery
1 From *The Adornment of the Spiritual Marriage by Jan Ruusbroec*, translated by C. A. Wynshank (London: John M. Watkins, 1951).
2 From *The Nag Hammadi Library in English*, translated by members of the Coptic Library Project (New York: Harper & Row, 1977).
3 From *Early Fathers of the Philokalia*, selected and translated by E. Kadloubovsky and G. E. H. Palmer (London: Faber & Faber, 1954).
4 From *The Luminous Eye: The Spiritual World Vision of Saint Ephrem*, by Stephen Brock (Kalamazoo, Mich: Cistercian Publications, 1992).
5 From *Henry Suso: the Exemplar, with Two German Sermons*, edited and translated by Frank Tobin (New York: Paulist Press, 1989).
6 Isaiah 6:3.
7 Cited in *Christian Spirit*, edited by Judith Fitzgerald and Michael Oren Fitzgerald (Bloomington, Ind.: World Wisdom, 2004).

Chapter 1
1 John 6:44.
2 From *The Homilies of St. Augustine on St. John's Gospel*, in *The Divine Office* (London: Collins, 1974).

Chapter 2
1 John 14:6 RSV.
2 From *The Prayers and Meditations of St. Anselm with the Proslogion*, translated and with an introduction by Sister Benedicta Ward, S.L.G. (Harmondsworth: Penguin, 1973).

Chapter 3
1 John 12:24–26 New Revised Standard Version.

Chapter 4
1 Mark 13:37 RSV.
2 Cited in *The Mystical Theology of the Eastern Church*, by Vladimir Lossky (Cambridge: James Clarke, 1957).

Chapter 5
1 From *On the Suprasensual Life*, by Jacob Boehme, translated by William Law (London: Printed for M. Richardson, 1764-1781). Edited and adapted by Lorraine Kisly.

Chapter 6
1 From *The Kitchen Saint and the Heritage of Islam*, translated by Elmer H. Douglas (Allison Park, Penn.: Pickwick Publications, 1989).

Chapter 7
1 From *The Other Gospels: Non-Canonical Gospel Texts*, edited by Ron Cameron (Philadelphia: The Westminster Press, 1982).
2 From *The Other Gospels: Non-Canonical Gospel Texts*, edited by Ron Cameron. (Philadelphia: The Westminster Press, 1982).

Chapter 8

1 John 6:12 King James Version.
2 From *The Beginning and the End* by Nicholas Berdyaev, translated from the Russian by R. M. French (New York: Harper & Brothers, 1952).

Photography Credits

Cover Photo
Saint Catherine Monastery at Sinai Photo © Jean-Luc MANAUD/ RAPHO/Imagestate.

Page xvii
Portrait of Christ from the *Book of Kells* (c. 800), fol. 32v. Trinity College, Dublin.
Photo Art Resource, New York.

Page xix
Virgin and Child (Madonna Hodegetria). Russian icon (16th century). Russian State Museum, St. Petersburg.
Photo Scala/Art Resource, New York.

Page xx
Ceiling of Notre Dame la Grande. French Romanesque vaulted ceiling (12th century). Poitiers, France.
Photo by Adam Woolfitt, © Adam Woolfitt/CORBIS.

Page xxiii
Trinity of Uglic by Andrei Rublev (1360–c.1430). Russian icon. Rubliev Museum, Moscow.
Photo Scala/Art Resource, New York.

Page xxiv
Saint John Evangelist and Prochoros (1484). Prochoros takes notes while Saint John dictates, gesticulating with his hands. Behind them is a blue sky, clouds, and text. From an Armenian manuscript of the four gospels. British Library, London, ID: Or 2681, fol.217 b.
Photo by Erich Lessing Art Resource, New York.

Page xxvii
The Deposition from the Cross by Duccio (di Buoninsegna) (c.1260–1319). Panel from the back of the Maesta Altarpiece. Museo dell' Opera Metropolitena, Siena, Italy.
Photo Scala/Art Resource, New York.

Page xxviii

Story of Charlemagne. Stained glass window (13th century). Northern Ambulatory, Chartres Cathedral, France.
Photo Giraudon/Art Resource, New York.

Page xxxi

Christ (Deesis). Mosaic (14th century), Hagia Sophia, Istanbul. The first Hagia Sophia was built in 532–537 by command of Emperor Justinian. The present cathedral is the third on the site. Provincial governors were asked to send the most beautiful parts of ancient monuments from the Byzantine Empire for incorporation. It was the most important church in Christendom, but is now a museum. Photo by Robert Frerck, © Getty Images.

Page xxxii

Capital with the Dream of the Magi (c. 1120–1130. Cathedral St. Lazare, Autun, France.
Photo Scala/Art Resource, New York.